Speak My Words
Unto Them

A History

of

UFM International

(Unevangelized Fields Mission)

By Homer E. Dowdy

SPEAK MY WORDS UNTO THEM
A History of UFM International
© 1997 by Homer Dowdy

Published by UFM International, Inc.
306 Bala Avenue
Bala-Cynwyd, Pennsylvania 19004

Printed in the United States of America

Printed by Register Graphics
Randolph, New York 14772

ISBN 0-9656830-0-1

Contents

To
all those missionaries
whose lives, labor, and love
made this book possible

Philippians 1:3-6 (KJV)
I thank my God upon every remembrance of you,
Always in every prayer of mine for you all making request with joy,
For your fellowship in the gospel from the first day until now; Being
confident of this very thing,
that he which hath begun a good work in you
will perform it until the day of Jesus Christ.

Foreword

To write the history of some organizations, you start with headquarters. With UFM International, you start at a remote station at the end of some jungle trail or in an out-of-the-way provincial capital, then go on to another, then to still another, and finally arrive at headquarters. That is because UFM has always been — and still is — a field-oriented mission.

More than sixty individuals contributed directly to the writing of the history of UFM International, not counting missionaries and nationals of several fields who over the years were my hosts, interpreted for me or journeyed with me in canoe or camion. Among the many giving invaluable help are missionaries, both active and retired, mission executives and office staff. They responded in numerous ways to my requests for information: Letters, audio tapes, books, manuscripts, phone calls, typed recollections, folios of prayer letters, a station log and face-to-face interviews. In addition, I had the use of back copies of *Light and Life*, the mission's journal which later became *Lifeline*, and other important documents from the archives.

There are some persons I must mention in particular for their unusual degree of assistance. Dr. James H. Nesbitt, general director of UFM International, and John W. Miesel, associate director, now retired, started me on this project, and their interest and encouragement sustained me throughout. Al Larson, retired general director, and Jean his wife helped immensely by answering my many questions and talking one whole day into a tape recorder and by offering a multitude of authoritative documents. Jim Hively uncorked the flow of information from Irian Jaya. Mary McAllister and Effie Sarginson provided much detail about the Belém field of Brazil, as Mary Hawkins did about Roraima in that same country. Joy Brown helped make Haiti come alive and Majil Odman Wilson gave insights into the years in which Ralph Odman led the field of Haiti and then UFM in North America.

Priceless were the letters, journals and memoirs in manuscript form of Congo pioneer missionary Herbert Jenkinson, known by all as Kinso. The writings of Edwin and Lilian Pudney told about the early days of UFM in Canada and the United States. Brief books by Leonard Harris, Horace Banner and David Truby were very helpful, as were longer works on their own mission activity by Rosemary Cunningham, David Scovill, Marguerite Harrell and Shirley Horne, and scholarly writings of Douglas Hayward, Rowland Davies and Charles Stoner. A number of veterans went over the drafts of chapters pertaining to their fields. I have cited specific sources for each chapter of the history, but I myself must accept responsibility for any errors, misinterpretations or omissions.

I would be remiss if I failed to mention Lois Combs, a staff member at headquarters in Bala-Cynwyd. She did much to help, sometimes on an almost daily basis, putting me in contact with various missionaries, finding materials, keeping the project on track. Having been a missionary in Brazil, she could appreciate the field's perspective and quickly she learned how to reconcile that position with my incessant demand for more particulars.

A chronicle of this sort cannot be complete. The work of a man or woman that is between only himself or herself and the Lord may be just as essential to the planting of seed or nurturing of the tender shoot as a deed acclaimed by all. Some names may not be mentioned in the narrative, but the hundreds of unheralded laborers and their day-to-day efforts appear in God's record right along with those of greater visibility.

Before Messrs. Nesbitt and Miesel suggested a history of UFM, I had been somewhat acquainted with the mission's work and several of its people. Dr. Henry R. Brandt, a friend of both the mission and myself, introduced me to UFM back in 1958 when I as a newspaper reporter accompanied him on a three-week trip to Haiti. Later, I wrote books on the Wai Wai Indians of the Amazon and the martyrdom in Congo. But it was not until I began digging into UFM's sixty-plus years of worldwide service that I realized how much the mission has been used in the growth of Christ's Church. I trust that readers of this attempt to record UFM's history, an effort faulty at best, will gain an appreciation, as I have, of what God has done and is continuing to do through these dedicated people.

Homer E. Dowdy
Annapolis, Maryland
July, 1996

1

Eternal Life for the Dani

I
t was Sunday morning, and few in the village had slept.
The pigs hosting the spirits that people hoped to appease
had been butchered, and on these the Dani had feasted
throughout the night. These were pigs once dedicated to the
spirit world, their consecration a guarantee against all forms of
evil attack. With the creatures now dead and their flesh con-
sumed by every man, woman and child in the valley, who could
tell what might happen? It was enough to cause bad dreams,
whether asleep or awake.

"This is the day! Up, up, my friends!"

From peak to mountain peak, the call echoed through the
valley.

"This is the day we discover eternal life!"

Eternal life? Wasn't that what generation after generation
had sought, but the search had led only to disappointment and
discouragement, even disgust?

"Hurry! Prepare yourselves!"

Darkness gave way to dawn and the rising of the sun. That
bright image began its daily march across the sky, and scarcely
had it climbed above the valley's east wall when from clusters of
thatch huts scattered all over the scene came people — thousands of people — their lines weaving toward one central spot
like so many gliding snakes.

1

Ten, twenty, a hundred, a thousand, they headed for a towering pile of firewood at the end of a small airstrip. The day before, the pyre had been built up, layer on layer, in eager anticipation of its burning. Yesterday, the people had brought tree limbs and dried branches; today, they carried or wore around their necks or dangled from the tips of long sticks a bone or a swatch of hair or another variety of fetish that for all their years had ruled their lives.

One who was there, who was not one of them but who was a part of their lives, listened to the calls bouncing back and forth across the valley, announcing that this man's clan, or that one's, was on its way. From the modest bark house near the airstrip that he and his family lived in, he watched the lines slither toward the giant wood pile. But there was more than sight and sound; tension also filled the air.

"Our spirits soared to God in ecstatic joy and thankfulness, " he later wrote, "but also in apprehension and a certain tinge of fear."

"Then," he went on, "I felt it! The house began to shake. At the same time, I heard the thud of hundreds of feet on the turf. I looked out through the clear plastic which served as the glass in the window to see the paths, grass, foliage and stream beds almost literally disgorge themselves of the people waiting within their shelter. At a signal, they poured forth onto the airstrip, running, dancing and chanting.

"Smaller groups merged with the larger body until there was a single, solid mass of some seven thousand black, perspiring bodies. They raced madly up and down the airstrip in their dance patterns.

"Each person was decked out in all his or her finery of leaves and feathers. They had painted their bodies with designs of red clay. Most bodies glistened with a freshly applied mixture of pig grease and soot. Some of the men had let down their long hair from their traditional net bags and swished it back and forth."

A great many carried bows and arrows and long spears, some

measuring fifteen feet, and scarcely a one lacking the dried blood of an enemy, and some waved 'spirit dusters' whose purpose was to ward off evil spirits. Others boldly lifted above their heads the long poles from which dangled their spirit charms. Then the observer of this captivating scene heard the start of a chant that mounted in crescendo as the crowd took it up:

"*Ayu uugwe. Ayu uugwe,*" roared seven thousand voices. "We want heaven! We want heaven!"

The people of the Dani tribe, who inhabited one of Dutch New Guinea's numerous nearly inaccessible valleys, longed for the immortality they had lost centuries before.

This huge, swaying, shouting throng was not yet at its maximum. Smaller villages dotted the fringe of the valley, and it was to these the mass moved with the intent of leaving no one out of the day's momentous activity. Entering a commodious neighborhood men's house, where communal living for the adult males contrasted with the smaller huts of their wives and children, a leader would exhort, "Hold nothing back."

What they were about to do would be successful only if all fully participated.

The exhortation directed at the women was particularly acute. Why should it not be? The men feared the women; they had special powers of black magic. The women, in turn, feared the men for their brute strength — and for spectral secrets hatched in off-limit lodgings. If the men burned their protective charms and openly spoke of their shrouded rituals and the women did not, the men would have made themselves vulnerable; and were it only the women taking this unprecedented step, they would stand defenseless before the men.

Once back at the airstrip, a shaman began to speak. For years, he'd served the particular spirit that fed on the bodies of the dead, and to the dread of the people, this spirit was always hungry. Now, the sorcerer vowed to his listeners that the symbol of his power — some said it was a piece of human flesh — would be thrown on the fire. Following his example, others pledged polished stones, shells, fur headdresses, bits of string, pieces of cane, necklaces, nose bones, pig tails, stone and bone knives. Men reassured each other they were coming clean. Each person's symbol of the supernatural affected all the others; only by the willingness of each individual to reject the past and destroy the things that threatened another would the goal they aimed at be achieved.

Personally validating confession and renunciation was the last step before the burning. Family by family, neighborhood by neighborhood, the people approached the wood pile and on it tossed their charms, amulets, spears, bows and arrows, all relics that tied them to the past.

One man displayed his shells before his young son. His collection had been assembled over many years. Dividing the shells into two heaps, he said, "This one must go on the pile to be burned. This one we may keep. This one must go. This one's all right." To an outsider, one shell might appear little different from another, but he knew which ones had been used in demon feasts and black magic.

Dumped on that pile were the gods that had controlled every area of their lives every day.

Ralph Maynard, one of the first missionaries to this valley, and his colleague, David Scovill, whose notes recorded the scene, pressed close as man after man threw his fetishes on the pile. Scovill described one tribesman as a charismatic, influential community leader.

"He stood at the edge of that pyre already loaded with fetishes, and in a very dramatic gesture began to methodically strip himself of all his paraphernalia: his bundle of arrows along with the bow in his hand, his headdress, the pig's tusk in his nose, the plugs in his ears, the necklace and amulets which hung from his neck, the pretty colored leaves and feathers in an armband with which he had wooed women, the armband itself, gifts promoting animal pleasure in place of grief during the crises of war and death, the special net bags with all their exotic pieces of stone, wood and glass. Then, in a moment of rare grandeur, he pulled a long bone dagger from his other armband. Unsheathing it, he held it up for all to see.

"'Folks,' he said, 'I've killed over one man's hands (ten people, plus or minus) with this bone dagger. Today, I'm taking eternal life. I don't need this any longer.'"

He flipped it onto the pile, then in disdain for what had held him captive for so long, he turned and spat several times on the things he had shed. His resolve having been clearly demonstrated, he quietly retired to his place among his own group, becoming one of the whole as the sweep of bodies swallowed him up.

Nothing now was left but igniting the brush. Who was to do it?

Several men confronted Ralph Maynard. Would he start the fire? He refused. It was their place to burn their fetishes, he advised. As their teacher, it was his, the men maintained. For a half hour the stand-off continued, and it appeared that perhaps there would be no fire and Satan might, after such a promising overture, claim the victory.

Maynard then suggested that Ambenggwok, the valley chief, and himself together set fire to the huge stack of fetishes. This solution pleased everyone. As the people sat or squatted in anticipation, the chief walked forward, holding a bunch of dry grass. The missionary set fire to the grass and the chief, in turn, placed the burning grass under the firewood. In a very few minutes the pyre yielded to a blazing inferno.

But some of the people were not satisfied. As the fire burned, a group accosted Maynard, urging him to be responsible in terms of *his* "badnesses," which needed to be thrown into the fire alongside theirs. The two missionaries were at a loss to know just what the men had in mind. Thoughts then were stated frankly. Had they not seen Maynard purchase arrows to take to America? Were these not hidden in the rafters of his house?

"Oh, but I'm not going to use them to kill people," he quickly explained. "They are to show my friends in America what you folks here at Mulia do."

The Dani were not convinced. Those arrows had been used in war and were thus tainted with spirit power. They had burned theirs, why should he not burn his? Maynard pulled down his souvenirs and became one of the crowd by heaving them on the fire.

The blaze was at its height when one of the Dani leaders rose to his feet to give a cry of victory: "Witness this fire devouring our badnesses!" He pointed to the burning fetishes.

"Today is the day we embrace the 'living words'; today is the day we take to ourselves the words of eternal life. *Ninogoba wa!* Our Father, thank you!"

More than seven thousand voices joined in a mighty response of affirmation, which reverberated between the mountain walls. Then one by one the groups rose to their feet and without looking back, seemingly aware that now there could be no turning back, slowly and with absolute silence walked the paths to home.

There had been burnings in other areas. The first occurred in 1955 among a settlement of the Damal people, who were loosely related to the Dani, and a part of whom lived a two days' walk at the opposite end of a Dani valley. A maverick Roman Catholic teacher had urged these Damal to burn their fetishes and prepare for a millennium of peace and prosperity. They burned their fetishes, but the teacher was reprimanded by his superiors and the group was left alone with unfulfilled hopes. The following year missionaries of the Christian and Missionary Alliance arrived in Ilaga, the site of another community of Damal that had been infected with the millennial fever. They had entered a heavily primed atmosphere. They lived among the Damal for only seven months and were in the beginning phase of learning the local language and customs when an outside trading party dropped in. Among the visitors was a Christian named Widiabi who exhorted the Damal to follow Jesus Christ as his fellow tribesmen, the Ekagi, had done. It was impressive to hear a tribesman like themselves speak with such certainty about the things they cherished but which seemed so elusive.

Over the years, the Damal had tried on ten occasions to gain a taste of paradise, joining one messianic movement after another, but all proved illusive and merely the path to failure. What they were hearing now, however, seemed different. By the hundreds the Damal assembled to hear Widiabi speak, drinking in his new but intriguing message. Like the Dani, the Damal were people of group action. For several weeks they debated Widiabi's testimony, comparing his urgings to their own aspirations. Then one day they settled the matter. They would burn their fetishes and turn to Christ.

Word of the burning was carried by traders and travelers to other Damal concentrations and to tribes in other valleys. The Western Dani at Ilaga held a massive burning. Repeated often was the astounding message: "The people of Ilaga have traded their fetishes for immortality."

Destruction of spirit charms soon exploded into wildfire.

Like the old game of "Gossip," the message became distorted as it moved from valley to valley. Spellbinding speakers assured their hearers that death was now conquered, there would be instant wealth (didn't the missionaries' plane zoom in from heaven loaded with good things?), there would be no more sickness, black skins would turn white. But like the spirits of their old life, the God of Heaven must be appeased. Minor points of the message were twisted into major hallmarks. Many of those who burned their fetishes were still tied to them in their minds.

One self-ordained preacher went about proclaiming that salvation came through him; he had purchased it with pigs, thus it was his to confer. Others designated the clearing on a mountain top as the site of Christ's second coming. It was the preferred place to be baptized.

The Maynards and the Scovills at Mulia and other missionaries of their sponsoring organization, Unevangelized Fields Mission (UFM), saw danger in the rapid sweep of theological error that the burnings were bringing. Missionaries of several agencies reckoned that since the supposedly "true word" regarding immortality had come from the Ilaga Valley, correction could come only from Ilaga. Responding to their plea, two missionaries among the Western Dani and two Christians in that tribe, Butikabua and Yimbituk, set out on a tour that would last forty-six days and take them throughout the North Baliem valleys and over the mountain range to Kelila, Bokondini and Swart Valley. Their purpose was to separate truth from error.

The team stayed two days at Kelila, a UFM station where Leon and Lorraine Dillinger had taught the basics of Christianity and could only wonder whether the contagion that had reached their village was merely tribal hysteria. Perhaps the Dani were looking on the Gospel as the white man's legend, even though admittedly a better one than their own legends, just as at the beginning of the contact they had viewed white men as additions to their roster of spirits.

"Are you sure about the burning?" the Dillingers asked the leaders of the village. "This is a very big step. Don't you want to wait until we can teach you more, and then you can decide if you really want to make this decision?"

The people of Kelila made their decision. More than five thousand gathered to burn everything that had been dedicated to the worship of spirits. The Dani chiefs of Kelila lit the fire. At that moment, their bondage to the evil spirits was broken. Now they had freedom to follow God's path. The fire raged and, matching its intensity, the people ran en masse from one end of the airstrip to the other, shouting endlessly with ecstatic joy.

As the fire died down, the people swarmed with excitement to the large houses in the center of their villages where until today only men had been permitted to enter. Now, these dwellings were opened to women and children. With enthusiasm, the villagers filed in, milled about, reviewed what they had just done and talked about the words of eternal life.

On that clarifying expedition thousands of Dani heard the Gospel in its purity, and the burnings that followed in each location appeared to reflect a deliberate choosing of the Christian message over the old ties to animism.

At Mulia, where the burnings did not occur for yet another year, the missionaries there, too, were concerned lest people convert without counting the cost. They needed teaching if they were to understand the demands that faith would make of them. And not least, the missionaries' grasp of the Dani language was tenuous. How did one express the truths about God, salvation and commitment in the rudimentary nouns and verbs they were just now beginning to handle?

But finally the Dani couldn't wait any longer. They sensed the heat of cleansing fire blowing over their fetish piles. One day several Dani chiefs sat in a circle on the grass before Scovill's house. Their spokesman asked him and Maynard to sit with them. As they did, this leader pointed to the small bag of fetishes that hung from the shoulder of each man.

"My fathers," the spokesman said, "the things we do and worship are in direct opposition to the living words you give us from that big book. We as a people have made a decision to do away with our life of killing and worship of the spirits and to live the way that big book tells us to live."

That was the beginning.

More was said at other times. Still the missionaries were hesitant. They had been trained in one-on-one evangelism. Now a large part of a tribe — perhaps in all the valleys as many as one hundred thousand souls — was wanting to come to Christ . . . *now!*

"These are new and heavy words," Scovill said, much as the Dillingers had said at Kelila. "When you really comprehend their meaning, ridding yourselves of your weapons and fetishes will be fine, but not yet." Had not the Lord spoken of a house swept clean only to be infested with even more wicked spirits than had been there in the first place?

"Then don't bother any longer to teach us from the big book," replied the men, "because there is a veil over the eyes of our hearts. It does not allow us to take in any more truth."

Those in the circle explained that that veil was the things in their net bags they wanted to get rid of. They added that their implements of war would go, too.

For a different reason, the missionaries doubted the wisdom of their intentions. Some months earlier Scovill had pleaded with the group not to attack an enemy settlement two days' journey down the valley. They listened politely, but went ahead with their raid, returning from the fight with sick and wounded for the missionary's medicine to heal, but boasting that they had killed men, women and children and had forced some to jump to their deaths from a high cliff.

"What if your enemies down there hear that you have burned your bows and arrows and the fetishes that make your warriors so fierce in wars?" Scovill asked. "They will seize the opportunity to come up and return the attack. You will be powerless against them, fleeing like women out of your homes and sleeping like possums in the forest. Your villages will be burned, your pigs killed, your gardens ravaged and your women raped and killed."

"That is true," one replied solemnly. Fact was fact. What the missionary said could not be denied. Silence followed. The men drifted into smaller huddles to weigh the issue. They had no answer — but did they?

One of the chiefs turned from his group and confronted Scovill.

"*Tuan*, you have talked to us from that big book. If that Being up in the sky who made the world and who made us — if He can heal the sick, if He can cast out demons, if He can raise the dead and quiet the wind and the waves, can He not control our enemies so they will not attack us, or at best protect us if they do?"

What was there to say? Their logic had won the day. Word spread rapidly that the fetish burnings at Mulia were on. The valley began to prepare.

There was no stemming the tide. Some called the phenomenon a cultural explosion. Life certainly changed for the Dani. Intrigue, fear, warfare — all gave way to a peaceful pursuit of God's truth. For the missionaries, the mass turning was somewhat frightening — how could a handful of missionaries shoulder the responsibilities that now lay upon them? But they had learned from the experience. One reasoned that in Christ's earthly ministry He never turned people away because of their "impure" motives. He was willing to accept inquirers as they were and to lead them into deeper truth and purer motives — example, the Samaritan woman at the well.

Perhaps the Dani *had* counted the cost. Destroying their fetishes was without recourse. Some might create new ones, but these could not take the place of the old whose ghostly power evolved from age and tradition and the immersions in war and mystical experiences. Certainly the destruction of their weapons left them vulnerable — except now these people expected none less than God Himself to shield them.

Throughout the valleys of Dutch New Guinea two attitudes toward the burnings and turnings prevailed. One looked on the events as the experience of salvation. The other, among whose adherents were the UFM people, saw the wave of change as a step — perhaps a mighty first step — in the right direction. Each individual would have to believe, but the burnings had freed them up to believe. All were agreed that the people had lost their confidence in the old gods, so now were teachable. Teaching was the huge task before them all.

The outside world heard of the transformation taking place in the interior of the world's second largest island. It may have appeared that the decisions were headlong, perhaps even fickle. They were not. They did not come about suddenly.

The change wrought in the Dani, the Damal, the Ekagi and other tribes came through what missiologists term a "people movement." Such movements result from a core of people acting together in a "multi-individual" context. Never in modern church history had there been so large a people movement as the fetish burnings of the Western Dani.

For days on end — even weeks — tribal leaders met together to deal with the most minute implications inherent in changing their beliefs. The opinions and reasonings each person had to offer were important. But in the end it would be a group decision. They had always acted this way.

The missionary was in no position to cajole the leaders into accepting his teaching. His familiarity with the language limited him to the simplest of concepts. The elders would decide, based on the discussions, on their own thoughts and on the degree to which they knew people would follow them.

Not everyone at first favored the burning of their charms. Even those eager to burn still feared that the spirits would maim or kill them through sickness or war. But the talks went on until every angle had been probed and, at the end, unanimity was reached.

Even though the Dani at the western end of the Ilaga Valley were sure what they wanted to do, they held off their final decision until they conferred with their relatives in another valley. Only when their approval was won did they commit themselves.

Was there fruit now, or was that which had appeared only the promising blossom before the fruit? Writing some years later, David Scovill evaluated this marvel of Christian history as one who had participated in it and who for many years had assisted in the nurture, direction and oversight of the Dani mission.

"Was their experience real — that is, have they continued

in the faith?" he asked. "I must record my answer to be a resounding *yes*. It was real then, and its impact is obvious in the changes which have permeated the structures and daily life of the society, continuing even to this day."

And change there was. At Mulia, Kelila, Bokondini, Ilu and Wolo and at stations of other mission societies change came about not through admonition of the missionaries, who merely taught the Word of God, but as the principles of the Word began to settle in the lives of the people. Anything having to do with the old spirits was banished, including sacrifices, cutting off fingers, killing supposed witches, the magic in the long hair of men.

The old men who had cherished their long black locks now crowded Melba Maynard and the other missionary women, eager to have them cut off the offensive hair. No more sorcery by means of their hair — and, to their personal relief, no more haven for the lice that had been life-long companions.

Warfare ended. People were now able to travel about freely, and reconciliation between clans took place. Medicine was more readily accepted, and sanitation improved. Cremation of the dead continued — a health expedient, inasmuch as the rock under the soil prevented graves from being dug deep enough to escape the uprooting of bodies by the pigs. .

Having pointed to real change, Scovill went on to say, "Such change was not, nor is it yet, without its trauma, as the culture experiences and learns how to handle new influences that move into its life. But by and large, the momentum generated by this wave of change precipitated by the conversion experience has continued until now in a positive direction."

In their areas of work among the Dani, some mission agencies baptized the new believers immediately or shortly after the burnings. Unevangelized Fields Mission took the position that teaching was necessary first, and the convert's life had to reflect change as a result of that teaching before the administration of baptism.

Whether green or ripe fruit, or merely a blossom, the cause of the fragrance that quickly filled those New Guinea valleys was not produced without the seed having first been planted.

Tilling the ground and planting the seed started long before in Papua, the eastern half of the island that was divided between Australia and the Netherlands and today between Australia and Indonesia, the latter's west sector known as Irian Jaya. Papua's south shore lay just eighty miles from Australia's northern coast; it naturally was the more prone to colonization and outside influence. Early missionary activity concentrated there; in the Netherlands' territory only a few Dutch churches were established on the north coast and a scattering of Roman Catholic activity on the south.

The interior of Dutch New Guinea was first penetrated by mountain climbers in 1909. Other climbing expeditions followed occasionally, and in 1926 Dutch and American explorers ventured where outsiders had not gone before. The Dani had been discovered, but with contacts brief and interest in such people seemingly faint, they were all but forgotten by the civilized world.

The Dani did not forget, however. Their customs unchanged by these fleeting visits, they nevertheless were affected by them. The coming of outsiders prompted, or at least gave new meaning to, a legend that some day a white man would come to stay and bring with him some very important words for the Dani people. This man they called Bok. A giant, he was their creator. Some thought they had picked out his footprints in a rocky part of the mountains. Was Bok to be their next visitor?

In 1938, another explorer, accompanied by several scientists, established a base among the Dani. The group stayed almost a year. Then they, too, left, and the Dani failed to hear the words they had hoped for. But the world heard, or rather, saw and read about, these "stone-age" people, some of whom

14

were headhunters and others cannibals. An article in *The National Geographic* presented "Unknown New Guinea" to readers everywhere.

The world took note that a large primitive population existed in the interior of New Guinea, and Christians became concerned that they were people without a knowledge of Jesus Christ.

The Dutch might have turned inland in an attempt to evangelize these people except at that time the meager work that had been conducted along the coast for a hundred years suddenly sprang to life. It was all the church could do to minister to the thousands of coastal dwellers who flocked to their churches to learn that Jesus Christ was their sole hope of salvation.

In neighboring Papua, missions were going full tilt. The Australian branch of Unevangelized Fields Mission had in 1931 sent Albert Drysdale as its first missionary across the Torres Straits to the Fly River in Papua. It was the area where thirty years before James Chalmers, the renowned Scottish missionary to the South Sea Islands, his young colleague, Oliver Tomkins, and twelve Papuan Christians were clubbed to death and their bodies cooked and eaten by their killers. Operating from a base that had miraculously come into possession of the mission, Drysdale and others who joined him later pushed up the Fly into areas that even then were populated by wild and dangerous men of the Gogodara tribe. They built schools and a hospital, but evangelizing was always their main effort. Response was good. Hundreds flocked to the simply-built churches that soon dotted the region, and pleas came from unchurched villages to not overlook them.

The Fly River in one stretch separated Papua from its Dutch neighbor. The UFM missionaries often peered across to the far bank and longed to extend their contact to the vast numbers they knew lived there in the darkness of demonism. The lost tribes of Dutch New Guinea lay heavily on the consciences of others as well, none more than Robert A. Jaffray of the Christian and Missionary Alliance. Jaffray had gone as a missionary to China in 1895, and in 1911 crossed the mountains into what today is known as Viet Nam to pioneer the great work of the C&MA there. In 1931 he reported to his home board that people in the interior of New Guinea were in need of the Gospel, and he began training men in the Dutch Indies for the task of taking it to them. Seven years later he traveled to New Guinea to confer with Dutch officials about opening mission work among the Ekagi people around the Wissel Lakes. China, French Indo-China, Borneo, Java, Sumatra, the Celebes, and now New Guinea — each was a part of his vision. The C&MA opened a station at the lakes, but it, like the Australian UFM work on the Fly and other mission efforts, was closed by the outbreak of World War II.

United States airmen flying out of Hollandia on the north coast rediscovered the interior of this great island. War correspondents aboard their planes dispatched stories about the Baliem Valley below them. They called it Shangri-La. Soon military personnel made low-level flights over the valley a favorite Sunday afternoon recreation. They wanted to peer down at the strange, naked but highly decorated people — "God's forgotten people," they called them — their villages of closely compacted thatch houses and their neat gardens drained by a grid of canals. At flight's end, they could boast membership in the "Shangri-La Society."

One day a sightseeing C-47 plane carrying twenty-four persons crashed in a pass of the Oranje Mountains, killing all on board except a WAC and two GI's. Nearby Dani who had often seen such planes overhead and thought them strange birds of the spiritual world, converged on the crash site, hoping they'd find steel for knives and axes, a precious commodity the visitors of other days had left with them. They found mangled bodies, fearfully reminding them of death. But discovery of three survivors led them to overcome their fears. With sympathy, they

16

built a fire to warm the injured, built them a shelter and made frequent trips to supply them with food.

More than two weeks went by before the Americans could rescue their own, first having to parachute men to build a strip on a mountain top where a glider could land and in the evacuation be snatched by a C-47 tow plane. Dina Reimeyer might have died on that flight, but at the last minute gave up her seat to another WAC. Hearing of the kindness the tribespeople had shown her replacement, she wanted to meet them, hoping she could one day when the war was over. She did return — with her UFM missionary husband David Cole. They started the work on the Iluwaggwi River, just over the divide that separated them from North Baliem Valley — Shangri-La.

After the war, the Dutch opened their colony to missions. The Christian and Missionary Alliance station in the lakes area was reclaimed by men who had been challenged by Jaffray before he died in a Japanese prison camp. They pressed into Dani territory. The Australian UFM entered the interior from the north coast. The Evangelical Alliance Mission settled in the Bird's Head, the western-most part of the island. The Australian Baptists and the Regions Beyond Missionary Union selected other areas. With an estimated half million tribespeople living in the interior, there was ample work for everyone.

Robert Story, who after sapping his health as a missionary in Brazil's jungles had returned home to become general secretary of Australian UFM, received an invitation from the United Dutch Missions to enter the untapped areas of Dutch New Guinea. He and Fred Dawson, a recent graduate of Perth Bible Institute, set out in 1950 on a survey of possible work sites, going with the chiding of a Dutch official ringing in their ears — the interior was too dangerous for a white person to live in, they'd enjoy no government protection there and, besides, there was no way to get to it. By air the two men got a picture of the broad landscape. By hard walking through dense rain forests, Dawson, along with his bride of three months, arrived at the spot they believed suitable for a base station.

Sengge was fifty miles into the interior, but a long way from the Dani, who were the objective in UFM's plans. The struggle to get that far convinced Dawson that air transport was the only method to achieve their objective. Mission Aviation Fellowship, which had been assisting UFM missionaries in Papua, agreed to provide service.

But first, landing strips had to be cleared from the thick-set forests. Overland treks were the only way to reach the potential sites and hard hand labor the only method to clear the ground for air transport. To this end, Dawson, Hans Veldhuis and Russell Bond, accompanied by carriers who were converts of the UFM mission at Sengge, cut their way through rain forests, crossed swift-flowing rivers on flimsy rope bridges, endured the threats of suspicious tribal warriors, staved off hunger, and in some thirty days arrived at an appropriate location for an airstrip.

Cutting a swath from the forest and leveling the land became the first task at every new mission station. Throughout the 1950's Christian witness spread to most of the Dani areas. Some twenty permanent stations by a half-dozen mission societies were opened. Obviously, some guidelines and strategies had to be worked out.

After much discussion, in which each agency adamantly protected its doctrinal stance and traditional values, comity was reached. Geographic areas were agreed on and remaining areas were left to any group having the personnel to open them.

When America read of its army's Shangri-La rescue, leaders of the North American branch of UFM assured the Australian UFM that they would come in if the Aussies started a work in Dutch New Guinea.

"Once you begin," Edwin Pudney replied to a query from the Australians, "We'll provide workers to help." In reality, his statement was restrained. Pudney was eager for North America to get involved.

The pledge was fulfilled in 1958 as the first three UFM

missionaries from the United States joined one from Australia in walking four days from the nearest airstrip into Mulia's valley. Ralph Maynard, David Cole, Leon Dillinger and Bert Power, the Aussie and only veteran missionary among them, opened the work there. Some went on to pioneer other locations and soon another American, David Scovill, became a member of the team.

Just who were these Dani?

The largest of New Guinea's tribes, they numbered some two hundred twenty-five thousand, and were split among Western Dani, the most numerous, and those in the lower Baliem Valley. The steep, almost impenetrable mountains isolated the Western Dani from civilization, and even sub-tribal groupings were in large part cut off from relatives over the ridge. A walk of a day or two marked the limits of each colony's world.

Missionaries who came to know them intimately describe the Dani they first met as aggressive, curious, daring, arrogant, independent — and loving the spotlight. They were not to be intimidated by their neighbors nor by the outside world as it gradually moved in. Their attitude toward the missionary was fashioned by the benefit they believed he could give them. They were black and well-built, their bodies often smeared with pig grease and soot. Naked except for a gourd or grass skirt that hid their genitals, they compensated for clothing by painting themselves in bright colors and hanging strings of cowrie shells around their necks, the shells a type of bank account. The men dangled a small net bag from the shoulder, and in it carried tobacco, needles made from the leg bone of a bird and other small items. The woman's carrying bag, fit for a child or potatoes, was worn on the back, suspended from a head strap. The men, especially in times of war or spirit ritual, stuffed pig tusks in the pierced cartilege of their noses, and it was a man's pride to remove the mesh net from his head and let his long, matted black hair hang to his waist.

In times of grief, such as at the death of a relative, ears were clipped and fingers of a child cut off at the second joint, these measures calculated to appease the offending spirit and delay its return. Warfare seemed to be the Dani religion, dominating life until it was time to stop and plant their potato crop. War could start because a man in a neighboring village stole someone's wife or pig — which, it mattered little. At some point long-range shooting of arrows and throwing of spears gave way to hand-to-hand combat. These duels often appeared to be a ritualistic dance, but they were a deadly dance. In their wake were strewn many wounded and dead. The dead were cremated, except for enemy dead. More common among the Eastern than Western Dani, the victors would carry a fallen enemy off the field of battle and in sight of the vanquished stomp on the body and, to show the utmost contempt, cut it up, roast and eat it.

The outcome of a battle always left the score uneven. Eventually, revenge would renew the fight. But temporarily peace was regained through a reparations feast. Stone axes and pigs and highly prized special stones representing debt were paid over by the losers. For this truce, the warriors donned flamboyant headdresses of bird-of-paradise plumes and danced long into the night.

Attempting to appease the spirits that ruled them was their way of life. They had never known a good spirit, and all their striving was aimed at persuading the spirits to be a little less venomous. The people practiced magic, honored taboos and governed their thoughts and hopes with tribal legends. They huddled nightly in their round houses whose sides were wood slats shaped by stone axes and whose roofs were thatch. Seeking shelter from the cold, and from stalking marauders and the ever-present evil spirits, a family would repeat once more the folk tales that all knew so well. While the women turned the potatoes baking on the embers for supper, the children would ask of their fathers, "How did our ancestors come to be?

"From the bowels of the earth they came," the fathers would begin. "Ants bored a hole, and through it one followed another, all spilling out from the darkness into the sunlight. After them came the snake, making the hole bigger. Then the Dani people scraped away the earth, enlarging the hole, and pushed their way through to the outside."

The people saw that the snake every so often slipped out of his dead skin to become a new and shining creature. Each time he shed his skin, he seemed to be able to put off death and renew his life again.

"He was immortal," the fathers said to their children. "He held the secret of eternal life and intended to pass the knowledge on to man."

A race, however, was staged one day, to see whether the snake or a bird could reach man first. The bird, possessing only the lighter weight of mortality, was the faster, and as victor touched man with its death. The defeated snake was thus unable to bestow on him his immortality.

Death brought weeping and wailing, cutting off fingers, pulling out men's hair and tossing it on the roof of the house, covering bodies with white clay. It also caused the mourners to curse bitterly a common, little bird, the *pirigoobit*. Seeming to know where death had struck, this sparrow-like creature sat on the roof of the distressed house or on the pole that was driven into the ash of the funeral cremation, and there screamed at the living. It hurled a mocking reminder that they had lost eternal life. The ash before them was a mute confirmation of that fact.

The white men who entered Dani land — the transient explorers and later the missionaries who settled among them — were relevant to their legends. From them they would obtain an improved strain of pig, steel for their weapons, medicine, especially penicillin for yaws. One man even attributed his victory in war to his association with the "ghostly" outsiders.

21

But what produced awe and wonder was the belief that the missionaries' words were fulfillment of that prophecy that from the outside would come instructions for regaining their lost immortality.

Yet, acceptance of the message, and at times of the messenger, was in the beginning doubtful. At times the lives of the missionaries were endangered. At Wolo, Walter Turner, an Australian, took an arrow in the chest; it pierced a lung and hit perilously close to his heart. Others were at some time attacked, most lost property to thieves and all suffered numerous indignities. But perseverance paid off in the wide-spread burning of fetishes and the turning of thousands to the Gospel.

The day after the Dani at Mulia burned their spirit charms, several men returned to the airstrip, dug a hole where the fire had raged and buried the ash, putting it forever out of sight. Within a few days one of the men planted a tree there, saying in words of dedication, "May you confirm our decision by growing, spreading your branches, and providing shade and shelter for those that come and sit under you."

The tree grew, resisting natural impacts that might have killed it. Symbolizing the rooting and growing of the Gospel in the land, it stood twenty-three years. Only after it had grown so large as to jeopardize airstrip safety was it removed.

There were later burnings, somewhat along the lines of a clean-up. At Bokondini, the Dani not only destroyed the weapons of war that had escaped the first burning, but threw in their ceremonial stones that had functioned in weddings and cremations and served as blood payments for debts. For the first time they broke an ancient taboo that decreed sickness or other retaliation by the spirits if one spoke aloud the name of his in-laws. Now that they no longer feared the power of the spirits, they confessed the names of the ancestral demons to which from time to time they had sacrificed a pig, and by so doing had inherited the demons' power.

A number of writers who explored the phenomenon of Dani

conversion, several of whom were present and participants, emphasized that it was the Holy Spirit who, as David Scovill wrote, fused all the elements present in the action: The personality of the Dani and his receptivity of change, the desire for material wealth, a philosophy of life that raised within him a longing after eternal life and disillusionment with the old, futile ways of obtaining it, the coming of the missionary and the prayer of Christians throughout the world. Douglas Hayward, referring to the mass turning, pointed to "the timely arrival of a band of missionaries, uniquely prepared to accept and to encourage and to direct the movement as a movement toward Christ."

The work was accomplished by a large number of missionaries representing some half-dozen mission organizations. The Australian and North American missionaries of the Unevangelized Fields Mission were among them.

It took the presence of women and children as well as missionary men to break the old mode of Dani life. Before they became Christians, Dani men held their women in little respect, and love was scarcely known. Yet they developed a certain reverence for the missionary wives. One day Melba Maynard fell ill and this upset many of the people.

"Not Mommie!" cried one of the chiefs in anguish. (Some of those who called her "Mommie" were old enough to be her father.) "Our women get sick, but it shouldn't happen to *your* wives."

The personal interest the missionary women took in the Dani, along with their patience and perseverance, filled in the cracks often left by their more aggressive, task-oriented husbands. By their practice as well as their words, the women taught the Dani much about the attributes of God and the qualities He wanted to see in His people.

The children, too, contributed to the conversion of the Dani. They simply filled the universal role of children by just being children.

SOURCES, Chapter 1

Dani Legends, Unpublished manuscript, edited by David Scovill, translated by Douglas Hayward

Dillinger, Leon and Lorraine, *Experiences of Leon and Lorraine Dillinger in Dutch New   Guinea / Irian Jaya*, unpublished paper, undated

_____, Notes on early draft, 1966

Hayward, Douglas, *The Dani of Irian Jaya Before and After Conversion*, 1980, Sentani, Irian Jaya, Indonesia, Regions Press

Hitt, Russell T., *Cannibal Valley*, 1962, New York, Harper & Row

Hively, James, Audio Tape, 1995, comments to author

_____, Notes on early draft, 1966

Horne, Shirley, *An Hour to the Stone Age*, 1973, Chicago, Moody Press

Huff, Grace, *Danis Round My Door*, Unpublished manuscript

Light & Life, UFM Periodical, London, England, February-March, 1932; November, 1940

Light & Life, UFM Periodical, Melbourne, Australia, September-October, 1940

Papua's New Day, Pamphlet, Unevangelised Fields Mission-Australia, no date

Maynard, Ralph and Melba, 1996, Notes on early draft

Scovill, David L., Thesis, *The Dani World View*, 1984, Columbia, South Carolina, Columbia Graduate School of Bible and Missions

Steiger, E. Janet, *Wings Over Shangri La*, 1995, Self-Published

2

Beginnings in Brazil

Perhaps on only one other field in which UFM works has there been the proportionate turning to the Lord equaling that of the Dani in Irian Jaya — the Wai Wai Indians of South America, though their numbers fall far short of the Dani. Most other efforts have by comparison been uphill plodding, calling for unbridled faith and steadfast faithfulness.

Brazil's is among them.

Brazil is larger than the forty-eight contiguous US states, and has a population today of nearly 150 million. For four hundred years until modern times it was a citadel of Catholicism, breached only by a current of secularism and, among the Indians of the vast equatorial forest, the spirit worship of animism.

Protestant missionaries were at work in Northeast Brazil — in the region of the gigantic mouth of the Amazon River — before there was a UFM. In 1924, the London-based Worldwide Evangelization Crusade (WEC) sent four missionaries to the state of Maranhão, and the work was incorporated as the Heart of Amazonia Mission. The going was hard and rewards were seemingly few. While these trail-blazers went where others had not gone — up the coastal rivers and tributaries of the Amazon — Protestant Christians had entered Brazil before them, taking the Gospel to other parts of the largest and most complex country of South America.

The French Huguenots, those beleaguered Protestants of the Sixteenth and Seventeenth Centuries, first attempted a bridgehead in 1555 when three hundred of their number settled where now is the city of Rio de Janeiro. They might have succeeded in planting a Protestant colony that possibly would have given the country an evangelical foundation, but for the fact that their leader, Admiral Villegagnon, revealed himself to be a Roman Catholic and, turning on his Protestant friends, began persecuting them. The settlers either returned to Europe in unseawothy vessels and on the way nearly died of starvation, or escaped to the wilderness. The last of those who fled inland was captured and executed in 1567.

A second attempt by the French followed in 1594, but it too was snuffed out. The Dutch fared scarcely better, their foothold on the Brazilian coast lasting from 1624 to 1654. Hostility toward evangelicalism continued, propelled mainly by the Jesuits, though the government and much of society moved rather steadily away from ecclesiastical dictate. Immigrants came from many European nations and they were allowed their churches, but for the most part non-Catholic faith and practice were confined to the isolation of an enclave. This, however, began to change with the arrival in 1837 of an agent of the American Bible Society. He and later representatives distributed the Bible throughout the settled areas of Brazil. They found the Brazilians eager to buy and read the Word of God. Outside of heaven, who knows how much their labor softened the earth for the seed that was later sown?

The first permanent Gospel work in Brazil is attributed to a Scottish physician. Dr. Robert Kalley, who along with Mrs. Kalley, arrived in Rio de Janeiro in 1855. Despite harassment by clerics and sometimes local authorities, he worked steadily to win souls to Christ. One historian described his mission as "clandestine, something of a Protestant underground." This approach was no doubt an effort to avoid the harsh persecutions his converts had received in Madeira, his first mission field.

Believers he had brought from Madeira worked wherever they could find employment, and while on the job quietly sounded out their fellow workmen. Finding one open to the Gospel, they would instruct him, and in time invite him to their worship service, which resembled more a circle drawn up for family devotions.

Kalley baptized his first convert in 1857, and a year later organized a congregation with 14 members, a church that continued into the present day.

Colporteurs sent out by Dr. Kalley carried the Gospel to the Portuguese speakers of Northeast Brazil. But it was the people who lived beyond the fledgling towns, out under the endless green canopy of the mysterious forest, that caused the blood of a few intrepid men to race through their veins. Here were souls — how many, one could only guess — whom no one had yet approached with God's message of salvation.

One such pioneer was Fenton Hall, an Englishman who as a new WEC missionary in 1924 quickly plunged into the region of the Guajajara Indians on the Pindare River. Barefoot and stripped to the waist, battling inhuman heat as well as dangers of the jungle, he tirelessly tramped the trails, waded streams and slogged through mud past his knees, sparing neither health nor safety in his urgent effort to tell the Indians of Jesus Christ. After only five months he was stricken with disease common to the area and died on Christmas Day. He was buried in a lonely Indian village deep in the forest.

Ernest Wootten was another groundbreaker. He arrived at São Luis, capital of the State of Maranhão, in 1909, and with a small band of missionaries formed the Maranhão Christian Mission. The work centered on the small city and its suburbs. Wootten opened a school, beginning with one little fellow. Soon there were five boys, then in a short time a room full of both boys and girls. He sought help in teaching them, and one of the volunteers who arrived became his wife.

He was a tireless worker, carrying on the school, gathering

children for Sunday school, distributing tracts and Gospel portions house-to-house and in the prison. After six years he felt God's urging to move inland. In stages he moved deeper into the remote regions until reaching the Tocantins River. There for another six years he did what he had done in town, colportage work house-to-house, teaching school, visiting distant settlements, always assisted by Ninoca, his wife. Then help came from England and the Woottens were able to push deeper into Indian territory. They settled on the Araguaia River, a major tributary of the Tocantins. There they came in contact with the Kayapo people.

The Kayapo at this location were a branch of a large tribe and, unlike their relatives somewhere in the surrounding jungle, were somewhat domesticated. The Indians were friendly, but the malaria the Woottens came down with was not, neither were missionary friars in the region nor the floods that submerged their house.

UFM, which had been formed out of WEC, gained information on the kinsmen of Wootten's Kayapo. The mission began praying particularly for this wild and ferocious band. Years before, these Kayapo had met the fringes of civilization and turned their backs to it, choosing to roam the forest and pit themselves against man, beast and the spirits that plagued them. Eventually ecclesiastical and political pressure forced Ernest and Ninoca from their home on the Araguaia, and it was then that the mission asked him to look for the warrior tribe. They were somewhere in the upper reaches of the Xingu River, a thousand-mile tributary of the Amazon. For five days he rode muleback through jungle and sun-baked open country from the Araguaia to the Fresco, an affluent of the Xingu. He reached Novo Horizonte, a once thriving rubber center, but with the price of rubber having fallen, now a lonely desert.

The Kayapo he sought were known as the People of the Big Lips. Horace Banner, who later was to spend his adult life among them, recorded this observation on his first encounter: "Each man had inserted into the flesh of the lower lip a disc of wood as much as two and one-half inches in diameter. The original perforation must be made in early years, the hole being gradually stretched by the substitution of one disc by a larger one. One can only conclude that this practise is calculated to strike fear into an enemy. Both speech and eating are severely hampered and drinking, in the normal manner, is quite impossible. The warrior must either pour the water straight down his throat or, using both hands as a scoop, throw it into his mouth and retain as much of it as he can. Some of the men were just able to close their mouths by bringing the disc right up to the nose, but others were unable to control it and it hung, a pendulous rim of red flesh down over the chin."

Hideous as it was to see these disfigured warriors lounging about, it was horrifying to witness them in frenzied attack. Their lips clapped to accentuate the curdling screams they hurled against the enemy. Their long hair flowed and their naked bodies glistened with the black paint that covered them from head to toe. The Kayapo were expert with bow and arrow, club, wooden sword and bone-tipped lance.

The few residents of Novo Horizonte lived in constant fear. An invisible line of demarcation purportedly separated Indians from *civilizados*, but often the Kayapo crossed this imaginary line and killed village residents. The Brazilians described for Wooten the raids on their homes by the Big Lips. Day or night, the Indians would attack, burning houses and carrying off their contents. Men returned from their work in the rubber tracts to find their wives and children butchered, bodies impaled on lances and battered by the weapons that had been abandoned once these had accomplished their bloody tasks. Sometimes the women and young girls simply were not there; they had been carried off into the forest. It was in Kayapo thinking that all men different from themselves had come to kill them; so it was only prudent for them to kill first.

Wooten soon learned that the wildness of the Indians he

sought was equalled by the hatred the Brazilians had for them. Preach to Indians? How foolish! The red man was a wild beast without a soul. Only bullets would tame the Kayapo. Banding together, tracking down the murderers, shooting as many as their ammunition afforded — this was the rubber hunters' method of dealing with the Big Lips. On both sides, retaliation was the law of the region.

The missionary found no Kayapo on the Fresco, so continued his search, riding the river down to its junction with the Xingu itself. No one would help him seek out the Kayapo. After nine futile months, Wootten, weary and sick at heart for the darkness covering the region, headed back for the Araguaia and the domesticated branch of the tribe. He needed a rest.

But his heart never left the Xingu. After nine months he journeyed again through jungle and blistering plain to renew his quest. This time he was accompanied by a man and his wife from the tame Kayapo. One day they came across a group of Big Lip men. What promised to be a friendly encounter turned to tragedy. The woman was abducted, and the rest of Wootten's hopelessly outnumbered party had to flee for their lives. Still, the intrepid missionary pursued every lead that might produce another contact. But it was not to be. After sixteen months he was forced by ill health to leave the Xingu and return home.

It would be several years before Protestant missionaries again penetrated Big Lip territory. When they did they heard from the Brazilians the full story of Ernest Wootten's tireless efforts, and, as Horace Banner once wrote, "of his endless journeys, in small canoes without shelter from sun and rain; of his quiet courage in the face of unspeakable difficulties; of his cheerfulness in loneliness and long separation from his wife; of his contentment, even when, through lack of communications and mails, funds were exhausted, and even food was scarce; of imperturbable patience in the tribulation of bodily weakness, in sickness, and at times when mosquitoes and sandflies were so numerous as to be well-nigh unbearable."

This compassionate man, who never spoke unkindly of anyone, was known as "the walking saint."

Whoever Wootten was with became an object of missionary endeavor. He distributed and explained the Scriptures, reading to hardened rubber hunters at night by the light of a smoky kerosene lamp or the fire. He taught young people to read the Bible for themselves. His faithful, earnest demeanor overcame much of the prejudice and suspicion which opponents of the Gospel had spread against the Protestants, easing the way for those who were to follow.

Perhaps one of his greatest contributions to the eventual evangelization of the Big Lips was his lexicon of the Kayapo language. Years later it would prove invaluable to those who took up his cause, those who left the tranquil Kayapo on the Araguaia for their unpredictable kin on the Xingu.

Wootten composed a number of hymns and choruses in the Indian language. His health finally broken, a leg crippled by an ulcer, but still a man strong in spirit, he was all but ordered home by mission headquarters. After more than twenty years without a furlough, he went, leaving, of necessity, the work he loved to others.

New missionaries arrived in Brazil. Some took up the evangelizing of domesticated settlements along the Amazon and its lower tributaries, as well as inland areas reached by other rivers in Northeast Brazil. There they started churches and opened schools. Opportunities for ministry appeared limitless in this developing region. Discussions arose regarding UFM's objective in Brazil — should it be only the native Indians, the original target or should there be a double drive, reaching out to the civilized Brazilian as well as the Indian?

The issue traveled to London, and there it almost tore apart a conference called to set future policy and procedure.

The Indians were dying out, one side said, and if the Mission restricted its activities to only Indians, eventually the work would also die. And was not the need of the interior Brazilian just as desperate as the red man's? In getting to the Indians, how dare they stumble past the Brazilians and ignore their souls? Many mission societies, came the counter argument, had been diverted from their goal of winning South American Indians by the more responsive fields among the Brazilians. They had abandoned the lost sheep in the remote fever-laden areas. Was this to be true of Unevangelized Fields Mission?

Consensus was reached. The Brazilian work would continue, but the vision of salvation for the Indians should never be allowed to dim and every effort would be made to win them to Christ before their tribes died out. A few years later, reporting to the Home Council in London, Leonard Harris, who some day would lead the mission, remarked on the unity that prevailed at the Brazil field council meeting in Belém. Gone was the controversy over priorities; he, however, was concerned over outside criticism which said that the mission's efforts might better be directed to more populous continents.

"Some have criticised and spoken of the limited character of their vision (the missionaries in Brazil)," he wrote, "but to do that is to find fault with the Giver of the vision. It is true that the missionaries in Brazil are dealing with but a few as compared with the millions of Asia, and that they have none of the cheer of seeing mass movements towards Christ, yet they have the assurance that 'every creature' includes the vanishing Indians and the dwellers in the widely scattered Brazilian villages. Their God-given vision may not be blotted out by the multiplication table . . . "

The world would focus on Brazil — on Indians who were not so much dying themselves as bringing death on other people. And focus, too, on the missionaries who followed in Ernest Wootten's footsteps in trying to reach that killer tribe for Jesus Christ. Three men, each bearing the name Fred, would provide another stepping stone — a very large rock — in taking the

Gospel to the Kayapo. Their thrust into the jungle to find the blood-thirsty Kayapo would be UFM's first deliberate effort to pacify a people. The plan held risks, but those who would carry it out had, from the first day they signed on to a missionary career, counted on risking their lives for the sake of the Gospel.

Fred Roberts and Fred Dawson (not the Fred Dawson of New Guinea) were from Australia, Fred Wright from Ireland. Two Aussies and an Irishman, wrote Fred Wright in a letter, "a strange combination. Still, without the Lord even such a combination is doomed to failure, so I correct myself — we are four."

Dawson and Wright were newcomers to Brazil, Wright having completed his study of Portuguese and Dawson half-way through his. Fred Roberts had spent ten years among Indians. Roberts' first venture came in 1926 when, accompanied by Pat Symes and George Sharp, he cut through the territory of the hostile Timberas tribe to Sapucaia, a village of the peaceful but indifferent Guajajara Indians in the upper reaches of the Pindare River. It was there that his hero Fenton Hall was buried. From Sapucaia and Bacuri, its neighbor, the three men made sortie after sortie to discover villages, some of them populated only by Indians, some having Brazilian rubber hunters or traders living among them. Everywhere they went, the missionaries preached, speaking Portuguese and as much of the tribal language as at the time they had learned. They started schools. They took a census of Indians.

Sharp became desperately ill and to save his life was sent home to Australia. Roberts went out to the coastal city of São Luis in 1928 and there married Mabel Green. He brought her back to the jungle where she worked faithfully alongside him. In six months she died, and her grave was dug next to that of Fenton Hall.

Prophetic of his own future, Fred Roberts replied to the question asked by Joe Glenn, a fellow missionary who had joined him at Mabel's grave, "Fred, do you think it is worth it?" Fred said, "Joe, if ever God should give you the task of laying me to rest beside her, I should still count it well worth while. True, it does not seem that we have accomplished much as yet, but I believe that God will give us fruit from these lives laid down."

By his own service and stirring letters, J. C. Wright prompted much of the vision that sent his younger brother, Fred, to serve God among Amazon Indians. Fred arrived in Brazil teeming with Irish humor, saying with a twinkle that when he might be found wrong, he would always be Wright. He possessed the energy of a rough and ready rugby player, swimmer and boxer. Ever the enthusiast, he seemed to know no fear. Scarcely any man could have been more fit for the work of a pioneer missionary than Fred Wright. Soon after arrival, he won his first soul in his adopted land to Christ.

Fred Dawson was born in Tasmania and orphaned while quite young. His future lay in farming — until God laid on his heart a burden for the Indians of South America. He had grown to be a huge fellow and powerfully strong, but was gentle, humble and had a childlike faith. Like Fred Roberts, he had been influenced by Fenton Hall's brief but intensive work. Walking on a Sunday afternoon with another missionary, Dawson was reminded that advancing the Gospel to the Xingu would be a life or death job.

If the Lord ordained, he was willing, he replied, to lay down his life for Christ and the Indians.

Fred Roberts had done the preparatory work for the upcoming venture of the three Freds. After years of work on the Pindare and Gurupi Rivers and in the rugged land between them, he put off going home on furlough until he could reconnoitre the situation on the Rio Xingu. With Joe Wright, he made the trip to Nova Olinda, and from there the two paddled up the Riozinho, setting out from the rubber town where the "Little River" emptied into the larger Xingu. The Riozinho, they determined, was the heartland of the Big Lips, and though they encountered none, Fred went home to Australia, promising God that his second term would be given to the evangelization of the wild Kayapo.

To this end he had spied out the land, assembled all available data, made plans, and scoured his native country for people of God who would prayerfully intercede for the commission he so strongly felt God had entrusted to him. While at home he was asked to visit UFM's work in Papua. Eager to return to Brazil, he found a substitute. Spending several months in New Guinea no doubt would have been profitable, but Roberts looked with suspicion on anything that would delay his mission to the Kayapo.

In the Spring of 1935, the three Freds joined for the venture. They were alike not only in name but in devotion to their Savior. Eager, courageous, selfless, they were of one mind — to take the Good News of God to yet another people among earth's many tribes. Nothing seemed lacking in their preparation, their baggage even contained six sheets of galvanized iron, a supply of rivets and some strong tincutters — for the making of steel shirts. What the three felt more reliable than man's armor was the promise that the prayers of God's people both in Brazil and in their home countries would cover them.

Fred Roberts had been back in Brazil only four days when their fellow missionaries bade the trio farewell. River steamers transported them up the Amazon to the Xingu and a hundred miles up that great tributary. From Altamira a launch took them past numerous rapids far upstream to the village of São Felix. There they bought the only available boat, enlarged it and set in the motor they had brought along. Each evening they held a Gospel service, and with medicines treated some two hundred sick people. Finding their revamped craft entirely reliable and their motor equal to whirlpools and rapids, they reached Nova Olinda on May 16. This settlement on the Fresco opposite the mouth of the Riozinho was to be their base. They were well equipped and needed only to pick up interpreters, rowers and carriers to start their trip further inland. But the residents of the little settlement gave them the same puzzled look they had given Ernest Wootten years before. What motivated these Britishers to make these repeated, persistent, yet fruitless attempts to contact a tribe of wild and bellicose Indians?

In recent months the Kayapo had murdered four Brazilians, one felled by a bullet. Arrows and clubs could certainly fly again. (The mosquitoes and sand flies surely would.) The rapids on the Riozinho might be too swift for their motor. One cataract certainly would be unconquerable — to get around it, they'd have to drag their boat and its load overland for nearly a mile. And in this dangerous area, if they took no guns, how would they defend themselves? Neither did they wear their iron shirts. They had given up the idea of making them — too cumbersome and probably ineffective.

Each of the Freds dispatched letters before shoving off.

Fred Roberts wrote: "Maybe you will not hear from us again for some time, but keep on praying. Stand behind us as fellow-soldiers in the Lord's battle to win these Indians for Christ. Pray harder, brethren, not only that God will work out here, but that He will also move those at home to do their share in the work. If we are going to reap together, we must sow together."

Fred Dawson said in his letter, "The assurance of the call of God to this land is strong indeed. I have never doubted my call, but now I am more fully persuaded that the call of God is a rock on which to cast my anchor. Whatever the future may hold of disappointments, I will remain with the conviction that God brought us here, is responsible for me, and will keep me all the days."

In his letter, Fred Wright concluded, "As far as we can ascertain, the Kayapo are very numerous. We are quite aware that, humanly speaking, we are as good as dead men, but brethren, stand by us as one man. Do not criticize. We are beyond criticism as we go forward in the Name of the Lord and under His command, after having fully counted the cost. Finally, it is well to remember that Calvary was and is the greatest victory of all times. Death to the Christian is not defeat. Should the Lord will that we be taken, our prayer is that more men and more money be rushed out to follow up this advance . . . I should like to say that the day we set out I received a letter from my mother, who was then quite unaware of our proposed advance. She sent me the command and promise contained in Joshua 1:11, 'Go in to possess the land which the Lord your God giveth you to possess it.'"

The trio had decided on an exploratory run up the Riozinho in hope of making a first contact with the Kayapo. Their baggage light and their motor boat quite capable, they had no need for crew, so cast off the mooring line and their last ties binding them to home, friends, fellow workers and the curious. In their letters they had said not to expect further word from them for six months. After a wait of nearly twelve months, the long-expected letters never came. No news filtered out of the jungle. The three Freds had been seen chugging up the Riozinho. They had not returned.

SOURCES, Chapter 2

Banner, Horace, *The Three Freds and After!*, 1975, London, Unevangelized Fields Mission

Cunningham, Rosemary, 1996, Notes on early draft

Davies, Rowland, *Highlights of the Religious History of Brazil*, 1959, Unpublished manuscript

Harris, Leonard F., *Our Days in His Hands*, Undated, London, Unevangelized Fields Mission

Hough, Florence, Letter to author, 1996

Light & Life, UFM Periodical, London, June-July, 1932; January-February, 1933; March, 1934;   June, 1935; October, 1935; March-April, 1955

Poultney, S. V. (Editor), *Battle for the Big Lips*, 1965, London, Unevangelized Fields Mission

Pudney, Edwin J. and Lilian G., *Miracles Multiplied*, Undated, Unpublished manuscript

_____ , *Sacrifice of Praise*, Undated, Booklet

Roberts, Fred, Unpublished manuscript, c. 1927

Stoner, Charles G., *Indians, Institutions and Churches*, 1987, Unpublished manuscript

3

Kinso and the Congo

As a new first-term missionary, Herbert Jenkinson walked into Congo. Not long out of the trenches of the First World War, this young Englishman would have walked and swum from his home in Surrey, if need be, to get to the mission field. He and his two companions, fellow neophyte missionaries, had steamed up the Nile River to Rejaf in Sudan, and from there motored over a mountainous road to the Congolese border town of Aba. To get from that point into the heart of the Belgian Congo — the heart of Africa — it was foot-slogging twenty miles a day through elephant grass and forest, wading through streams and marshlands, sleeping in vermin-infested huts when one was available and camping out when one was not.

Jenkinson attributed his call to the mission field to two influences in his life. As a youngster he joined the Boys' Brigade. This connection rescued him from bad companionship and challenged him to commit his heart and life to Jesus Christ, and often the Brigade Bible study dwelt on the lives of Carey, Morrison, Livingstone, Paton and other legendary pioneers, and their histories never failed to stir the boy. On that foundation came an encounter when he was sixteen with a famous English cricketer who had helped England retake the game's glory from Australia and who, beyond university, went on to become an even more famous missionary — C. T. Studd.

While training with a machine-gun regiment before going to war in France, Jenkinson felt duty to country called for his immediate full effort, but that the rest of his life was to be lived in service to God in Congo. One evening while strolling in the Surrey town of Pirbright, where he was stationed, he entered the village churchyard and there noticed an unusual headstone. Going over to examine it, he discovered with surprise the grave was that of Henry M. Stanley, the man who found David Livingstone and was the first white person to travel the length of the Congo River. Congo — even in His Majesty's forces he could not get away from it.

This solid conviction that God would someday send him to Congo steered him through many dismal and at times dangerous experiences in the trenches in Flanders. Men at his side were killed. He had no doubt God was sparing him for a future mission, and in the trenches was rehearsing him for life in Congo — hardening his body and banishing fear. Theological training followed the war's end, but when an invitation came to forego ordination and leave promptly for Congo, he did just that, casting off from England on February 23, 1920.

Shortly after the war's ending, many others sailed for the mission fields of the world, some, like Jenkinson, having heard God's call through Studd's challenge. George Kerrigan and Edwin Pudney were among those going to Belgian Congo. A born pioneer this Irishman, Kerrigan worked where the going was rough and the need was great. Not recognized like others as a leader, he nevertheless plowed his furrows deep. He soon came to know the African well. He understood the fear and resignation that dogged the people every day. For guidance of missionaries in animistic cultures he wrote a treatise on the *Mambera*, the particular cult of deadly witchcraft among the people he served.

Kerrigan was sent to the village of Bomili in 1924. At some time in early missions history, hundreds of people there had turned to the Lord, but the lack of workers denied them Biblical teaching, so Satan moved in and the people swung back to their old witchery, only a very few standing true in their Christian faith. Kerrigan found an empty mission station. He and others then tramped from village to village, proclaiming the Word once again. He discovered the tenets of *Mambera*, and helped the Christians to stand against its secret rites of maiming and murder.

The woman who was to become his wife reached Congo in 1926 and they were married two years later. Dora Kerrigan was just as faithful and hard-working as her husband. Another wife who with her husband made a forcible team was Lilian Pudney. In 1923 she and Edwin settled among the Babinga tribe, who not only killed their enemies in warfare, but in triumph roasted their bodies over a fire and ate them.

"Jenkinson" was too tongue-twisting for the Congolese, so he became Kinso, not only to them but to all who came to know him. Hardly had he checked in at mission headquarters deep in the jungle when he began teaching in the boys' school — an opportunity to learn the local language, he was told. Trekking village to village provided practice for his learning. But that was just a start. He later would describe mission work from his own experience:

"A well-balanced field programme is bound to include a range of activities. To go from village to village to sow the seed and reap a partial harvest is of limited use if not followed by a building-up work. Whatever else it entails, it demands that believers shall have the Word of God to read for themselves. Translation work is therefore necessary. Even if we have the Scriptures in a language people understand, that advantage is so much the poorer if they do not know how to read them. Hence the indispensability of schools. Further, Paul advised Timothy to commit the Word 'to faithful men who shall be able to teach others also.' So we must have Bible schools. All these things, like the plain proclamation of the Gospel itself, entails contact with people, and, not seldom, large groups of people. Some will be sick from time to time, so a beginning must be made with dispensary work. And that, once started, always grows. When we learn that our Lord went about the villages teaching, preaching and healing, we feel we have good precedent for all these activities, for they are all means of communicating the Gospel to people."

At times, Kinso accompanied C. T. Studd, or "Bwana" as the aging leader was known, on safari to unevangelized villages. At one place the elderly chief listened as the two missionaries explained the Gospel. After a long while he broke in:

"If all that you tell me is true about God loving us and sending his Son to this earth to save us, why didn't you come long ago to give us this news? I am now an old man and I find it hard to take in new ideas and to change my manner of life."

His rebuke produced no satisfactory answer, and he himself failed to accept the message.

On some of his trips Kinso courted the dangers of the jungle; once while traveling in a canoe barely escaping the jaws of a mammoth hippopotamus. He met tribal chiefs and slaves, strong warriors and lepers, one day a chief who was a leper and who, before the encounter ended, became a trusting child of God. In most areas large crowds turned out for his meetings; the people were eager to hear a message from God. If God was greater than the spirits of evil that possessed them, they wanted to hear more.

So ingrained was their dread of the spirits that even Christians found it not easy to shake off the old fears that once held them. One day a man who had confessed Christ approached Kinso quite distressed. He explained his dog had been bewitched and so would die. This deeply grieved him for the dog was a good hunter. Kinso reminded him that now he was a Christian he should know that the Lord was able to look after him.

"Oh, yes," the man said. "I believe in Jesus and know He can keep me from harm. But my dog — he is not a believer."

A few days later the dog died.

Polygamy caused much sorrow and suffering. A man's wealth was reckoned by the number of wives in his harem. The junior wives were veritable slaves, especially the girls who had been captured in raids of enemy tribes. One who turned to Christ was beaten and tortured maliciously by her husband, but accepted her punishment without a murmur. Eventually her life of faith bore deeply into his soul. One day he suddenly stopped thrashing her and declared she was the only wife he wanted. He began attending services with her and joined the inquirers' class. He became another among Congo's masses to emerge from darkness into light. The threats of a spreading government had some effect, but as the Gospel and its life-changing message penetrated further and further under the canopy of the vast forest, coming to rest right where people lived, the welfare of women dramatically improved. Faith was found where fear once ruled.

Early on, one of Kinso's assignments was to go to the Sudan border or, in the other direction, to Stanleyville at the cataracts of the Congo River, to meet new contingents of missionaries. This meant slow plodding along jungle trails, and where villages were happened on to preach and teach. In a matter of weeks he would arrive at his destination, only to reverse route and on the way to headquarters immerse his uninitiated party in the ways of the tropical forest. The new missionaries were indoctrinated by Kinso's stories. He himself had sat around many a night fire in the villages, absorbing history and customs as the tribal storytellers spun out their tales. In one group of newcomers was Miss Alice Renn, a nurse and midwife from Kinso's own Surrey in England. She was to become his bride, and thereafter would be known as Ma Kinso.

Kinso became Studd's right-hand man, his trouble-shooter, and Ma Kinso his housekeeper. Kinso even nursed the ailing Bwana back to health.

There were more treks for the couple, more evangelizing, more nurturing of new believers, more instances of miraculous intervention in the affairs of the Congolese, such as the time two tribal chiefs, once warring enemies, were baptized within a week in the sight of each other, a far different way to achieve peace between their clans than the offering in a prior day of a human sacrifice. Both Kinso and Ma Kinso treated ills they had never heard of and at times fell severely sick themselves. En route to Leopoldville, now Kinshasa, from where they were to go back to England for furlough, Kinso came down with blackwater fever and she with dengue fever. They began their furlough as patients in London's Hospital for Tropical Diseases.

A missionary's furlough is no cessation of doing the Lord's work. The Kinsos filled their time with engagements that acquainted the home churches with the Lord's advances in Congo. At a weekend of missionary meetings in Warrington they met a young man who, as a result of attending the sessions, heard God's call to dedicate his life for missionary service. He did not go to Congo, but to a field just as needy, Brazil. No one would be more identified with the evangelization of that country's Kayapo Indians than Horace Banner.

"Do you really want to go back to Congo?" the Kinsos were asked over and over the year they were home. But for both, the call to Congo had been strong enough to enable them to overlook the difficulties and dangers of the first term and to increase their determination to overcome any future trials. In September of 1926 they sailed again, accompanied by five women, all to serve under the recently renamed society, from Heart of Africa Mission to Worldwide Evangelization Crusade. WEC now extended its work into South America and Asia.

The last five days of the trek to headquarters in Congo wound through dense forest, and the traveling was exhausting. But that was physically enervating. What awaited at journey's end would be a mental and spiritual struggle that took its toll on the Kinsos and their colleagues. The authority of their venerable leader was now exercised in the erratic manner of a very sick man, which Studd was. Relief came for the Kinsos when they were moved to a station some distance away. They found on their plate a full menu of mission activity.

The new work was to bring them both joy and the learning of many lessons. In an "unopened" territory, meaning ungoverned by Belgium, they came under the jurisdiction of one of Congo's many autocratic chiefs. Unlike the despots of some areas who treated their people as personal slaves, imprisoning, torturing or killing at will, and standing firmly against the Gospel, Chief Misa provided the Kinsos with a house, encouraged the start of a school and permitted the preaching of the Gospel.

As for the house, this mud and stick structure was fully occupied when the Kinsos moved in — first by jiggers, then fleas and later four-inch millipedes. These worm-like creatures were everywhere, dropping from the rafters into their food, covering the floor, in every hole, of which this house had many.

"Our sympathies," wrote Kinso, "were with the Egyptians in Moses' day, but we persevered and eventually overcame all our plagues!"

The school attracted children from a wide area. That meant each day they had to be fed . But money was always short and the Kinsos were constantly thrown on the mercy of God. They marveled at the way He worked in their behalf.

People came for medical treatment. They both heard the Gospel and saw it in action. Sunday services became well established. Sometimes after church the people built a bonfire and in it burned their witchcraft charms and fetishes as a testimony to their faith in Christ. There were battles against witchcraft, which still prevailed in much of the village. Sometimes this was a race against the poisoning of a person, or if death was not the aim, to prevent the dropping of a certain tree sap into a cursed one's eyes, thereby causing blindness.

The experiences of the Kinsos were not altogether different from those of other WEC missionaries in Congo. The Edwin Pudneys, G. F. Buckley, D. V. Evening, the George Kerrigans, among others, endured trials, outlived dangers, prayed much, practiced faith and joyfully watched as fruit ripened on the trees of their labors. But a cloud hung over the sector of Congo which they were given to work in. Strange occurrences at Ibambi, C. T. Studd's headquarters, could hardly be allowed to continue without attention given to them. If their work was not to be disrupted and lost, what course of action should be taken? It was a problem that could no longer be ignored.

SOURCES, Chapter 3

Harris, Leonard F., *Our Days in His Hands*, undated, London, Unevangelized Fields Mission

Jenkinson, Herbert, undated, unpublished manuscript

_____, January, 1986, personal letter.

Larson, Alfred and Jean, 1996, interview

_____, 1966, Notes on early draft

4

How UFM Began

A group of respected Christian leaders in Africa, representative beyond the Worldwide Evangelization Crusade, visited C. T. Studd, but could do nothing to resolve either his personal problems or those between him and his mission staff. WEC's Home Council sent an emissary to Ibambi, but the conflicts abated none. Still contentious were Studd's dependency on morphine — the sedative of that day for killing pain — the shocking title of a booklet he had written and his arbitrary behavior toward his missionaries.

The Home Council became greatly concerned when dissension with the way the mission was going surfaced in Brazil as well as Congo. Studd dismissed the Council. Many missionaries resigned.

The Council members felt responsible for the welfare of those they had recruited, trained and dispatched to the field. These missionaries now were without an organization, without a home base and without a field in which to work. WEC and C. T. Studd, its founder and director, were seen by the Council members as one and the same. They felt they had no alternative to forming a new mission.

On June 29, 1931, the members concluded an historic resolution thus: "We resolve further that we set about forming at once an entirely independent Missionary Society, which shall continue the present activities of the Council in Amazonia and the other occupied areas, and by other extensions to be adopted."

Two home deputation secretaries and a dozen missionaries home on furlough — five from Brazil and seven from Congo — penned their allegiance to the Council's action.

The new mission took the name Unevangelized Fields Mission. It was the designation given by Dr. Thomas Cochrane, director of the Movement for World Evangelization and one who had attempted to arbitrate the disputes within WEC.

Less than three weeks later Studd died. The new mission, as well as Christians generally throughout England and much of the world, suspended business and laid aside judgments to pay tribute to the man who for almost a half century had been on a mission to the lost world. Abandoning his wealth and fame as an English sportsman, he became one of the Cambridge Seven, a group of young men who submerged themselves in the task of winning China to Christ. During his long career as a missionary to China, India and Congo, he inspired hundreds of young people to volunteer for service across the globe. In his prime, he truly had been a giant among the Lord's men.

Looking back on this period, Leonard Harris, both a missionary and an executive of UFM's British branch, wrote thirty years later, "The storm abated as both sides (WEC and UFM) were reminded of a Higher Court to be faced than man's limited one. The storm between the two societies never arose again. To the parent Society the separation gave the opportunity to develop along the lines they had wished, which God has honoured and blessed. To the new Mission it gave an equal opportunity of laying new foundations and rethinking methods and policies, which have equally been owned and blessed of God. The years have but deepened a respect for each other's work."

According to tradition, UFM at its beginning consisted of thirty-two former WEC missionaries, each with five to fifteen years of experience, and a small home staff. A 1931 list numbers thirty-six. A modest office was opened in a dwelling in the Upper Norwood section of London. Operations were on two fronts — a number of missionaries at work in Brazil and one couple in India's Kashmir. Two other fields were eagerly contemplated. The Australians were ready to send a man into Papua New Guinea. There were UFM missionaries in Congo, but as yet no place for them.

In a few days two UFM representatives, W. J. Roome and A. V. Thynne, returned from Africa with the news that the Baptist Missionary Society had turned over one of its stations to the new group. It was the start of UFM's work in Africa and promised to be the departure point for wherever God might lead on that great continent.

The territory that now was the mission's responsibility covered some sixty-thousand square miles and its half-million inhabitants were almost totally unevangelized. Its chief occupants were the Babari tribe. In the report brought back by Roome, a missionary who had visited the new ground said, "The Babari are a very lovable people and their affections are easily won. Unlike the tribes of the Nepoko district, who live apart in scattered hamlets, the Babari build large villages and live together in communities. Their villages are very similar to those in England, and consist of a long street with backyards and outhouses. The resthouse for Europeans is usually about midway up the village and during a stay you have the feeling that you are quite one of the community. On either side you hear the chatter of the women as they pound meal in their mortars or tend their cooking-pots, and appetising odours float in from time to time. In the village street kiddies romp about, or come to gaze with round eyes at the mysterious white man and his strange belongings. Goats and dogs are just as companionable as the natives, and one is kept busy evicting them from the living-room or kitchen. Altogether, one gathers the idea that the Babari are a very friendly and hospitable race.

"There is a keenness for the Gospel amongst them that is

not often found in Congo tribes, and as a rule every man, woman and child in the village turns out to the meeting, and they show a real interest in the messages. Often they will come and ask if it is now time for the service, as they are all anxious for it to begin. Unfortunately, they are not without their failings, and kindly and light-hearted as they usually are, they can on occasion manifest a very ugly spirit. One of the greatest curses of the Babari tribe is the *Mambera* witchcraft society."

Another missionary familiar with the Barbari predicted that "the *Mambera* cult will be one of the main enemies of the Gospel in these parts and we shall need special prayer."

This first station of UFM was at Boyulu, in the center of the tract ceded them. It was an old town, set on a trail once used regularly by slave traders. The missionary passing through Boyulu saw the town jail crowded not with slaves, but with Barbari who, it appeared, had manifested very ugly spirits. They were accused murderers.

While Congo was the direct cause of UFM's birth, Brazil figured largely in it. A few WEC missionaries there elected to stay with the old society and thus left the country. Most, however, shifted to UFM, and WEC handed over its operations to the new mission. The work continued without disruption. Leonard Harris published an account of a trek he and George Thomas made to the Guajajara Indians who lived around a town called Barra do Corda.

"The first night we slept in the town of Coroata," Harris wrote. "When I passed through the town in 1929 there was hardly one believer in the area and I remember how I lifted up my heart to God in prayer, at that time, that He would begin an evangelical work there. God answered that prayer in a remarkable way. Our kind host was converted in Caxias, and at the same time his brother entered into the joy of salvation; but tribulation soon began, for their employer told them that no Protestant could remain in his business. Our host renounced the business without renouncing his Lord, while his brother denied his

Lord and stayed in the business. Having little capital and an unconverted wife, who told her husband that she repented of their marriage, it was only natural that he (our host) should seek fresh fields to begin work. He left Caxias, and arrived in Coroata, not because of the commercial advantage of living in Coroata, but because of the town's need of Christ, with practically nothing in his pockets. We found him with over thirty believers, with a flourishing business, and, best of all, his wife rejoicing in the Lord."

Harris told of village after village where his colaborers had planted the Gospel and where at the time of his journey abundant fruit was clearly visible. Ernest Wootton, Myrdden Thomas, Miss Lily Giles — these and others had kept doggedly at the task, praying and working, working when they could, praying when they couldn't work. There had been suffering and sacrifice. Two missionaries on a long and wearisome evangelistic journey had been accompanied on the trail by two gold prospectors. The hardships of swollen streams and muck had been so great in the final two days that they (one of the two missionaries being a woman) had to travel barefoot. The gold hunters remarked at the end of the trip, "We would not do that journey again for all the gold on the Amazon." One of the missionaries replied, "No more would I — but I would for Christ."

In UFM's beginning year a party of five missionaries sailed for Congo. In the same month, December, 1931, Albert Drysdale left Australia to open the mission's work in New Guinea. Intrepid trailblazers penetrated further into the Brazilian jungle to establish a witness among the savage Urubu tribe and at numerous landings along the Acara, Gurupi and Pindare Rivers. Gospel meetings were inaugurated, churches launched, schools set up. Older stations were turned over to less experienced missionaries, freeing their founders to explore further into the great Amazon forest.

Of no less significance was the London Council's step of faith in commissioning Mr. and Mrs. Edwin J. Pudney as its envoys to North America, replacements for the Reverend W. F. Roadhouse, the first representative whose poor health had forced him to retire.

The couple sailed on September 16, 1931, on the Empress of Britain, having had an enthusiastic send-off at London's Waterloo Station.

"Never," wrote Leonard Harris, "was a 'Farewell Message' more prophetic than the one given to Mr. and Mrs. Pudney. No one knew then that, as the years were to unfold, these devoted workers were to see evolve from one rented room, Headquarters both in Toronto and in Philadelphia. It was not known then that they were to be used of God to send hundreds to UFM fields, that they were to develop work in Haiti, in the Dominican Republic, in British Guiana and help forward the arduous task among the savages of New Guinea. It was not seen that when England was slowly bleeding to death after Dunkirk during World War II, North America was going to maintain some British workers through the dark days of war, and that these intrepid workers were to travel thousands of miles, visiting one field after another, ensuring the right foundations were lain and indigenous churches founded."

Edwin and Lilian Pudney may well have been typical of young English couples when they married in 1921 after his four years of service in World War I. They both enjoyed promising business careers, he as an accountant. Furnishing a new home in a London suburb was a delightful adventure. In one way this couple was different. They had consecrated their lives to Christ.

This led to giving of their free time to a mission in the slums of London's East End. There they met two young men who were enrolled in the Interdenominational Missionary Training College in a suburb near where the Pudneys lived. These students gained practical experience at the mission where Edwin and Lilian served, and the mutual friendship forged brought the men rather frequently to the Pudney home. The fellows shared their vision for God's work in Africa, and it is not to be surprised that in a matter of months their hosts began to share the vision.

Lilian spoke up first.

"I believe the Lord is calling me as a missionary to Congo," she said to her husband of nine months.

Edwin had also felt the call. He had been praying that the Lord would deal with his wife. He had wanted to be sure that she was willing to leave their new home and prayed that she might be the first to speak.

They gave up their home, sold their furniture, quit their jobs. They entered training and he went on ahead to Congo. After she joined him there, they served in Central Africa from 1923 to 1931, with a single furlough in that period. They worked under primitive conditions. Some of the people to whom they ministered were cannibals, and witchdoctors brought fear and terror to their villages. In many areas they were the first heralds of the Gospel.

The Pudneys were home in England for a furlough year when UFM was started. They felt they should not return to Congo while her father, who had been a faithful minister in numerous Methodist parishes, suffered from a critical heart condition. His recovery would take at least a couple of years, they were told, and the church he served in Middleton, near Manchester, invited Pudney to supply the pulpit for this interval, which he agreed to do.

Lilian's health was such that a return to the tropics was inadvisable. Thus, this pastoral assignment seemed to be the Lord's answer. Then her father died. The church extended a regular call to the Pudneys. Continuance in the pastorate was most logical. The day before they were to give their affirmative answer to the church board, Lilian accompanied her mother on a trip into Manchester, and Edwin, left to himself, went for a walk in the country to think things through. He was not fully at peace in accepting this pastorate, and while walking felt an urge to return home. On the doorstep lay a telegram instructing him to call UFM's London headquarters immediately. He did. The London Council requested that he and Lilian sail as soon as possible for Canada to establish a headquarters for the mission in Toronto.

Was this what God really wanted them to do? In accepting the church's call, they would enjoy a secure, even attractive, future — a home provided, a stated salary and loved ones near at hand. Go back to Congo, yes they would, if that were possible. But to Canada to establish a mission whose name was completely unknown and the entire continent was in the throes of an economic depression? Many churches could not support the missionaries already known to them and some even their own pastors. What could a man and his wife do, given these conditions, to advance the mission's cause there?

"If your father were here, he would say, 'Go to Canada,'" Lilian's mother told them. "I say the same; the Lord will take care of us."

The church found it hard to understand their decision to go. The Pudneys found it hard to leave people they were beginning to know and love. Some in the congregation questioned, "How can you leave the country under such circumstances, a recently bereaved mother and family, and a church with all the work awaiting?"

The couple could not expect others to understand the leading of the Lord for *them*.

They sailed for Canada, not knowing one person and having no experience in the administration of a mission, but with the Biblical message pounding in their ears, "I AM hath sent me unto you."

Arriving in Toronto on September 26, 1931, the Pudneys determined that the North American branch of the mission should not accept financial help from British headquarters. Starting with only $40, they in that first year went through many testings, and the future was uncertain. It was a time of holding on. Toronto headquarters consisted of two rooms — an office-sitting room and a bedroom for the Pudneys. Their landlady provided meals. Once at a women's Bible class, Mrs. Pudney contributed her last fifty cents toward a layette for an impoverished mother-to-be, but before she left that afternoon, a member pressed a dollar bill into her hand, saying she had intended to give it the previous Sunday, but by the time she got around to it, Mrs. Pudney had disappeared. Now Lilian had twice what she had come with. Rent and board money, gifts of clothing, other bounties arrived from the Lord, often "just in time."

Unevangelized Fields Mission was founded as a faith mission, and by its practice of looking to God for all resources, and its personnel likewise dependent on His provision, it would remain one.

Pudney traveled a great deal to make the mission and its needs known, but especially to raise up prayer for the one missionary they supported on the field, a Canadian by the name of George Thomas, who had served in Brazil since 1928. Somewhere in his travels, the North American director picked up a severe skin infection that in his judgment would not allow him to stay in the homes of other people. Forced into inactivity, he and Mrs. Pudney reduced even their minimal life-style to save on expense, and looked back on as almost luxurious those days in Congo when they paid no rent for their mud house and could always grow potatoes in the yard. Pudney was asked to pastor two small rural churches outside of Toronto, which he agreed to do for a limited time. From the heat of Congo to the comparative mildness of England to a very frigid winter in Canada, the couple adjusted and made it into spring, though on several nights they had had to lift their mattress onto the dining room table next to the heating stove to survive the freezing temperatures.

After nine months in the country his health was restored and they returned to Toronto, vowing to start once more the UFM headquarters there. If they could not make it this time, they agreed they would return in defeat to England.

But make it they did. His ministry of the Word to the two

rural churches had refreshed Lilian and him. One of the churches answered the missionary challenge they had given. Others, too, responded, churches and individuals. Five women met faithfully every Tuesday afternoon to pray for the UFM's one North American missionary, George Thomas. The mission's cause began to prosper. A particular friend was found in Dr. Oswald J. Smith, pastor of Toronto's People's Church, which was noted for its emphasis on missions. Dr. Smith reserved a place for Pudney in the church's outstanding annual missionary conference, enabling him to acquaint the Christian public with UFM. The pastor personalized his connection with the new mission. From his wide-world experiences, he was able to advise on many fields. Among other counsel, he suggested that the Australian branch concentrate its efforts on the field closest to home, New Guinea, which it did. People's Church would also over the years take on the financial support of a good many UFM missionaries.

Another good helper was Dr. Isaac Page, the honored head of the China Inland Mission. He opened many doors. The American Keswick conference in New Jersey welcomed Pudney to its platform. Small churches, many of them without ties to a strong denomination, were drawn to UFM's work.

One day Mrs. Pudney picked up from the mat at the front door of their tiny apartment an envelope containing a check for one thousand dollars. Such an amount had never before been received. She wanted to telephone her husband, who was in New York. But she thought of the call's expense, so wrote him instead. It meant that George Thomas, on furlough and with Pudney in New York at the time, could now sail for Brazil.

Lengthy separations from each other were a cross the Pudneys had to bear in much of their many years of ministry. While he traveled the length and breadth of Canada and sometimes into the United States as well, she stayed home, representing the mission as best she could in their own community. She also had the care of the office and their home. At times as she pushed a mop around the floors she thought, with longing, of the Boys' School, the Girls' School, the women's work, the bush itineration in Congo, all of which she had revelled in. She confessed she did not like her present job, being a home representative. She did not like the thought of spending the rest of her life pushing a mop over the floors. Then one day the mail brought a letter from Fred Roberts, later to be known as one of the Three Freds of Brazil. He told of a trek to contact the wild Guajajara Indians, saying he and his companions had taken along a mule as an aid to the journey. But to start their trip, how to get the mule into their canoe? They urged and coaxed, pulled and pushed, but the mule was in no way willing. They overcame his obstinacy by tying two long poles to his body and carrying him into the canoe. After negotiating rapids and long stretches of river, they came to the landing where from then on the mule would be useful. After the first day's journey they put him out to graze, tying him to a tree. But the next morning the mule was not to be seen. For three days they hunted for him, then gave up and went on. Fred Roberts wrote this sentence in his letter, "Well, the mule was a great loss, but he was a rebellious creature from the beginning and rebellion is not of any use for the Lord's work anyway."

If a missionary could write that under the circumstances he was in, surely, Lilian Pudney told herself, she should not rebel in pushing a mop around, if that was what the Lord had in store for her. She accepted as fact that household chores were a part of home missionary work. And such work had to be done to keep the missionaries on the field, both they and she having non-glamorous tasks to accomplish.

Meanwhile, in London the Unevangelized Fields Mission had been incorporated on May 19, 1932, and its first Council elected in May of 1937. Progress there was in evidence on several fronts — the number of missionaries, field expansions, administration and finances. In time, Canadian headquarters moved to Pacific Avenue in Toronto, and from there the first North American missionary was sent to UFM's vast field in Belgian Congo. Miss Verna Schade, a United States citizen, tackled the educational problems of a people passing through a rapid transition from crude paganism to civilization. Toronto then sent Miss Viola Walker, a Canadian, to Congo. The next year others were assigned to Brazil, and thereafter new missionaries were sent out every year. Once again the office in Toronto was moved, in 1937 to 18 Howland Avenue, where it was to remain for many years. This nine-room house was purchased by the mission in 1955. It was turned into a comfortable home for furloughed missionaries and candidates by the gifts of furniture, appliances, tableware and linens from many in the growing constituency of the mission. Friends and missionaries alike filled the large living room for the weekly prayer meeting and the monthly Day of Prayer. Besides these special times, prayer was a daily feature of the home. Each morning after a portion of Scripture was read, there followed a season of prayer covering the fields and special needs. After the noon meal, one person prayed for financial matters and countries and missions other than UFM's own. In the evening, a page of Daily Light was read, and prayer made for families, pastors and churches, missionaries on furlough, the children of missionaries, deputational workers and the radio ministry.

Daily prayer times and special Days of Prayer became standard procedures on every UFM field. Wherever they might be, UFM people knew that each day their fellow workers were reading the identical page in Daily Light. The favorite song — "UFM's hymn," *Great Is Thy Faithfulness* — was sung around the world.

Candidate school was started in Toronto, though in the beginning it merely meant receiving into the fellowship of the home a young man or woman who had heard God's call to one of the fields. For a month the potential missionary would work and live in the home in order that the staff might get to know the person and, perhaps more importantly, for that person to get to know those who pledged to stand behind him when on the field. During this time the candidates learned about mission history, the organization's constitution, working principles at home and on the field and warnings of possible temptations and failures on the field. It became a month of joy through singing around the piano or kneeling in prayer time or working in the kitchen. Candidates passed from being strangers to becoming integral members of the corps of Christ's ambassadors sent out by UFM.

In their travels for the mission, with more than two hundred engagements annually, the Pudneys touched at many places in the United States. But whether in Canada or the US, Pudney, when traveling alone, made it his practice to never spend more than a dollar a day for a bed to sleep in and another dollar for his day's food. As the mission grew and became more widely known, US support increased greatly. By 1941, it appeared the time was right to open a headquarters across the Canadian border, and Philadelphia was considered the most suitable location.

War raged in Europe. Atlantic crossings were nearly an impossibility. Financial dealings between nations had grown complex. Opening an office in the United States was seen as an absolute necessity.

After ten years in Toronto, the Pudneys were to move to Philadelphia in 1941, leaving the Canadian office and residence completely furnished for the convenience of those who would succeed them there. Starting up in the US would mean starting from scratch, much as they did when first arriving in Toronto. There was a difference, however. The mission now had friends in the United States, particularly in the Philadelphia area. Led by Miss Mary Zimmerman of Lancaster, Pennylvania, a band of loyal supporters showered the Pudneys with kitchen equipment, and before they moved to the city members of Aldan Union Church, in the Philadelphia suburb of Aldan, completely outfitted the big twelve-room house on North 63rd Street that for some years would be the mission office and home. Valuable help also came from the Overlea Baptist Church of Baltimore, which later was named Perry Hall Baptist.

Aldan Union and its pastor, Dr. William Allan Dean, and Calvary Independent Church at Lancaster and its pastor, Dr. Frank

C. Torrey, stood by UFM from its earliest days in the Philadelphia area. Also contributing significantly, Dr. Donald B. Fullerton recruited young people for the mission's ranks. As an alumnus of Princeton University, Dr. Fullerton formed the Princeton Evangelical Fellowship in 1931 and in the years to come pointed a number of his students toward UFM, believing it to be the best foreign society for church planting open to the men and women who found Christ at Princeton. Some rose to leadership, and several served on the mission's governing board. Moody Bible Institute and Grace and Dallas Seminaries became other prime sources of missionaries for UFM.

The first guests at the new home in Philadelphia were Verna Schade and Viola Walker, on furlough from Congo. Because the house was a better choice than a previously selected property which had suddenly become unavailable, and because the rent of the second house was only two-thirds of the first, the women from Congo named it "The Miracle Mansion." The first party of new missionaries to go out from the US headquarters left within two months of the opening. Going from "The Miracle Mansion," they called themselves "The Miracle Party."

SOURCES, Chapter 4

Harris, Leonard F., *Our Days in His Hands*, London, Undated

Letter, H. A. Jenkinson to Alfred Larson, January 10, 1986

Larson, Alfred and Jean, Interview, 1995

_____, 1969, Notes on early draft

Lifeline, UFM Publication, Bala-Cynwyd, *February, 1981*

Light & Life, UFM Publication, London, October-November, 1931; December 1931 - January 1932; February-March, 1932; June-July, 1932

Nesbitt, James H., 1996, Letter to author

Pudney, Edwin J. and Lilian G., *Sacrifice of Praise*, Bala-Cynwyd, Undated

Pudney, Edwin J., Audiotape, 1961

Rabey, George, 1996, Letter to author

5

The Three Freds

The three Freds were murdered. They had been killed by Kayapo warriors at Smoke Falls on the Riozinho, a feeder of the Xingu River.

Their bodies were not recovered, but convincing evidence of their deaths was discovered by Horace Banner and Will Johnstone in a search for the three missionaries a year after the trio had last been seen. Displaying as much courage as the three Freds who sought to contact the wild Kayapo in order to win them to Christ, Banner and Johnstone traveled the route of the Freds, constantly scanning the banks of the Riozinho for any possible clue left by the missing men. Their crew, made up of Brazilian rubber tappers, looked for any excuse to turn around and flee back to the safety of the village of Nova Olinda. They found such grounds the day the search party portaged around a particularly menacing cataract and on the trail came across the charred remains of a crude wheel. Made from a slice of tree trunk, it was pierced in the middle by a perfectly round two-inch hole. Suggesting wheel and axle, not something an Indian would contrive, it was presumed to be the only remains of a simple conveyance to truck the three Freds' laden canoe to the upper end of the falls. Likely the Freds had hidden their make-shift trolley for use on the return trip, but the Kayapo, after killing the men, discovered it, and following tradition, destroyed it and everything else belonging to their victims. Believing that a horde of savages had indeed killed the earlier party and at any moment would swoop out of the forest and do the same to them, the crew could not be stopped in its retreat downriver.

Banner and Johnstone, however, were not to be thwarted in their determination to learn with certainty the fate of the three Freds. With a fresh crew, they set out again and this time went farther upstream, reaching Smoke Falls, a thousand miles, more or less, from the mouth of the Amazon. Here the Riozinho swept in a mighty gush over a high ridge of rock and many feet below dashed against innumerable stones, sending up a cloud of spray before rushing off downstream in waves of foam. Only momentarily did the missionaries train their attention on the falls, nor did the crew long scan the surrounding forest, a possible shade for wild Kayapo. Rather, attention quickly shifted to a shallow backwater in which someone had picked out the shape of a submerged motor boat.

Raising it, they saw the craft, that of the Freds, had been slashed, its bow broken, the motor bashed and stripped of its lighter parts and the rudder wrenched off and pitched under some bushes. A search of the land nearby turned up a pile of what was once clothing, though it had provided ample meals for voracious ants. A shred of weather-beaten cloth still showed a stain — was it motor oil or blood?

Fred Roberts, Fred Wright and Fred Dawson — their names were soon known to the world. News accounts of their martyrdom in the service of Jesus Christ circled the globe. Some criticized them as foolhardy. Others commended their daring and selfless dedication. UFM remained unswayed in its determination to penetrate the Xingu with the Gospel. The last communication of the three had been a plea to carry on where they left off.

"Three of our best had no graves or burial service," wrote J. C. Wright, brother of one of the Freds, "but they had a triumphant entry into the presence of Him whose command 'Go ye . . . ' they gladly obeyed.

"Some asked, 'Is it worth while?' I answer with my brother Fred's last message: 'Remember, He died for the Indians of South America.'"

The trio's hope had been that "should the Lord will that we are taken . . . more men and money will be rushed out to follow up this advance." It was fulfilled. Men and women and money did reach Brazil. In the wake of a memorial service in London and services of remembrance in North America and Australia, hearts were touched and wills surrendered to the Lord, and the ranks of volunteers swelled, not only for Brazil but also for other fields. Some of those stand-ins for the three Freds remained with UFM for many years and their names became well known to later generations.

Following the discovery at Smoke Falls, Horace Banner turned back toward his Urubu Indians on the Gurupi River. For some years he had felt they were his responsibility, the call to search for the three Freds only a momentary diversion from a lifelong labor. After confirming the deaths of the Freds, the search party paddled down the Riozinho toward the protection of Nova Olinda En route, a phrase from Ezekiel pounded in Banner's ears, "Thou shalt speak my words unto them." He had no doubt that the words he heard so distinctly were not just a command spoken to the prophet around 600 B. C., but they were God's distinctive message to him, and "them" meant the Kayapo.

At one point on the return trip the party came across a tree on the river bank blazoned with the initials of the three Freds. It had been their way of marking a campsite of their upriver trek; they probably planned to use it again on their way down. Banner and Johnstone and their men were tired from incessant paddling through the night, and an unavoidable long fast, due to running out of food, had further sapped their strength. What should they discover at the site but a sealed tin of farina, the staple of interior Brazil that had only to be moistened to make a satisfying meal! The Freds had deposited it in a clump of bushes, no doubt intending that it replenish their supplies on their return trip. The Freds did not need food now, but their search party did. Though a year old and stale and foul-smelling, to the famished it was sweet nectar.

Back in the rubber town of Nova Olinda, the base for the Freds' endeavor, Banner and Johnstone had the task of going through the boxes the three had left in storage. On top was a hastily scrawled message in pencil on a couple of envelopes detailing their bequests should they give their lives to the undertaking. Apart from a few personal items, they had stipulated that in the event of their deaths, all else among their effects was to go "to those who should continue the attempt to reach the Kayapos with the Gospel."

The three Freds had taken for granted that their foray into the Xingu jungle was only a stepping stone by which others would proceed.

And for Horace Banner, linked to their expectation was the command that continued to throb in his brain, "Speak my words unto them."

About a year later Banner and Leonard Harris were in Belém, then called Para, buying and packing stores for an exploration up the Araguaia River. A headline in the local newspaper arrested their attention, XINGU TOWN INVADED BY 600 INDIANS.

Brazil-nut merchants just in from Nova Olinda, the town of the headline, confirmed the report, some saying the number was more like a thousand. Here, Banner and Harris declared, was the answer to not only their prayers, but the prayers of many over many years. The killer Kayapo had emerged from the forest and these ferocious Indians, evidently defeated in an intertribal battle and fearing their enemies, were seeking refuge among the Brazilians of the outpost town. Kayapo seeking peace? It was a miracle.

The two missionaries changed their plans and set out immediately for Nova Olinda, which sits on a bank of the Fresco River opposite where the Riozinho enters it. Twenty-eight days were required to reach the town, and on arriving they found many of the Brazilians had fled for fear of attack by the Kayapo, who were encamped on the opposite bank. Those days were difficult because the Kayapo, though professing a desire for peace, still were threatening, disgustingly crude and totally erratic in their behavior. At the first encounter the missionaries were roughly handled, unable to understand the commands thrown at them by five hundred agitated men lisping all at one time through the two-and-a-half-inch disks that hideously stretched their lips. Each day Banner and Harris crossed the river from the town to the Kayapo encampment to decipher the tribe's unwritten language. It was the beginning of a task that would occupy the rest of Banner's life.

Eventually others shared in the mission to the Kayapo, among them Frank Houston, an early partner with Banner. They and the others experienced untold frustrations. There were a lack of workers at critical times, official opposition from those who believed that Indians should be left to perish in their pagan superstitions and a constant battle with the powers of spiritual darkness.

As a schoolboy in Britain, Horace Banner had once debated the better state for the Indian — civilized or untamed? Horace championed the savage. Years later he came to know the Kayapo as no other outsider had known them. He could only lament that too often more mature thinkers never got beyond the conclusions of an uninformed, idealistic youth caught up in romantic fancy. The lot of a Kayapo was hard, his life filled with fear, hatred and cruelty. To teach the concept of a loving and forgiving God, it had first to be shown, then verbalized. In doing this, Banner cared for one of the known killers of the three Freds, built him a house in which to die. Perhaps he was prompted by remembrance of a message he once had heard at the Keswick Convention on the theme, "He (Jesus) went about teaching and showing the Gospel of God."

He taught them. He showed them a photo of their victims. In awed silence, the Kayapo passed it around. Banner spoke of why the three had sought them out. One of the killers surrendered his club to the missionary.

Another called to the task through the martyrdom of the three Freds was a Canadian, Robert Angus Cunningham. He became Banner's partner at Gorotire. There on a high bank of the Riozinho, Banner had built his house and it was now surrounded by the dwellings of one branch of the large Kayapo tribe. Cunningham had wanted to marry Rosemary Anderson and bring her from Altamira, her station further down on the Xingu River, but a post among the Kayapo was considered too dangerous for women, and besides, the mission had a rule that marriage of missionaries on the field was permitted only after they had been there for at least two years.

Both restrictions were overcome, time taking care of the one. The fact that neither Banner nor Cunningham had yet been killed suggested that a woman, after all, might live there safely, too. The Cunninghams began a school for the Kayapo boys, though it was an effort to persuade the fathers in the tribe to let their sons study rather than initiate them in the prowess of war. They took in orphaned children. The "gathering room" of their house was the setting for many palavers among the men, but not the women. Rosemary was welcomed in the homes of the women, but none would set foot in hers. This was because when Angus went out to claim his bride a child had been killed in the house and, the women believed, the tiny spirit still spooked the place. The Cunninghams learned that some of the men enjoying their hospitality were the very ones who had killed the three Freds. One day one of them turned over a revolver that had belonged to one of the murdered missionaries. Horace Banner went home to England and married during his furlough. He brought back Eva with her nursing skills and they moved to open work among another branch of the tribe. During certain seasons the Kayapo became somewhat nomadic, so periodically left the encampment at Gorotire. The Cunninghams thus found opportunity to travel downstream to Brazilian settlements for short rests. For the equivalent of eight and a half American dollars, they bought an adobe hut in Nova Olinda and there held Gospel meetings for the twelve families of the village. One time they journeyed about a hundred miles down to São Felix. While there, they were given an emergency message by the pilot of a Brazilian trader launch. A mortal enemy of the Kayapo had moved on Gorotire. Cunningham, possibly the only peacemaker, must return quickly.

At one time, perhaps fifty years previously, the Kayapo was one large, unified tribe. But quarrels among local factions led to warfare that was as bitter and bloody as any among unrelated tribes. The Kayapo had been fractured since. The branch known as Kuben Kran Ken, the Shaved Heads, were fierce warriors; it was the KKK who had descended on Gorotire. Unless something or someone intervened, they no doubt would slaughter their more peaceful brothers. Cunningham jumped on the launch and headed upstream, hoping he would be in time to prevent the killing.

Reaching Gorotire, he was met by a young man he knew well.

"The Kuben Kran Ken are here," the fellow said.

So, the story he'd heard downriver was true.

"I brought them."

This fellow *brought* them?

"They want to palaver with you."

Ladeira, the youth whose astounding words were delivered with unaffected calmness, had indeed brought members of that feared tribe to his home village. To Cunningham, he explained why.

He had been in the forest a long way from home when, stricken with influenza, he curled up against the trunk of a tree, too weak to look for food or to even move. There he expected to die. How long he had been asleep or unconscious, he didn't know, but barely rousing he heard footsteps. Managing to prop up his head, he looked full into the scowling face of an enemy Kuben Kran Ken. "Don't kill me yet," Ladeira stammered.

The Shaved Head crept closer, looking about for a trap.

"See, I am weak. I cannot move. Before you kill me, I have something to say."

"Speak!"

"I have no enemy spirit. I die now. My tribe has new talk. We do not want to kill. Let us be friends. I lie not."

He said again that his tribe had new talk.

Two more KKK hunters suddenly appeared. The three of that clan talked among themselves. Was this fellow being foolish?

"Let us be friends," Ladeira pleaded. "If you let me sit by your fire and eat some of your manioc and fish so I can get my strength back, I will tell you the new chants."

Some weeks later Ladeira arrived at Gorotire with three Kuben Kran Ken, an event that sounded the alarm all the way down the river to São Felix . Cunningham, arriving at Gorotire, was tired from the journey, hungry and thirsty. He felt a siege of malaria coming on. But these brutish warriors wanted to palaver. They wanted to hear the new talk.

That was what Cunningham had dedicated his life to. Sharing the new talk with any who would listen. The Kuben Kran Ken — never before had there been contact with them, and now Ladeira's sickness and plea for his life, and his sharing the new talk with an enemy, had opened the door. Truly, nothing less than God's own doing.

Yet, it was not to be easy. Winning the Kayapo, any branch of them, was slow, plodding, painstaking work, with as many steps backward, it sometimes seemed, as steps taken forward.

"Sowing in tears," was the way Banner characterized those days.

"Reaping in joy," portrayed the endeavors of more than one missionary whose target was the Brazilian, in either coastal city or inland village.

The missionaries who formed the Brazilian field of UFM had as their original thrust the evangelization of the Indians living far up the rivers and in deep forest, the Red Indian as they called these wandering, elusive and often hostile people. But in the region there were also Brazilians, most of them a mixed breed of European and American Indian and sometimes African origin. They lived in the towns along the Atlantic and in the lower reaches of the great rivers, and in numerous clusters farther upstream where they wrested a minimal living from the region's dying rubber industry or from Brazil nuts or trade with the Indians. By and large they came under the hegemony of the Roman church and generally looked on Protestants as heretical in their beliefs if not outright dangerous in their practices. It was to such that more and more UFM missionaries were drawn through a conviction that the souls of these poor, rough people were as precious and as accountable as those of any race or culture.

The origin of Gospel work in the interior of the state of Maranhão can be traced to a crippled and harshly persecuted Brazilian evangelist, João Batista Pinheiro. He moved in 1893 from Recife on the coast to the inland village of Barra do Corda on the Mearim River. He influenced Perrin Smith, a Canadian with no mission agency affiliation, to settle there in 1905. Picking up the mantle, Smith traveled by mule-back from village to village, preaching the Word of God wherever he went. He invaded areas steeped in witchcraft, overcame the antipathy of its adherents, taught the villagers they could be liberated from sin and loved the people into the Kingdom of God. In the late 1920s he began gathering the believers scattered in isolation over his territory for an annual conference. At this assemblage they studied the Bible, learned to pray and to sing Gospel hymns and enjoyed much-needed fellowship. The curious started attending and some of these became convinced that what they heard was true. Out of this gathering grew a Bible school. Perrin Smith and his wife became spiritual parents to many UFM missionaries. He counseled them on a missionary's attitude toward local people and how to win their confidence. He was a source of answers to their questions. He and his wife opened their home to sick missionaries and she tenderly nursed them back to health. He tramped the forest trails with neophytes, demonstrating, rather than describing, the way to reach Brazil's interior for Christ.

UFM first planted a church among the Brazilians at Santa Isobel, near Belém, a work that was eventually turned over to the Pentecostals. Churches were established at Grajaú and Turiaçú in 1935, Pedreiros in 1937, Belém in 1939 and Altamira and Parnaiba in 1942.

Barra do Corda became the site of the mission's first Bible school, founded in 1936 by George and Blanche Thomas, the first UFM missionaries in Brazil from North America. Housed in a burnt and sun-dried brick building, the Bible Institute occupied a large tract about a mile outside the town. It was in the vicinity of Barra do Corda that a few years back Kayapo had butchered a number of Brazilians. At this time, Brazilians were enrolled in the school to prepare themselves to reach out to the Kayapo and to the other tribes. According to Thomas, only one of the early graduates worked among the Indians. Many of the others ministered through Portuguese-speaking endeavors, some joining denominations since no national church organization yet existed for non-sectarian believers such as those who came to the Lord through UFM.

The ardor of the students must be recognized. Regularly, they preached on street corners and in local jails. Meetings especially for women were held. In less than ten years the Institute noted that, despite opposition, some of it severe, a thousand souls had been led to Christ through the witness of the students. Many of these converts were among the five hundred or so Christians who attended the institute's annual Bible and Missionary Conference, an eight-day spiritual feast.

The mission's first endeavor in the important port city of Belém began in 1939 as an "extracurricular" outreach of Leonard Harris, the field leader. The church, Igreja Cristã Evangélica da Cremação — the church of the crematorium — stood in the shadow of the city's garbage incinerator. Though always small, the church was the first to become self-sufficient, requiring no subsidy from either the mission or other Brazilian congregations.

In 1940, forty-two missionaries served in Brazil under UFM, which by this date worked out of a field office in Belém.

It would be expected that only men could stand the rigors of the frontier. But wives and single women proved otherwise. Florence Hough arrived in Brazil in 1939 and was sent to evangelize the town of Cururupú in the state of Maranhão. It would be the base for most of her forty-nine year missionary career. In the early days, outside communication often did not exist, neither mail nor support money getting through. During some of the uncertain months of World War II, papaya from a tree in her yard was her only food.

Florence opened a boarding school. Trusting in the God that George Mueller had trusted for his orphanage in England, she, like he, experienced time and again the Lord's provision for her children when it was evident that help was not to come from any other source. A plaque in front of the school stated, "He abideth faithful."

The year 1940 was labeled one of advancement for the Gospel in Brazil. In it the first Kayapo convert was recorded. Churches among the Brazilians were started, established ones grew, schools opened. The schools were essential if the children of believers were not to be trained out of their family faith by hostile government or parochial teachers. The beginning of the decade served as the summit for an expansion that was slowed only by the outbreak of World War II.

In 1943 the government shut down all work among Indians. Citing security in war time, it allowed no foreigner to live in unpoliced areas — meaning the vast jungle areas where the work was going well among the Kayapo and other tribes. The ban would be in effect until 1955. The edict did not stop the work among the Brazilians, and Horace Banner was given permission to visit now and then a number of Indian settlements. Evangelism concentrated on the towns. Because Belém was on the flight path of American bombers flying to Africa and thence to Europe, US servicemen were stationed there. UFM opened a Christian center to accommodate them and to present Jesus Christ as their surety in the troubling times of war.

During the war years new missionaries were not allowed to enter Brazil, except a few from North America. The veterans from Britain or Europe could not cross the seas to go home on furlough. Sometimes malicious rumors flew about, hinting that the missionaries were actually spies and should be expelled. The churches united in defense of their foreign brethren, and the evangelicals not only survived, but their work prospered.

Horace Banner reported in January of 1946, "Things have certainly altered on the Xingu River since we first came here, unknown, unwanted, despised Protestants, not knowing a soul. Now we have fifty preaching points, and as many warm welcomes. Meetings are held somewhere along the river almost every night, while by day we call and leave Gospel literature for all who can read it."

The war having closed the interior rivers to UFM, Douglas and Mary McAllister were brought back from Altamira on the Xingu to the lower Amazon region. Leonard Harris had visited Abaete, later called Abaetetuba, a town that stood on a bank of the Tocantins River, a tropical watercourse fifteen hundred miles long and, at its mouth, ten miles wide. Finding no Gospel witness there, he asked the McAllisters to make the town their

71

new assignment. Indian work had brought Doug to Brazil, but he would not allow the long journey from his native Australia to be nullified by war. He'd work in Brazil wherever he could.

As a boy, Doug went to Sunday school much against his will. But one year he did achieve perfect attendance and for it was awarded a book, *Adventures with the Bible in Brazil*, which struck a chord in Doug's thinking. Missionaries were frequent guests in the McAllister home, and one in particular showed interest in the boy's spiritual condition. Doug did all he could to avoid him, but on the man's last morning with them could not escape taking a horseback ride with him. Expecting a sermon along the way, he was surprised to hear the missionary tell of his own rebellion against God and of his joy when he surrendered to the Lord. In church that night, Doug started a new life in Christ.

As a student at Melbourne Bible College, he heard the story of the three Freds, and he knew then that God had called him as one to take their place. UFM in Australia asked him to go to Papua, but he declined, sure of his call to Brazil. To go so far, he had to pay his own way, which he did. He went to Brazil by way of England, and there at a prayer meeting met the one who was to become his wife, a young woman born in Belgium of Dutch parents and who then was a student in missionary training in London.

Doug and Mary were sent to Altamira on the Xingu River. There they were involved in the church planted by UFM missionaries before them, and shuttled supplies to those who were working farther upriver with the Kayapo. Returning east where the government permitted missionaries to live, they looked for shelter in Abaetetuba. Word passed through the town that "heretics" were coming. No one wanted to rent to them. They finally obtained a small house with only one door and no conveniences. Here Mary started children's meetings and Doug hired a boat to take him up and down the nearby feeder streams to evangelize the residents of villages along the way.

Even the poor quarters they had been able to rent they had to surrender to families coming into town for the yearly celebration of the patron saint's day. They moved ten times, finally renting a house that was ideal for Gospel meetings. The village priest bought the house and turned them out. By this time the mission owned a boat, and the McAllisters made it their home.

Their boat, the *Colaborador*, had been purchased from the British and Foreign Bible Society. UFM sent Charles Sarginson a thousand miles up the Amazon to Manaus to bring it home. The mission was ready to begin in earnest a launch work that would produce spiritual victories for many years.

In 1944, the McAllisters opened a stretch of the Amazon delta to the Gospel. In their visits they came across a grannie who had no canoe and could not get to the church in town to confess her sins. When the tide lowered, she would kneel in the bush and pray, "God, send me light." She heard from Doug and Mary that Jesus died on the cross to forgive sin. "This," she said, "is the light I prayed for." She and her family accepted Christ as Savior; soon a small congregation was formed and the first church arose on the banks of the Maracapucu River.

In one place the McAllisters sold a number of Bibles to a local merchant. A priest visiting the man's little store seized them and threw them in the river, but villagers jumped in and fished them out. They were dried, page by page, and those who could read gathered in the evenings around an old can stuffed with a rag soaked in oil, the dim light enabling them to see the light on the pages that God had sent them. In time, an evangelical church was raised on the very spot from which the Bibles were thrown into the water, reminding one of the words of Jesus, "Cast thy bread upon the water and thou shalt find it after many days."

The McAllisters went on furlough in 1946 and Charles and Effie Sarginson took over the launch work.

Coming from Canada in 1940, Sarginson first engaged in

language study, then went to the Xingu River to join Horace Banner and Angus Cunningham in work among the Kayapo. Sarginson was given the boys to oversee. In the evenings they would gather in his room for lessons. The boys taught him as well, having fun in showing how they could filch his belongings without his knowing it. He loved the work, but was forced out of it when the government prohibited foreigners from living among the Indians.

The marriage of Charles Sarginson and Effie Parkhill was the only one ever to be "arranged" by mission headquarters. It was war time and the two were engaged, but having been denied a visa six times Effie was unable to journey from Canada to join Charles on the field. Edwin Pudney advised Charles to return home. He would marry them in Philadelphia, and then perhaps she could enter Brazil on the strength of having a husband with a valid visa. It worked.

When fully into launch work, the Sarginsons piloted the *Colaborador* from May to November along the tributaries of the Amazon, starting as far upstream as they could cover in three weeks, working downstream village by village. Leaving the launch in the care of a hired youth, they would lower a canoe and steer it to every home on that particular stretch of river. Most of the people were friendly and knew absolutely nothing about the Bible. Few had even seen one. There was keen desire to read it, but seldom did the missionaries come across a person capable of reading. In lieu of paying a few cents, many would trade a small chicken for a copy. Eventually, the Sarginsons, out of necessity, built a chicken coop atop the launch.

During the rainy season, when the rivers were too erratic to travel, Charles and Effie held children's meetings and did house-to-house visitation in Abaetetuba. They laid the foundation for later mission work in the town — the second UFM Bible school, a church and other efforts.

Returning from furlough, the McAllisters resumed their

launch work. Charles Sarginson received the votes of his fellow missionaries and became field leader, a post he was to hold for the next thirteen years. Doug McAllister began building a new launch, the *Araúto* (Herald).

Always a problem in river work was the fact that few of the villagers could read. Mary McAllister had sat under the teaching of Frank Laubach, the originator of the "Each one teach one" method of teaching illiterates to read. She put her training to work on the Amazon tributaries. One woman, a new convert, was eager to learn. In a short time she was able to read the Bible verses Mary gave her to memorize. She learned to read the Bible, but whenever she picked up a newspaper or another book she could not decipher one word. She was stricken with tuberculosis, and before she died had committed to memory one hundred twenty-five verses.

"Some of the seed we planted fell on hard ground," Mary McAllister once wrote. "But some produced fruit, and it is still growing." In their forty-two years on the field, eighteen of them in river evangelism, the McAllisters saw third-generation Christians take their places of leadership in the churches of the Amazon and its many tributaries.

The launches used in spreading the Gospel among the scattered river dwellers were in no way similar to what the term evokes for the average boat lover. Simple wooden structures twenty to forty feet in length, a minuscule deck in front of a tiny cabin, with or without glass in the windows, these craft were utilitarian in every sense of the word. The McAllisters used a kerosene pressure stove for cooking their food. It made quite a clatter as they pumped it up for their morning coffee. Someone hearing it for the first time thought it a kind of Morse code and reported them as having a clandestine radio, no doubt informing the enemy where along the coast Brazil could be invaded. The couple was investigated, but found not to be spies as suspected.

Abaetetuba became the operations base for the McAllisters.

With no evangelical church in town, the missionaries held meetings wherever they could and people came. Boys shot firecrackers through the windows, and many an interested listener was lifted off his seat by one exploding right under him.

"At least," quipped McAllister, "not many people sleep through the sermon."

Years later Abaetetuba would have a thriving group of churches in its environs, and one year the town's council would award the title "Citizen of Abaetetuba" to the residing missionary.

For several years UFM's launch work flourished. Among the vessels were the *Colaborador*, the *Herald*, the *Crusader*, the *Conqueror*, the *Ambassador*, the *Glad Tidings* and the *Aurora*. Wherever these vessels anchored, a witness occurred. One report said that in a little over a year a thousand isolated homes were visited. All up and down the rivers where they plied, churches were established. The Sarginsons, the McAllisters, Ted and Janet Laskowski, Angus and Rosemary Cunningham, Delbert and Marguerite Harrell, Leslie and Anita Jantz — all in some phase of their missionary service in Brazil had a part in the launch evangelism of the Amazon Basin.

Because churches planted by UFM missionaries accelerated so much during World War II, a need was felt for an independent alliance of those churches. Leonard Harris, before he was called to London to head up UFM there, formed a national church organization in 1945, The Alliance of Evangelical Churches of Brazil. Two years later, on July 17, 1947, six missionaries and sixteen national workers, building on his effort, formed a more effective successor organization. The group resolved to found an organization that would, among other tasks, coordinate and guide the work of the graduates of the Maranhão Bible Institute. George Thomas, founder and president of the Institute, was elected president of the new church organization.

This grouping of churches — ten of the eleven affiliates were located in the state of Maranhão — was first known as the Alliance of Evangelical Christian Churches of North Brazil, reflecting the early regional nature of the work. Fifteen years later, the "north" designation would be dropped to recognize the Alliance's presence in Brasilia, in the central region; it became known as the Aliança das Igrejas Cristãs Evangélicas do Brasil, or Alliance of Evangelical Christian Churches of Brazil, or AICEB.

Some missionaries who reflected nondenominational backgrounds opposed any standardization that would give the Brazil group of churches the appearance of a denomination. Evangelical denominations in Brazil were, however, absorbing many of the promising works begun by missionaries or by nationals trained in the Bible Institute. For graduates pastoring independent and autonomous churches, AICEB, as an alternate, provided a unity in doctrine and practice, identity and a structure for persons of like-minded faith.

AICEB was set up to hold every second year a General Convention to which the member churches would send their delegates. Accenting the national association's independence, UFM had only two voting members. This separate but cooperative arrangement proved workable. The national church was not a part of the mission structure nor was the mission an integral part of the church.

An agreement was drawn up in 1955 between UFM and AICEB. Revised from time to time, the basic document nevertheless governed how the two entities worked together. It stated that each agency had its own field of service and jurisdiction over its own workers. An important provision specified that UFM would begin, prepare and transfer churches to AICEB according to guidelines. AICEB agreed, in turn, to receive and care for those churches.

Missionaries in certain cases were permitted to become pastors of AICEB churches, thus placing them under the jurisdiction of the national church while retaining membership in UFM. Later, provision was made for missionaries and national workers to begin cooperative church planting efforts right from the beginning. Missionaries could work under the jurisdiction of local AICEB districts in pioneer evangelism and church planting, on loan to AICEB, and the resultant church would not need to request transfer to AICEB since it was an AICEB project right from its start.

A coordinating committee, made up of four representatives from each entity, was established to encourage discussion of new needs and problems and to make recommendations to the two governing bodies, AICEB and UFM.

SOURCES, Chapter 5

Banner, Horace, *The Three Freds and After!*, 1975, London, Unevangelized Fields Mission

Canfield, Mary Yvonne (Bonnie), Undated paper, *Our Testimonies*

Cunningham, Rosemary, *Under a Thatched Roof*, 1955, Toronto, Evangelical Publishers

_____, *There Is Singing in the Rain Forest*, manuscript in preparation

_____, Notes on early draft

Harris, Leonard, *Our Days in His Hands*, Undated, London, Unevangelized Fields Mission

Hough, Florence, 1996, Letter to author

Larson, Alfred, 1996, Notes on early draft

Laskowski, T., 1996, Letter to author

Lifeline, Bala-Cynwyd, February, 1981

Light & Life, Melbourne, November, 1940

Light & Life, London, January-February, 1944

McAllister, Mary, Letters to Author, 1995, 1996

_____, 1996, Notes on early draft

Sarginson, Effie, Letter to Author, November, 1995

_____, 1996, Notes on early draft

Sharp, Larry, 1996, Notes on early draft

Stoner, Charles G., *Indians, Institutions and Churches*, 1987, Unpublished manuscript.

6

In the Ituri Forest

T he Ituri Forest in Congo, now Zaire, ranks second in size only to the Amazon jungle among the rain forests of the world. Under this immense green canopy the newly formed Unevangelized Fields Mission was to do much of its work.

Boyulu, the station ceded to UFM by another mission society, sat in the middle of the forest, its few acres carved out of dense growth, like other villages that at the time the mission could only pray would some day have a Gospel witness. Although the *Mambera* witchcraft was widely practiced among the Babari tribe, the people of Boyulu nevertheless were open to the message the missionaries brought them. They were keen for the Gospel, and as a rule every person in the village attended every time there was a preaching session. Some were eager enough for the meeting that they continually asked if it wasn't time to begin. Yet, there was no massive turning to the Lord. Two years after the work started at Boyulu the first baptismal service was held. Twenty-nine converts were immersed, not many among the large and spread-out Babari tribe, but enough to consider whether other stations ought to be started.

It was a difficult question, for funds were extremely low and the missionaries already on the field often were asked to accept half-allowances. But the Africa Council, in making its recommendation to the Home Council, cited the UFM's stated policy, "We believe in the Will and Power of God to supply our every need in His service."

The Home Council agreed with their brothers in Africa, and a second UFM station was opened at Maganga in Stanleyville Province.

Maganga had lain heavily on the hearts of George and Dora Kerrigan. He had visited the village and found it completely unevangelized. It would, he believed, make an ideal center for reaching out to the several thousand people between Boyulu and Stanleyville. He and his wife prayed to that end — and in August of 1934 they moved to Maganga to begin what would be a twenty-year ministry there before transferring to other work. Over the years their endeavors at Maganga would include a church, a school and a medical dispensary and outreaches to numerous surrounding settlements.

A year before UFM was formed as a new and independent society, Herbert and Alice Jenkinson, known to all as Kinso and Ma Kinso, had moved from WEC headquarters at Ibambi to a village in a hitherto unreached area. They had a fruitful stay there and for a time saw no reason to join former colleagues who had resigned from WEC and now made up the Africa corps of the new UFM. But progressing into 1931 they sensed the situation changing, and obeying their consciences, tendered their resignations. For six months they lived at a small government post, for them a sort of safe haven, while they waited for the Lord to reveal their future service.

Three options appeared to them: Return to England, work among the Pygmy or continue in the evangelizing of Northeast Congo.

After five years on the field they were due a furlough, but to leave Congo they would have to find passage money on their own, and they had none. A missionary to the Pygmy, the little people of the Ituri Forest, had recently died and a committee searching for a successor thought Kinso was their man. But in the end, the door opened for further evangelization of Northeast Congo, in the area for which UFM was responsible, and he and Ma Kinso entered it. They never doubted their decision.

A man of the Babua tribe invited them to live and teach in his village, an invitation they accepted. They soon started a school and one of their pupils was a bright boy by the name of Masini. Who at the time could have foreseen that the churches spawned by UFM would some day cover a great deal of the Northeast and one of the outstanding leaders of those churches would be Pastor Masini of this insignificant little village?

This station of Bongondza, named for the clan of the Babua tribe on whose land it stood, was UFM's third in Congo.

More missionaries entered Congo, including the first two from North American UFM, Miss Verna Schade and Miss Viola Walker.

A two-week trip by boat up the Congo River from the national capital, with a stop each night at a shore village, indoctrinated Verna Schade in the ways of Africa. By the time she had quit the boat and traveled overland from Stanleyville to Boyulu she was prepared to go to work as head of a school for girls.

Operating a girls' school was not easy, especially getting girls to attend. Girls did heavy work around the house, drawing water, cutting wood, hoeing rice and cotton, cutting leaves for a roof, gathering food, taking care of children. A woman, even a young girl, walked miles with a burdensome load on her back, it sometimes weighed sixty to a hundred pounds. And girls were the wealth of a family. Father could sell his daughters or give one in marriage for the payment of a hundred or so knives or valuables equivalent to ten American dollars. To give a girl up to study for three hours a day was done only with extreme reluctance.

For years Verna worked to free one of her schoolgirls from the fervency of the girl's father to give his daughter to a rich and powerful but lecherous old man who already had six wives. When grown the girl fell in love with a young evangelist of a neighboring tribe. The youth tried to win the father's favor, but twice the girl was torn from him. Bloodily beaten and threatened with greater harm, she was rescued by her missionary teacher. His daughter's resolve to marry none but a Christian finally persuaded the father to negotiate with the young man she loved, and the story ended happily, the young marrieds going out together to carry the Gospel to another village.

Verna persisted for her girls, imparting to them the courage to "stand firm and pray without ceasing," and through her school many of them grew into fine Christian women. And as boys in their own school grew into responsible Christian men, woman's value developed far beyond the convenient and mercenary.

Verna Schade moved from Boyulu to Bongondza, about three hundred miles distant, and instead of girls there she taught boys. There was no scarcity of them. One evening she was called to settle a dispute between two young fellows and their supporting classmates. One insisted that in a certain month each year foreigners entered the forest to capture women and children and to make mincemeat of their bodies. She laughed and said no foreigner would think of eating an African.

Yokana Jean, the best student in the class, believed the story. Verna was completely surprised because even then this young fellow exhibited many of the traits that in years to come would make him a respected Christian leader as he traveled all over the UFM territory inspecting schools and preaching the Word.

"Not you," said the youth who had posed this case of foreign cannibalism. "Not missionaries, but other foreigners do." For proof he led her to the pantry where several tins of corned beef and finger-like Vienna sausages stocked the shelves. He was certain the cans were filled with his fellow countrymen.

"It's not difficult for them to believe that we eat human meat," Verna wrote home in a prayer letter. "Just think, these people are only one generation from cannibalism."

Missionaries in Congo went on trek rather regularly. Single women missionaries were no exception. During vacation from their schools, Verna Schade and Viola Walker hiked through the forest, stopping at village after village, dispensing the Word of God to people eager to receive it. The Babua people knew of a great, good God, Kunzi, but he was impersonal and because he didn't care about them could be ignored. It was the evil spirits that gained their attention. The everyday occurrences of life were entrusted to chance, and too often chance dealt unkindly, but the spirits had to be cajoled to avoid catastrophe. God's Word, however, told of a great, good God who loved his people too much to leave them to chance, and in overthrowing evil permitted His only Son to sacrifice Himself to obtain their eternal peace and joy.

The two missionary women had heard Kinso use a well-known story among the Babua to illustrate the shedding of Christ's blood to bring about man's peace with God. In an earlier generation clans would fight each other and remain enemies for years. In one instance when enough killing had gone on and peace was desired, a palaver between leaders was arranged.

"For as long as any one of us can remember we have been enemies," one chief said to the other. "If you injured or killed one of our people we were never satisfied until we had our revenge upon one of you. You took the same attitude toward us. Thus, we never knew peace. We are gathered today because one of our people killed one of yours and you are here with your spears and knives demanding revenge. Listen! Back in my village I have a slave girl. Let me bring her here and you can execute her and so your demand for our blood will be satisfied. After that let us live in peace."

The assembled warriors of both sides listened intently and soon agreed to the proposition.

Back in the village, the slave girl knew nothing of this arrangement, and when sent for went unsuspectingly. She was told to walk along the no-man's land separating the two opposing groups. As she obeyed, a warrior stepped stealthily from a hiding place and after she passed him swung a large curved sword. Advancing silently, he crept upon the girl and with one swift stroke severed her head from her body. With a shout of victory, the watching warriors grabbed their spears and leaped forward and bloodied them in the girl's body. Peace thus descended upon the area.

"An illustration," Kinso said each time he told the story, "of Hebrews 9:22: 'Without shedding of blood is no remission.'"

Many on that trip accepted the shedding of Christ's blood as so much better than the blood of an enemy. Taking an immediate stand in their new-found faith, many relinquished their fetishes. If the two women would stay and teach them, they would build churches, they said. But the two could not stay, and there was no one else to send. Verna had boys at Bongondza to teach and Viola girls. They also had to train Congolese teachers who came in periodically from their village schools in the bush. To follow up their trek, Kinso and Ma Kinso after several weeks made the same trip. They found three groups of new believers, true to their word, constructing churches.

Viola Walker had made other treks, among them trips to contact the Pygmy.

These little people — averaging between four and five feet in height — were an enigma to other Congolese. Animals, they were called. They lived in the thickest parts of the forest and seldom let themselves be seen by outsiders. Mainly nomads, they lived on wild fruits and meat obtained by their expert bowmanship. Their houses were tiny tepee-like huts of bamboo and leaves. Those living in the environs of the Ituri River were within reach of Viola's treks, and because they were she included them as part of the reason God called her to Africa.

Her interest in the Pygmy was shared by Lilian Pudney, wife of UFM's North American director. In the 1920s while she and Edwin served in Congo, Lilian Pudney heard of the shy, little people and against the judgment of those who said the Pygmy were incapable of believing, insisted that Christ had died on the cross for them, too. While her husband was busy with the affairs of a large mission station, she went in search of the Pygmy. She had only eight Congolese carriers to accompany her.

Penetrating the dense forest, they came upon a Pygmy village, whose inhabitants had scrambled out of sight before their arrival. Though lacking congregation, the carriers became a choir, Mrs. Pudney the preacher and the jungle their sanctuary. The men sang lustily, and faces began to appear in the forest around them, eyes peeped from behind the trees. Slowly the people emerged, curious children first. She spoke in the dialect she knew, and one of her men with some ability in Pygmy interpreted her message. Each pause for translation gave time for her words to sink in. At the conclusion, a great commotion broke out. The interpreter could not explain what was happening because the people talked too fast for him. Then, out of the solid foliage overhead dropped the chief and a dozen warriors. They had been there all the time. Having heard the message, the chief had at its conclusion asked his people what they thought of it, and their answer came in the ensuing hubbub.

The chief stepped forward, bow and arrows in hand, his warriors flanking him.

"White lady," he said, "those words were very sweet and we shall let you come back into our forest again."

After three months Mrs. Pudney returned to find the Pygmy as friendly as before. On a third trip she suggested that if they wished to hear of God's Book more frequently they should move the tribe to a dense forest nearer the mission station. Then visits could be made much more often. The chief and his people agreed — after all, moving about was common for them and as long as they had the protection of deep forest, it mattered little where they located. They moved to within an hour's hike of the mission station. Still, they were worried that the tall tribes might find them. To avoid detection, they made no trail, but marked a tree along the forest path indicating where the missionary was to turn off into the thick jungle and go for a half hour. The secret sign was sufficient, the going from that point onward difficult. But every week the contact was maintained and the Gospel was shared with them.

One day Mrs. Pudney could not find the marked tree. She thought she had arrived at the turning-off point, but with so many thousands of trees seemingly identical she was not sure. Suddenly, a small man stepped out onto the path.

"White Mother," he said, "we have cut down the tree and cleaned the forest path all the way to our village because we can see your shoes do not understand our jungle."

Precious words, Mrs. Pudney found his speech. The Word of God was boring into their hearts and understanding.

After a few weeks she said that while she had been many times to their village, the chief and his people should visit hers. They agreed to it. One early morning they came, men and boys, women and girls, all single file, to attend the worship services. History was made as the little people and the tall tribesmen sat under the same roof to hear a message from the Lord.

There were converts among the Pygmy, and they were encouraged to reach out to their own people in the hidden areas of the great forest. Following custom, the people eventually moved away, probably to wander again. Among this unusual ethnic group were those whose lives had been changed by God's Spirit and some who could read God's Word. Congolese evangelists began searching the Pygmy out and including them in their itinerant ministries.

In 1946, it was almost twenty years since Lilian and Edwin Pudney had worked in Congo, and now accompanying her husband on a director's trip to Africa, she looked forward to another contact with the Pygmy. She traveled with Viola Walker. They arrived at a large village and found a strange arrangement. A tall bamboo fence separated Babua tribesmen from the Pygmy, each living their own way of life, yet accessible to the other. At sunset the drum was beaten and the village gathered, including the Pygmy, for messages by the two missionary women. In the morning the drum beat was sounded again, but this time only one old woman among the Pygmy came. All the others, the women learned, were preparing for war.

Two weeks before a tribe living in that area of the forest had quarreled. They split into two groups. One night warriors from one of the halves stole a young woman from the other half. Surely there would be retaliation. The guilty sought a haven in the tall tribesmen's village.

Today the two parties would fight. Hearing the war horns sound from the forest, Viola Walker ran to the path at the village edge. Through the forest she saw a great file of diminutive but heavily armed men marching toward her. Lilian Pudney hurried to the other side of the bamboo fence. She found the Pygmy warriors there battle-clad. The chief was exhorting his men. She approached him.

"Why do you go to war? Blood will be shed and some will be wounded."

The chief replied, "When we go to war, there will be no wounded. We kill!"

For a couple of minutes the chief and Mrs. Pudney argued, "Kill!" "No!" "Kill!" "No!"

Suddenly Viola Walker appeared.

"There will be no war!" she exclaimed.

She had stopped the approaching army. Holding her ground and waving her arms, she had yelled "Stop!" and stop they did. Off into the forest the men fled.

Had they seen only a lone woman barring their route to the battlefield? Or had they also seen a host invisible to all but those whom God intended to see it?

The next morning the women prepared to depart. The Pygmy residents assembled with their fellow villagers as if nothing had happened the day before.

In saying good-bye, Mrs. Pudney shook hands with the chief and said, "Now, you won't fight will you?"

"No," he replied in all innocency. "Not until you have gone."

Mrs. Pudney went back to headquarters in the United States and Viola Walker went on furlough to her home in Canada. But on her return to Congo she again sought out the Pygmy.

"Where is your mother?" they asked, inquiring about the older of the two missionaries.

"She is at her home praying for you." Viola said.

The seed that had been sown bore fruit. A number of the Pygmy accepted Christ as Savior, including the chief.

Ekoko was UFM's fourth station in Congo. Hoping to induce missionaries to live in their village, the people there had built a church and guest house. A missionary assigned to Ekoko sent home this report in 1940, shortly after station work began:

"We have just returned from a trek to villages where we have never been before. The first village where we stayed, the entire village accepted Christ as their personal Savior, including the chief, who was an old man. How happy he was! We then went seventy-five miles deeper into the forest and found thousands of people. They lined the road on both sides for long, long distances, and begged us to stay and tell them the story of salvation. We just had to stop, for huge crowds stood in the centre of the road and would not let us pass. We went on and visited other villages, but, oh! what crowds!"

Boyulu, at this time a more mature station, saw no letup. Twenty-two services were held there each week and in a single year a hundred visits were made to surrounding villages. There were baptisms, evangelists were sent to eleven outposts and the medical work increased to the point that building hospital wards and a larger dispensary were priorities.

Good reports came in from Maganga and Bongondza. At the latter, nearly three dozen were ready for baptism, but it was dry season and the nearby streams were down to a trickle. Not to be hindered by nature, the church leaders set to work damming a small creek and when enough water had accumulated to form a pool the service was carried out.

"You will rejoice to know," the report to headquarters said, "five of those baptized were women."

The medical work at Maganga was said to be nothing less than amazing. The outstation work was "an inspiration and a joy."

But ominous clouds were beginning to cover the skies. In 1939 Hitler was on the march. Britain and France and their allies had decided he'd gone far enough and must be stopped. World War II began, and repercussions soon were felt even in the heart of Congo's Ituri Forest.

SOURCES, Chapter 6

Harris, Leonard, *Our Days in His Hands*, Undated, London, Unevangelized Fields Mission

Jenkinson, Herbert, Unpublished, undated manuscript

_____, Letter to Alfred Larson, January 10, 1986

Larson, Alfred, 1996, Notes on early draft

Lifeline, February, 1981, Bala-Cynwyd

Pudney, Lilian, *Discovering the Pigmies in Congo-Zaire*, Unpublished, undated manuscript

Schade, Verna, Prayer letters, Various dates 1937-1939

Truby, David W., *Congo Saga*, Undated, London, Unevangelized Fields Mission

Walker, Viola, *Congo Liana*, Undated, unpublished manuscript

7

Before and During the War

Kinso returned from a year's furlough in 1936 with some thing in the ship's cargo that depicted the changes that were rapidly coming to Congo — an automobile. He drove from French Camerouns to Bongondza, not always, it is true, on roads intended for Twentieth Century developments. Increasingly it was becoming easier to get around the area served by Bongondza — and Boyulu, Maganga and Ekoko as well — and that meant an acceleration in penetrating the hinterlands with the Gospel.

While on furlough he and Ma Kinso had prayed for more than a car. They had felt the need for a doctor in their area; the Lord answered by sending them George Wescott of the United States. In him they got not only physician and surgeon but engineer, carpenter, electrician and musician. In all these fields he displayed the customary skills and combined some to go beyond the conventional, such as applying his violin bow to his carpenter's saw and producing delightful music.

Dr. Wescott gave the station electricity by hooking twenty car batteries to an old generator, which he powered by an automobile engine. He constructed a water wheel and built a radio receiver and transmitter. In putting up his hospital, he equipped its operating room with a diathermy he designed and constructed, and he reversed the insides of a paint sprayer, causing it to suck instead of blow and this made for control of blood in surgeries. The hospital and other station buildings were built strictly with materials that were locally grown or manufactured.

The doctor's radio informed the station of the outbreak of war in Europe. Two Dutch missionaries were at the time working at Bongondza. On May 10, 1940, they listened as over the air came the news that the Germans had invaded the Netherlands and Belgium. They were distressed beyond words when four days later their beloved Holland capitulated. The other missionaries were taxed to console them. Though thousands of miles from the conflict, the missionaries in Congo felt as if they were involved. But what could they do? Fortunately, they each had their work, and of this there was more than enough to keep both body and mind occupied.

The Congolese eventually heard about the war. Believing all Europe was Christian, they could not understand why people there fought each other. Later, as the war dragged on, their comments changed to be more inductive.

"The Belgians need us to win the war for them."

This was not altogether glib patter. As the Japanese shut off Southeast Asian rubber to the Allies, old sources in the Congo forests were tapped again and villagers who had almost forgotten the ways of the jungle were pressed into collecting this vital substance once more. Congolese troops fought in Ethiopia and spent a lot of time in Nigeria and Egypt, some getting to Palestine where at least one Christian soldier was baptized in the Jordan River.

There were now no furloughs for missionaries, transportation to home having become impossible and travel within the country restricted, creating more isolation. Money often failed to arrive from the homeland. Those out in the bush were forced into many adjustments; they lived these years much as the Africans did. One example, they used white ants as cooking grease.

There were advancements during the war years. National pastors and teachers were now stationed in eighty-seven locations. Similar progress was made in Brazil, even while the fields there were likewise under restrictions. Thirteen major stations there were manned by at least two missionaries each during the war years. National Christians stepped forward to assume a greater share in the evangelization of their country. One, a man over 50 years of age, applied for training at the Bible Institute; his wife promised to keep his land productive to earn the money needed to maintain herself and to keep him in school.

Light and Life, the publication of the British UFM, said in one of its wartime issues, "At all costs we must continue to support our missionaries and not only support them but continue to extend our work. A war is not an excuse to go on holiday from our Father's business. We trust and pray that the greatest blessing our Mission has ever known may come upon us during this trying period."

In some areas of the world, that would prove true. In others, the doors on the work closed, temporarily for most, permanently, it eventually proved, for one.

Because of Japanese occupation, all sixteen UFM missionaries were evacuated from Papua, New Guinea. No Europeans could enter Brazil or Congo. French Morocco closed completely. Miss Irena Wenholz had been UFM's sole representative in work among the Berbers of that North African country. The war sent her home and no missionary was allowed to enter. On conclusion of the war UFM did not reopen the field.

At North American headquarters in Philadelphia, the Pudneys coped as best they could with shortages at home and restrictions abroad. This office, junior to the longer-lived London operation, took on the financial responsibility for some of the British workers as the demands of the war on British society became so severe that Britain could not support all her missionaries.

The big house on 63rd Street pulsed with activity. There were public meetings, especially prayer sessions, interviews with prospective missionaries, orientation of accepted candidates,

Council meetings, office work in behalf of the fields. The house also contained living quarters for the Pudneys. Returning missionaries, often with children, occupied rooms from time to time. What at the start had seemed like a huge, rambling castle had, so to speak, shrunk to something comparable to the shoe that housed an old lady and her offspring. A home two doors down the street was rented as an annex. This arrangement would do until post-war growth forced mission personnel to look for something larger and, if possible, in an area a little more quiet than what busy 63rd Street afforded.

Those twelve years in the Overbrook section of Philadelphia are remembered fondly by missionaries and others connected to UFM during and some years after the war. More than a few expressed the conviction that the atmosphere at headquarters would have been the same no matter where or in what circumstance the mission's center was located. Wherever Edwin and Lilian Pudney lived and worked, it became a place of prayer. Prayer for those laboring on the fields, for finances to keep them there, for wise decisions affecting the mission's present and future activities, for an effective witness to the world, for the salvation of Indians and river dwellers in Brazil and for both tall and tiny tribesmen in Congo and headhunters in Papua and for spiritual growth for the thousands who had professed faith in Christ.

Marion Hutchison started as a secretary in 1942. She commuted to the office daily, but stayed over on Tuesdays for the weekly public prayer meeting and whenever a Day of Prayer was scheduled. She enjoyed the times at the dinner table when missionaries were present. There was a relaxed atmosphere with good rapport; at the same time, with Mrs. Pudney as hostess, good English table manners were observed.

With Orientation came a thorough cleaning of headquarters by the candidates, an activity that measured the qualities of humility and industry so necessary for a missionary on the field.

In 1944, Helen Brown applied to UFM for service in Haiti,

but was disqualified because the use of quinine for the malaria of that country would certainly leave her deaf. Mrs. Pudney invited her to work at headquarters. She went through candidate orientation and signed on as cook and housekeeper. For sixteen years she proved that to be an integral part of worldwide missions a missionary is not limited to piloting canoes through cataracts or parsing verbs of an African trade language.

Ethelle (Lufkin) Gibbs also worked at headquarters as a housekeeper and cook. From the beginning she was convinced that the house — the entire mission — ran on prayer. Working closely with Mrs. Pudney as she did, she stood in awe of the mother of the mission. Not that the woman was without her faults, but that she took these faults to the Lord in prayer with far more haste than she spoke to God about the weaknesses of others.

It was during World War II that UFM entered Haiti, but only after the Pudneys traveled to that desperately poor and backward country to see whether the mission could possibly do the people any good. The war was a time to reflect on past accomplishments and missed opportunities and to review the policies that would govern activity when peace came again.

In retrospect, the policies of UFM were sound, and only application of them, rather than their substance, might change in the future.

Of prime importance, UFM was a faith mission. That meant that man's planning took second place to the revealed will of God, and how His will would be carried out by the mission were matters of faith and obedience. Faith in the unity of the Godhead, Father, Son and Holy Spirit, in the full inspiration of the Scriptures, in the necessity and sufficiency of the atoning sacrifice of Christ on the cross and the regenerating and sanctifying work of the Holy Spirit, faith in the personal and visible return of the Lord Jesus and the eternal life and glory of the redeemed and eternal death of unbelievers — these constituted the bedrock of the mission. Added to it was another article of faith — faith in the will, power and providence of God to meet every need, including finances, of His work.

Once it was customary for missionaries to pull their belts in tighter every time a new worker arrived on the field. Edwin Pudney changed that. He believed, and made it a basic principle of the mission, that a candidate's call by God was not sealed until the day his financial support was pledged.

In its history, UFM had carried out the original mandate "to carry the Gospel to those regions that are at present unoccupied by Evangelical Missions and to establish churches of the people as early as possible." There were medical clinics and schools and in post-war times there would be orphanages, printing presses, book stores and radio broadcasts. But always, church planting and nourishing would be the primary thrust. If there were to be an informed body of believers, Bible institutes and schools would have to be considered essential elements of the churches. But education without evangelism was not in UFM's prerogative.

Being a faith mission, UFM belonged to no denomination, and by this independence was able to practice an administration that differed greatly from the traditional foreign mission boards. While a global outlook had to be maintained and cultivated through wide vision and strategic planning, practical direction of the mission was controlled, not by headquarters, but by the missionaries on the various fields. Philadelphia, assisted by Toronto, and London and Melbourne were more coordinating than commanding agencies. Each national office existed for the benefit of the missionaries on the line and for sending out additional personnel or replacements. Every field was staffed by missionaries from two of the three UFM entities and a few by all three. Easily seen as a problem of nationalities, this arrangement was not. Once on the field, the missionary reported not to the home office, but to his field council. The chairman might be a Britisher, an Australian, a Canadian or an American. He was elected by his fellow workmen at the annual field conference. The national office was drawn in on a problem only if a field council believed such intervention was necessary and beneficial.

Another element in field-oriented management was added as the work matured and churches on a particular field banded together for mutual support and fellowship and as they themselves produced missionaries. National mission bodies were established in the countries to which foreign missionaries had been sent. These would become the governing agencies in their own land, and whether one was a Bible Institute graduate from Brazil or a doctor from America or England, he served under the organization that included both nationals and foreign missionaries.

Because of the war Kinso and Ma Kinso had gone eight years without a furlough. At last, in 1944 opportunity came for them to sail in a convoy for England. Each night Kinso joined the other men aboard in keeping watch for enemy activity, and the usual blackouts and zig-zag maneuverings prevailed. Without serious incident, they arrived in Liverpool in mid-summer. The landings on Normandy beaches had taken place and some analysts were calculating that a favorable end to the war was just a matter of time.

The Nazis, however, were in their waning days making good use of a heretofore secret weapon, raining terrible destruction on Britain. By the thousands they sent over "pilotless planes" or V-1 rocket bombs with deadly effect. Arriving in London, the Kinsos were introduced to the underground shelters as a place to sleep. Home less than a week, Kinso went out for a stroll one evening and heard the engine of a plane overhead cut out and seconds later a terrific explosion close by. Another V-1 had found a target. He rushed back to where he and Ma Kinso were living, thinking he'd find her remains among the rubble. She was alive and not seriously hurt.

Deputation during the nightly blackouts Kinso described as "not easy," and the furlough was far from pleasant. He and Ma Kinso were happy to set their faces toward Congo again.

The war did end to the relief of the whole world. Its conclusion ushered in a new era for missions. Thousands of young Christian men and women had seen and experienced places in the world which in their school days had been only pictures in an encyclopedia. New forms of communication and transportation had become commonplace. The promise of full employment in a world eager to catch up on years of material impairment would make money available for whatever cause once championed.

Most important, the Spirit of God was urging the Church of Jesus Christ to step into this new world and take the Gospel of redemption to those to whom it had not yet been preached.

SOURCES, Chapter 7

Harris, Leonard F., *Our Days in His Hands*, Undated, London, Unevangelized Fields Mission

Jenkinson, Herbert, Undated, Unpublished manuscript

Larson, Alfred and Jean, 1995, Interview with author

Larson, Alfred, 1966, Notes on early draft

Light & Life, Bala-Cynwyd, Unevangelized Fields Mission, January-February 1944

Pudney, Edwin J. and Lilian G., Undated, *Sacrifice of Praise*, Bala-Cynwyd, Unevangelized Fields Mission

8

Hope for Haiti

UFM entered Haiti in 1943. It was an old country, as countries in the Western Hemisphere go. The island of Hispaniola, part of which it occupies, was one of the first to be discovered by Columbus in 1492. It was off the shores of what is now Cap Haïtien that his flagship *Santa Maria* went aground. From the broken timbers and splintered planks Columbus built a small fort, La Navidad, and left thirty-nine of his crew as colonizers. Theirs was the first European settlement in the New World.

On his second voyage Columbus discovered the fort burned, the men dead, both the work of hostile natives. But quest for gold drew the persistent Spanish. They forced the Indians into oppressive labor and soon the native population perished. To continue their exploitation, the Spanish began in 1510 to import African slaves, these becoming the progenitors of the Haitian people. In 1697 Spain ceded the western third of Hispaniola to France. Building on a slave economy, the French developed their new colony into one vast sugar plantation and it became their richest possession.

The people rebelled, futilely at first, but by uniting in 1798 gained hope of freedom under Toussaint L'Overture, a freed slave. Toussaint died in a French prison, but his successor, Jean Jacques Dessalines, "The Tiger," drove out the French in late 1803, and the next year proclaimed the colony's independence and massacred almost all the remaining Europeans. The plantations, irrigation works, sugar mills and roads fell to wreckage. Dessalines was assassinated in 1806 and was succeeded by Henri Christophe, who in his attempt to rehabilitate his devastated country built himself an ornate palace and a massive citadel, whose spectacular ruins endure. Following his death, one military despot after another seized power.

Haiti, free of European influence, lacked the investment, the stability, the societal institutions and the preparation for independence that other colonies generally received from their governing nations, particularly the English. Thus, Haiti has always been a poor, isolated land, and today ranks near the bottom on the world's economic scale. Though poor in the pocketbook, the Haitian people are warm in spirit. That spirit has more often than not, however, been prey to the policies and practices that have kept the people in bondage.

Voodooism, with sorcery at its heart, is the prevailing religion, whether in pure form or fused with State-recognized Catholicism. God is recognized as good, one who harms nobody, thus may be ignored; it is the evil spirits who must be appeased, and this is often done through animal sacrifices demanded by the witchdoctors. In the past, human sacrifice was not unknown. The dead are believed to exercise great power over the living, so fear envelops the Haitian. Yet today, evangelical Christianity has a firm base in Haiti, and because of its sponsorship of education and medicine and its identification with the common people, its influence is greater than its numbers would suggest.

The Wesleyan Methodists entered the country from England in 1821, the Baptists from Jamaica in 1850. In 1923 the Reverend John Alfred Edward Pearce, an Englishman, began his labors on the north coast. He had good success, but his health deteriorated and in 1928 his mission board ordered him home. He declined, however, to surrender to the mere physical. Relieved of his church in Port-de-Paix, he founded the Haitian Gospel Mission on March 20, 1928. Taking two young Haitian preachers with him, he went to La Tortue, an island off the coast, and there began evangelizing one of the nation's strong centers of voodooism.

Three years later the church in Port-de-Paix, now severed from its British sponsors, recalled Pearce as pastor, and the work spread from there. Before his death in 1941, at age 74, some two thousand Haitians had become believers, and these were organized into six churches, with three capable pastors, Sem Salvant, Isaac Etienne and Jansénius Lange.

The progress the Gospel made on the north coast during Pearce's lifetime might be attributed to this pioneer's dedication and the enthusiasm he exhibited in his ministry. No doubt a part, however, could be traced to the prayers of a godly man in Los Angeles. An elderly physician, M. H. Chamberlain closed his office every afternoon at three o'clock and spent the rest of the day, not breaking for dinner, in reading the Word of God and praying for God's work. In 1936 he knew that at age 87 his time on earth would not be long, so called a friend to his side and said, "For years my heart has been burdened for Haiti and I have been praying for that needy people. Now I am going Home and shall no longer be able to carry the burden. I want you to continue to pray for Haiti."

It is not known that Dr. Chamberlain ever saw Haiti or a Haitian. He died in the year that the Lord began His miraculous dealings with that country.

Following World War I, fifty-to-eighty thousand Haitians migrated to Cuba to work in the sugar fields. For years they were content to earn money and enjoy relatively good living conditions, speak their Creole and maintain their own culture quite apart from their Spanish-speaking neighbors. Then the Great Depression hit Cuba. In their narrowing straits, thousands of the Haitians were driven to desperation, and it was reported that hundreds turned to the Lord. Through the 1930s the economy worsened; in 1936 and 1937 some forty thousand laborers were shipped back to Haiti. Though having nothing but their faith to sustain them, the Christians among the returnees dispersed over the country and spread the good news of salvation through Jesus Christ. One count in 1940 enumerated ten thousand evangelical Christians in one hundred congregations.

Following Pearce's death, Pastor Sem Salvant, who had gone to La Tortue with Pearce and worked closely with him for years, shared the responsibility for the Haitian Gospel Mission with his fellow pastors Etienne and Lange. They came to feel that missionaries from outside the country were needed to keep the work going. Salvant contacted Dr. Oswald Smith, pastor of the People's Church in Toronto, having heard he was a great supporter of missions. Smith proposed a director to him, a missionary already working in Haiti, Alexander Mersdorf who, with his wife Mary, ministered in the south of the country around Les Cayes. Mersdorf accepted, but felt there should be a broader base than merely Haitian. He was thinking of setting up a new board in the United States when Oswald Smith introduced him to Edwin Pudney of Unevangelized Fields Mission. Pudney advised against a new mission agency. Mersdorf then asked for inclusion in UFM and this was effected on May 7, 1943.

Six years before, Alexander and Mary Mersdorf and a single woman missionary from Cuba, Zeida Campos, all fresh from language training with the West Indies Mission, now called World Team, had moved to Les Cayes in the south of Haiti just days before the landing of a mass immigration of Haitian returnees from Cuba. They threw themselves into in a hands-on ministry that never diminished in their years of service with UFM.

A prayer of Alfred Pearce had been for missionaries to help in the work. He did not live to see its answer, but one of the pastors he had trained gratefully acknowledged the fulfillment during the first visit of Edwin and Lilian Pudney to Haiti..

The Pudneys were part of a large congregation that heard the pastor pray. With tears in his eyes, Isaac Etienne poured out his heart to God: "Today we see the answer to the many prayers offered by Mr. Pearce. He so often asked God for missionaries to help evangelize our people. In his lifetime this was not granted, but today we behold the answer. We have the Reverend E. J. Pudney, the mission leader from America, who promises to send workers that we may be adequately helped. Let us all pray and work without relaxation. To God be the glory forever."

The young mission was strengthened when shortly Dr. Hector Paultre, pastor of a large Baptist church in St. Marc, with sixteen outstations, led his congregation into affiliation with UFM. Two other churches joined in at the same time. Dr. Paultre, coming from a prestigious family, was an honored citizen of Haiti and besides being a pastor was a senator, a medical doctor and a recognized mathematician. His brother, Volny, was an import-export businessman in St. Marc and, noteworthy in the Haitian church's history, the father of Dr. Orius Paultre, who for many years would be one of its foremost leaders.

Haiti is a mountainous land of hurricanes and drought, soil erosion and, with seven million people living on less than eleven thousand square miles, two-thirds of the land non-arable, a crowded population. Despite destruction from the skies, parched earth, never-ending poverty and political turmoil, the church steadily grew. Church planting and Bible teaching remained paramount, but the needs of the people spawned new thrusts — into education and medical work, care for children, leadership training, printing and literature distribution, rural penetration, camp and conference work. Mersdorf bought land at La Pointe des Palmistes, about four miles from Port-de-Paix, for many of these ministries. La Pointe was to become a chief focus for UFM's endeavors.

In 1949 UFM entered into an agreement with the churches that recognized the prior existence of the Mission Evangélique Baptiste d' Haiti (or, in English, the Evangelical Baptist Mission of Haiti) and the autonomy of the local Baptist congregations. MEBH itself was reorganized that same year and Pastor Sem Salvant elected president. UFM was recognized as sponsor for the Bible school, girls' and boys' homes, medical work, and a printing press in the vicinity of Port-au-Prince.

Mary Mersdorf and Grace Gulick started a dispensary under a tree at La Pointe. Then they moved it into a tiny house of two rooms. From time to time a physician visited from Port-au-Prince, the capital city one hundred fifty miles to the south. It was not until Caroline Bradshaw brought her nursing skills to Haiti in 1943, however, that the clinic took on definite shape. She had wanted to go to Africa, but World War II eliminated that dream, so she went instead to a bit of Africa in the Western Hemisphere — Haiti.

Vance and Joy Brown who, along with Neoma Snider, had been candidates for Brazil until that field was closed by the war, arrived later that year, Richard and Martha Wilkinson in 1946 and Ralph and Majil Odman in 1947. John and Jackie Schmid, Lehman and Luella Keener and Catherine Froh were among eleven missionaries who joined UFM when their mission, the World Christian Crusade, merged with UFM in 1949.

This merger brought an embryonic Bible school and its partly completed building as well as work in central Haiti into the mission.

Florent Toirac, a Cuban, had begun the school after six years of fruitful itinerant evangelism in Haiti's Southern Peninsula and another six in Port-au-Prince. He had left Cuba as an independent missionary with two suitcases and sixty dollars, though his money was stolen before his ship departed. He and a Haitian layman worked tirelessly in fighting the grip in which witchcraft held the people. They planted churches wherever victories were won. Because he was considered a national and not a missionary, the American mission group with which he cooperated refused to permit his marriage to one of their young women. This prompted his separation from the mission. His fellow workers assumed responsibility for more than a hundred churches that had been opened, and Toirac moved to Port-au-Prince.

The capital city offered a great opportunity for evangelism. Toirac plunged in immediately. He soon married the young woman he loved and her church in Indiana asked him to head up the work it contemplated through its own new mission society. A couple had already been sent to Gonaives, a coastal city in the arid north. Besides planting churches, Toirac intended to start a Bible school. Before Gonaives came into the picture, he had only Port-au-Prince in mind as the site. Now he walked the road north, inspecting land and the environment all along the route to Gonaives. Nothing satisfied him. Back in Port-au-Prince he selected twenty-eight acres atop a hill in Bolosse, a community on the southern edge of the city. As it commanded a dramatic view of the sea, Toirac determined that the building should be worthy of the site — a solid, well-built two-story structure would cost about sixty-thousand dollars. The building fund contained six hundred.

But with that amount and a great deal of faith the work began. The ten students already enrolled in the Bible school, who attended classes in a rented house, pitched in and helped with the construction. Only window frames and doors and the final touches were lacking when Toirac's connection with the school — and his service in Haiti — came to a sudden end. The church that had started the new mission board took a turn in its doctrine that was unacceptable to the missionaries on the field. The missionaries voted to sever and the board dissolved. Toirac urged that they start their own society. The others preferred to join an existing board. They chose UFM, whose work they had seen in the north. Toirac, who was in Indiana voicing the concerns of himself and his co-workers, returned to Haiti only long enough to sign papers turning over the defunct board's interest to UFM. He went on to Europe to a major role in a Bible school in France and later had a wide-spread radio ministry among Spanish-speaking people.

In the north, at La Pointe and other locations to which the work had spread, the UFM staff and their national co-workers were extending the evangelical witness into areas where once the darkest of powers had reigned. War did not stop them. In fact, with new missionaries diverted to Haiti because of travel and financial restrictions for other places, more needs of a very needy people could be met.

La Pointe soon boasted of a church, an elementary school, a vocational school, homes for orphaned boys and girls and a small hospital.

Caroline Bradshaw, UFM's first nurse in Haiti, loved children. Knowing that she did, Ralph Odman felt free to bring home a child he came across on one of his treks to outlying small villages. He noticed in a dark corner of a lay preacher's home a young boy lying shriveled on the floor. The boy was crippled. Perhaps Miss Caro could help him? She could, and did.

Caroline thought she was seeing an unusual number of children with ailing backs, particularly severely curved spines. She was. They suffered from Pott's disease, caused mainly by tuberculosis of the spine. In her trips through the hilly countryside in back of La Pointe she saw many children with reddish hair. Not children of the Devil as superstition had it; these little ones, she maintained, were protein-starved. The TBs, the red heads and other children suffering from other diseases and deformities needed to be in the mission hospital. But where to put them? The children's room was always filled. She vowed to build a ward just for the children.

"House of Hope," she called it. And for the many hundreds this first structure and its successors housed, there was hope — hope for a cure and a normal life, hope for a loving family among those whom Christ had taught to love, hope for inclusion in God's own family.

Periodically, Miss Caro loaded up her car or a borrowed truck with children needing surgery for their spines or chests or limbs and drove them as gently as possible over roads that sometimes were not roads but washed-out tracks and through streams and across hot mountain ridges to a very modern hospital built and operated by Dr. Larry Mellon, of the famed Pittsburgh family, and his wife Gwen. There her children received the utmost that medical treatment in this very poor country could give them. In return, the House of Hope provided long-term loving care for many of the hospital's patients.

The Albert Schweitzer Hospital lay between La Pointe and Port-au-Prince. At times, Caroline drove beyond it to the capital city. It was there that Sister Joan Margaret, of the Episcopalian Hospital for Handicapped Children, provided her with braces and crutches for twisted little backs and legs. Help for the children came also from another source. Numerous physicians, many of them highly trained surgeons and specialists, traveled from their sophisticated hospitals and clinics in the United States over the rutted routes of Haiti to apply (without remuneration) their skills to the hurting among both the children and adults. Many of them came because of Caroline Bradshaw's power to persuade.

Miss Caro was much more than a medical professional to the children in her House of Hope. To her children, she became mother, teacher, evangelist and cook.

Kenny Vil was a poor boy whose family lived near the La Pointe mission center. To deliver him at birth, Caroline had crawled through a barbed-wire fence at night to reach his mother. He was a bright boy, but had no prospects of attending school. Miss Caro saw that he got what education the local community could provide, then sent him to Port-au-Prince for a five-year carpentry program. Kenny Vil eventually became administrator of UFM's Béraca Medical Centre next to his old home. He also directed a vocational program that gave men and women training in a trade, and he worked to set up a basic program of training for boys to help them escape from the snares of the street.

Linda Félix suffered a crippled body, and her family's voodoo beliefs were unable to help her. Caroline took her in, raised and educated her and she became a later director of the House of Hope.

He was only a crippled youngster, a worthless scrap of humanity in the eyes of his family, when Noser Poliard was abandoned in the street in front of the House of Hope. Miss Caro rescued him, cared for him, obtained surgery for him and guided him through school and on to Bible school. He became the bookkeeper and paymaster for the Béraca Medical Centre and a leader in the Béraca Church. Héclatant Pierre, a victim of polio, was another taken in, cared for, won to Christ and sent to Bible school. He became pastor of the church at Champagne.

To Miss Caro, her young charges were not crippled children, but normal, lively, sometimes happy, sometimes cranky, often mischievous youngsters trapped in twisted, ailing bodies. Doing everything medically possible for them, she and her associates went beyond the physical. The children loved to sing, and they sang lustily from full hearts. Their annual Christmas program drew an audience from all around. School was very important. Those who could not walk or maneuver on crutches still were part of a curious, heart-stabbing parade every morning. The more able among the children rolled the cast-encased tykes on their beds or carried them on boards, knowing that none must miss his lessons.

Caroline Bradshaw did not limit her compassion to the children in her wards. She offered herself as private-duty nurse for many an ailing man or woman. She took on a responsibility for new missionaries. Often she would counsel them to open their homes freely to pastors and other visitors. The spirit in which people were received was more important than what was served to them.

"They'll remember how they felt," she would say, "and how welcome you made them, long after they forget what you fed them or what color your dishes were."

Meeting Robert and Nona Bitner during the new couple's orientation at Bala-Cynwyd, she advised Bob to take the time to learn how to repair Jeeps before going to Haiti. The advice was practical, an experienced couple could attest. Driving Haiti's terrible country roads over a couple of decades, Vance and Joy Brown wore out five Jeeps, wishing at times they had stuck with the slow and bony but dependable mule of their earlier years.

Famine often stalked the Northwest Peninsula of Haiti. Caroline Bradshaw would load up her old Jeep with bread, rice, peanuts and whatever else she could put her hands on and drive out to that desolate area and dispense food along with medical care. Once in appreciation the head man of the village of Passe Catabois gave her five acres of land, though he was excommunicated by his church for doing so. Caroline had a small house built on the land for a Bible school graduate, and that was the beginning of a church that grew to be of considerable size. It became the mother church for five others and sponsored three drinking-water projects and a reforestation center. At one point Caroline turned the House of Hope over to others and moved into the arid Northwest to begin a new medical work. As she had done at La Pointe, she soon began training poor, uneducated people to some day take her place.

At the House of Hope, in the hospital and in the clinics conducted several days a week in the countryside and the island of Tortue, spiritual needs received attention along with the physical. For many years Klébert Duré served as chaplain. He is remembered as a "poor preacher but a matchless soul winner." The number of patients and members of their families who were won to Christ often reached the hundreds annually. Thus, not only were the sick kept alive, extending their opportunity to hear the Gospel, and the care provided served as an alternative to voodoo approaches to bodily ills, but the Béraca Medical Centre became a prime vehicle for the direct winning of souls to Christ. In numbers, some years it surpassed any other one endeavor.

Neoma Snider, Charlotte Dancy, Clara Hess and Loretta Eberly were indispensable to the medical ministry. Clara Hess set up a one-room laboratory for examining the tens of thousands of cultures she took over her long career. Yaws was a common ailment when the clinic began. Application of the newly available penicillin brought the problem under control. It soon became common knowledge that help could be had at La Pointe for stomach aches, eye infections, kidney failures and Mama's pregnancy. Families moved onto the La Pointe campus the night before a clinic. The times when visiting doctors came from Philadelphia or Lancaster, the lines wound far down the road.

Loretta Eberly realized that the missionary nurses could not do the job demanded of them. She began to train young Haitian women as nurses. The initial class numbered three. The program grew to a dozen or so trainees in a three-year course.

Dr. Orius Paultre joined the staff in 1947. The Béraca Medical Center acquired in him more than a skilled physician. He was a man overflowing with the spirit of Christ. Always having wanted to become a pastor, he studied medicine to please his father, and convinced that his father's wish was not unreasonable, equipped himself to help the poor among his people. But often he would say, "I am a preacher first, then a doctor."

Dr. Orius, as he was known, did become a pastor. He led the church at La Pointe while heading the work at the medical center. For seventeen years he served the UFM-affiliated churches as their national president. He was looked to as an impartial moderator, often bringing divergent factions together through his calm judgment, deep understanding of his fellow men and his daily application of God's Word to his own life. Some men in his position would have spent much of their time in the nation's capital hobnobbing with people of importance. While on appropriate occasions he spoke in behalf of the believers to government officials, Dr. Orius left the area around La Pointe as little as possible. He counted his work there among the ailing poor to be more important than almost anything he could be doing elsewhere. He knew just about every trail in the North. He covered them all on the back of a mule. After delivering babies and treating the sick and counseling folk all day and far into the night, he would arrive home exhausted. The next morning, however, he'd rise early, ready and eager to start another very full day.

His wife Nellie came from an equally high-class family. She was as dedicated to the Lord's work as he, and in whatever gathering she happened to be, set the spiritual tone. Her faith was practical and active; she gathered in the children around La Pointe, opened a school for them and devoted years to it as a teacher and superintendent.

One report during the 1950s gave the number of congregations allied with UFM as three hundred, with twenty-five thousand believers. Nearly three thousand children attended church-related schools. Medical treatments in a year exceeded thirteen thousand.

This progress had not come easily. The work was going well when one day a newcomer to Haiti held out the promise of easy money to congregations in one section of the North. More than a hundred left the association affiliated with UFM. Ralph and Majil Odman had come to Haiti to work with these churches. Their shock at the news was understandable.

"With no churches to serve, what are we here for?" they asked the Lord. His answer was to draw the wayward churches back to their first allegiance.

The voodoo environment that permeated every section was not easy to work in. The superstitions of many generations were difficult to penetrate, and the witchdoctors who enforced them were formidable foes of the Gospel. Yet it was from voodooism that converts usually came. Commonly, whole families made the decision, and it came not in a church meeting but in the home. Regular Bible teaching and constant encouragement by the believers were necessary to break the bondage that Satan through his earthly power had held them in.

Vance and Joy Brown arrived in Haiti in December of 1943. They were thought of as "general" missionaries. That meant they did everything, without particular notice, that missionaries were supposed to do. Week-ends were especially busy. Typically, on a different Sunday of each month they visited the four churches assigned to them. Building projects might occupy the week, or there would be teaching or helping in the dispensary or balancing the books — all of which the Browns did — or perhaps it was a week in which malaria had laid them low, but come the week-end, they pushed themselves out into the countryside, riding either a horse, a mule or in a Jeep.

"We have had a baptismal service at each of our four churches," wrote Joy Brown to friends in 1951. "We have also had the generator and movie sound projector all this month in order to conduct special services at the same time. The first Sunday we were at Jean Rabel (a town in the northwest of Haiti). Vance had arrived home from the church past midnight Saturday night, for it had taken him and the church committee that long to question the twenty-eight believers who were to be baptized the following morning. It thrilled us through and through to see so many young people take this important step. It is important in this country because each believer must pass at least six months in a class of instruction, then be questioned by the church committee, and finally be accepted by the membership before he can be baptized."

She described the visit to another of their churches.

"All day Friday Vance was away on his horse, going further across the peninsula in order to perform two marriages. He returned just after dark, but I had the projector lined up and we showed movies with Creole explanation to the crowd. Movies are entirely new to these people, and in a new way the Gospel was made clear."

Early Saturday, Vance rode his horse over muddy trails across the mountain to another wedding and meeting with believers, and made it back in time for another Sunday morning baptism. "It was a real thrill to see the number of Christians who waded through mud up to their knees, for almost an hour, to get to a water hole big enough for the baptism . . . I wish you could have seen the crowds in church that day — everyone in bare feet! What was the use of washing their feet when they had to walk home through the mud again? Besides, there was no water on top of the mountain!" Shoes were too precious an item to get wet. For many families, they were seen only on other people, and likely these were not their fellow villagers. All through its history, poverty has been the national epidemic of Haiti. Like politicians elsewhere, those seeking public office promised jobs and good times. Seldom did fulfillment come. A road started by one administration was abandoned by its successor. Changes in government happened too often for most people to keep up.

John and Helen Beerley arrived in Haiti in late 1955. In their first six months they experienced fifty-five revolutions and six changes of government. The climate stabilized when Dr. François Duvalier was voted into the presidency in 1957, but at a price. Seven years later he was declared president for life, but already there were consequences almost everywhere of his despotic rule. The secret police were feared. Killings eliminated much of his opposition. No one was safe. "Papa Doc," as Duvalier was called, died in 1971, and was succeeded by his son, "Baby Doc," whom many saw as a faithful reproduction of his father.

To pastor a church in these times of poverty, superstition and political oppression required a man to be brave and determined in his calling. Missionaries had to walk a tight apolitical rope, and at times leaving the country for a period was necessary, especially for the women and children.

"The killings were not easy to take," said Beerley, "but knowing that he (Duvalier) would one day answer to the Lord for his conduct helped keep our sanity."

Pastor Isaac Etienne worried about the children of believers. They needed to be educated, but to send them to schools of another religion would surely lose many of them to the faith of their homes. The solution was the same as in Congo and other fields where this problem existed — each local church to conduct a local school. Teachers had to come from the congregations and salaries from tuition — ten cents a month. Blackboards were made by mixing whitewash and charcoal dust. Textbooks were in French, so the children had to be taught that language.

Catherine Froh, one who came into UFM by the 1949 merger, had been a teacher in the United States. She brimmed with ideas on how the Christian schools of Haiti should develop. She, Nellie Paultre and Majil Odman called the teachers to La Pointe for a first Teacher's Institute. No theoretical session this; they helped the teachers find pictures and other useful materials and taught them teaching methods as few of those attending had had many years of education themselves.

Verna Schade was a war-time transplant from the Congo field. At La Pointe she taught children and also men in the Bible school. She encouraged a new missionary to pursue her dream of an orphanage for girls. Ethel Donor started that work in 1945, gathering in street children from the area, and along with Marjorie Arnott taught them in the shade of a tree.

A boys' orphanage followed. Started by Wilfred and Grace Gulick, its leadership passed to Stanley and Gladys Hanson. As needs changed, the orphanages evolved into boarding homes for the various schools at La Pointe. The Hansons made hosting the boys their life work. For forty-three years, La Pointe was Ethel Donor's home.

Richard Wilkinson was a product of a Christian camp back in Ohio where speakers such as Isaac Page of the China Inland Mission and UFM's Edwin J. Pudney stimulated his interest in missions. It was natural that he wanted to launch such a camp for the young people of Haiti. But there was hesitation on the part of some missionaries — did they have the leadership, the facilities, the money to make it work? With their hesitant approval, Dick went ahead, along with Clara Hess, who took time out from her lab chores to minister to young people. Camp Bethel at La Pointe was successful. It was repeated in subsequent years, and the program expanded to include camps for younger children, older youth, women and church leaders. Eventually, camps were conducted at nine sites, and from them many Haitian young people went on to secondary and Bible schools and became valuable workers in their home churches.

Dick and Martha Wilkinson possessed the gift of encouragement for young missionaries. Whether in charge of the work at La Pointe or pastoring churches in St. Marc or Gonaives, they helped the new arrivals with French and Creole, languages Dick had easily mastered. He helped start a chapter of Intervarsity Christian Fellowship at the university in Port-au-Prince. As he rode the circuit to churches outside St. Marc, he set up classes for Bible training of pastors and lay leaders. And he pulled teeth. Having learned this specialty from an American dentist, he always carried his forceps in a pocket. Everywhere he went, pulling teeth became a part of his ministry.

Significant in his service were the years devoted to evangelism. Using a tent, he held meetings in Port-au-Prince and the larger towns, and often the educated and business-class people attended the meetings. He became a Paul to his Timothy as he rescued a discouraged, almost failing missionary and thrust him into an unusual type of evangelistic preaching.

Peter Golinski had intended to work in printing in Haiti. But that line failed to work out for him. What else could he do? He had no formal training in theology, though he read widely.

"Why not use another of your talents?" challenged Wilkinson.

Golinski was a natural artist. And he discovered he could preach very well. He combined these two skills through chalk artistry. Soon, Peter Golinski, the chalk artist, was in demand all over Haiti. His unique ministry extended beyond the UFM-affiliated churches, with emphasis on a deeper life for the Christian as well as salvation for the one who had not before heard the Gospel.

One of the first UFM ministries in Haiti was the printing of Christian literature. When a small, simple printing press arrived, Donald and Florence Evans immediately put it to use. They shared the upstairs of a building in Port-de-Paix with the Mersdorfs; the press went below. At the outset there was no electricity to drive its motor, so it was worked by a foot peddle — twenty-one thousand times a day. Tracts were a prime product; these were sent to all parts of the country through a monthly tract club. A periodical, *The Morning Star*, appeared in both French and Creole every month. Circulation was among pastors, missionaries and other Christian workers.

The Evanses moved the press out of Port-de-Paix and south to

Pétionville, a high-elevation town just west of Port-au-Prince, then into the capital itself.

Ten thousand copies of a hymn book were produced. A machine that could spew out such huge quantities of printed matter was naturally of great interest to the Haitians. Crowds gathered as the press started up each morning, and when Evans deemed the numbers large enough, he would begin a Bible class, teaching his curious on-lookers the simple message of the Gospel—while under his hand the same message was repeated over and over on paper for countless others. The hymnal, *Chants d' Espérance*, became the most popular product of the press. The songs of hope and joy found in the book met the Haitians' love for singing. Soon this hymnal was in use in most of the nation's churches, either in French or Creole.

The Evanses found it necessary to leave Haiti, and when they did, the printing press went idle. It was not until 1957 with the coming of Ed and Elsie Mae Kettleson that production of literature reclaimed an importance among field activities.

"A printer from birth," Kettleson describes himself, his father having had such a business in Chicago, this giving him ample on-the-job training. As an adult he worked at the Moody Bible Institute print shop and at a newspaper in Wisconsin. He was shocked when one day a letter arrived from UFM asking him to apply his trade for the Lord in Haiti. One year from the day that letter was received, the Kettlesons landed in Haiti, ready to begin work.

Before they could print even a postcard, a huge amount of work had to be done. Outside, the press building looked like an abandoned outhouse on the UFM compound. It was no more attractive inside. Rats, cockroaches, termites and rust had damaged much of the equipment. Supplies did not exist. Rather discouraging for someone who had just left modern, spic-and-span press-rooms. But, Kettleson reasoned, and brightened as he did, the Lord had led him to Haiti so there was no alternative to putting this shop in running order.

Scrubbing, patching, repairing eventually enabled wheels to turn. Funds for equipment and supplies came from the Back to the Bible Broadcast in the US. Rollers began transferring impressions onto paper. La Presse Evangélique was again in business.

Over the years other donations in money and equipment arrived, and even the building housing the press was doubled in size. Kettleson trained Haitians as printers with the thought that some day they would replace him and other missionaries in this phase of the work.

One outlet for this printed matter was a bookstore that not only sold Bibles and books but frequently was the scene of personal evangelism. It was begun in 1950 as part of Haiti's Bicentennial Exposition. The downtown portion of Haiti's waterfront was converted into a shoreline boulevard and new commercial building were erected on its land side. The mission approached the authorities, asking to buy land and their request was granted. UFM erected a small but attractive shop and crowned it with a sign in the shape of an open Bible. Its French-language text proclaimed to all passers-by, "For the wages of sin in death but the gift of God is eternal life through Jesus Christ our Lord." In the first year, the citizens of Port-au-Prince bought nearly eighteen thousand pieces of literature.

Alexander and Mary Mersdorf, the first leaders of UFM in Haiti, departed the field at the end of 1946 and were succeeded by Wilfred and Grace Gulick. As the Mersdorfs had done, the Gulicks stamped their mark on the work. Then poor health sent them back to America. Ralph and Majil Odman had been in Haiti only six months when they were chosen the new field leaders. But they were still in language training. So Murdeen McIver became the interim field leader. Possibly the first woman to fill this responsibility for the mission, she entered it well qualified. Not only was she an all-around missionary, but a multi-talented person. She taught in the Bible school at La Pointe. She was persuasive in guiding the break-away churches to reaffiliate. Her gifts ranged from writing poetry to leadership. Murdeen guided UFM in Haiti at a critical time.

Ralph Odman knew he had a solid foundation on which to build. That there would be much building of the ministries in Haiti was not doubted by anyone knowing him. He was said to be a man of many visions and one whose visions habitually became realities.

SOURCES, Chapter 8

Annual Reports, 1990 and 1995, Bala-Cynwyd, PA, Unevangelized Fields Mission

Beerley, John A., 1995, 1996, Letters to Author

Bitner, Robert O., 1996, Letters to Author

Brown, Joy, 1996, Letters to Author

_____, Undated, Unpublished paper

_____, News & Prayer Letter, November 5, 1951

Conference, Retired Haiti missionaries with author, May, 1996, Lancaster, PA

Courier Evangélique, Le, Port-au-Prince, UEBH, February 1979

Donor, Ethel, Undated, Unpublished paper

Harris, Leonard F., *Our Days in His Hands*, Undated, London, Unevangelized Fields Mission

Kettleson, Ed, 1995, Letter to author

Light & Life, Bala-Cynwyd, Unevangelized Fields Mission, February 1944; January-February 1947; First Quarter 1952; Third Quarter 1958; Fourth Quarter 1958

Loyer, Gloria, 1993, Unpublished paper

Pearl of the Antilles, Audio-tape script, Undated, Bala-Cynwyd, Unevangelized Fields Mission

Piepgrass, Charles, 1995, Letter to author

Pudney, Edwin J., *Haiti, White Already to Harvest*, 1944, Philadelphia, Unevangelized Fields Mission

Pudney, Edwin J. and Lilian G, Undated, Bala-Cynwyd, Unpublished paper

Pudney, Lilian G., *God Which Worketh*, 1953, Bala-Cynwyd, Unevangelized Fields Mission

Toirac, Florent D., *A Pioneer Missionary in the Twentieth Century*, Undated, Self-published

Wilkinson, Richard, Audio-tape, 1996

Wilson, Majil Odman, Letter to author

9

The Wai Wai Story

Having just completed graduate school at Columbia Bible College, Neill Hawkins, a lanky, perceptive, intuitive Texan, wanted nothing quite so much as to take the Gospel of Jesus Christ to jungle Indians. The fire in his soul had been fed continuously all through his life.

While a student at Wheaton College, he had been drawn toward missions by a guest speaker, Dr. Robert C. McQuilkin, Columbia's president. Earlier, he had read the biography of C. T. Studd. Of course, there was also the inner spark fanned by his parents. His mother had expected to become a missionary until marriage redirected her field of service to being the wife of an old-fashioned evangelist and radio preacher. Bearing three sons, she raised them with much prayer and spent Sunday afternoons immersing them in the lives of missionary giants who had made history. William Hawkins was no less influential, having covenanted with the Lord that his sons should one day take up his mantle of spreading the Word of God.

At Wheaton, Neill followed a pre-med course, thinking of a possible career in genetic research. But midway through, news came of the murder of the three Freds on the Riozinho and the martyrdom of Arthur Tylee and his infant child in another part of Brazil. The battle for the souls of Indians had lost front-line soldiers, he reasoned. He felt compelled to step forward and place himself in the gap.

While pursuing a course in Bible and missions at Columbia, he fell in love with an undergraduate girl whom he wanted to marry and take with him to South America. With two years to wait until Mary McMahan's graduation, Neill temporarily took the position of general secretary of the Student Foreign Missions Fellowship, whose headquarters was in Philadelphia. There he became acquainted with Dr. Frank Torrey, pastor of Calvary Independent Church of Lancaster, Pennyslvania, and a board member of the Fellowship. Being also a member of UFM's Home Council and knowing of Neill's determination to evangelize Amazon Indians, Dr. Torrey introduced the young staff head to Edwin and Lilian Pudney. Although he traveled much in his job, Neill began attending the UFM prayer meetings whenever he was in Philadelphia on a Tuesday night. He liked what he saw in UFM, and after Mary's graduation and they were married, the couple went to Brazil under UFM in 1942.

For a year they studied Portuguese at the mission base in Belém. Neill researched the locations of the various Indian tribes in the Amazon basin. He gained a personal knowledge of Indians by visiting Horace Banner among the Kayapo, some of whom had killed the three Freds. As Neill added tribes to his roster he thought about the uncounted people in the jungle who had not yet heard of God's salvation. He determined to build a bridge to at least one of those tribes — at the time he made no decision as to which tribe. But build his bridge he did, and it was the Macushi, a partly acculturated tribe whose area ranged across the Brazilian frontier territory of Roraima and into Venezuela and the savannas of British Guiana. After an extensive survey of Macushi settlements by truck, horseback and foot, he moved Mary and their infant daughter to Cuntao, a village reached via the Branco River town of Boa Vista.

Home was a thatch-roofed, mud hut ten minutes outside the village. This burned down. The apparent tragedy turned to blessing when the Macushi invited Neill and his family to occupy a vacant house in the very center of the settlement. Here they became a part of village life, gaining friends and learning the Macushi language, which to this time had not been reduced to writing.

Neill preached and taught, in the Portuguese he had already learned, and on land and in buildings given by a Christian rancher twenty miles from Cuntao started a school for boys. But he kept alert, hoping for word of a forest tribe having no contact with the outer world.

One day he heard of Indians called Wai Wai. Some of them lived in the deep jungle beyond the open plains of British Guiana, near the source of the Essequibo River. The rest of the tribe lived in Brazil, their ancestral home, across the mountains. Neill soaked up every available bit of information about the Wai Wai. A few men among neighbors to the Macushi, the Wapishana, had from time to time entered Wai Wai land to trade colorful glass beads and salt for the simple boards the Wai Wai made for grating the ubiquitous manioc tuber. From them he learned that the Wai Wai were a troubled people, slaves of witchcraft, fearing a world of spirits, lovers of strong drink, practitioners in promiscuous orgies, killers of unwanted babies, extremely dirty, possessors of many dogs and apparently fated for extinction. One positive thing about them — they were not noted for attacking outsiders.

Whatever their characteristics or reputation, these were people to whom God had called Neill Hawkins.

Sending Mary and now their two daughters ahead to the States, Neill delayed his first furlough long enough to survey the approaches to Wai Wai country and to look for a guide. In Georgetown, British Guiana's capital, he met a government ranger who had made a trip to the Wai Wai. Andrew MacDonald was half Scot, half Wapishana. He told Neill that there lived on the Essequibo only twenty-six Wai Wai, plus two of the Taruma tribe, whose kinsmen had been wiped out by measles. Neill was forced to ask himself, With millions in the world without a knowledge of Christ, should one devote his efforts to so few? His answer was yes. They were worth it. Besides, there were other Wai Wai across the mountains who sometimes came to the Essequibo to drink and dance, and perhaps some day permission could be gained to extend the witness to them in Brazil.

Neill's two brothers had also prepared for missionary careers. Rader and wife Ann took over the boarding school at Cuntao, and when that was turned over to Baptist Mid-Missions he would go on to British Guiana to establish a base for the advance to the Wai Wai and to work among the residents of Georgetown and along the coast. Robert was still at home, thinking of going to Morocco, but no suitable opportunity opened. Neill invited him to join in pioneering the Wai Wai work, and after much deliberation the younger brother accepted.

The brothers encountered a problem in Georgetown. The government absolutely forbade contact with the Wai Wai. The three battered the door of one bureaucracy after another. Each time, the answer was the same. No entry. For a year one obstacle piled on another. With his methodical and trap-like mind, Neill studied the colony's legal code. He asked to be shown the law that prohibited entrance into Indian territory. There actually was none. Then for whatever reason, permission was given — with the proviso that a government ranger accompany them on their journey. His job would be to see that the brothers did not alter the customs of the people.

Neill knew whom he wanted to make the trip — the man who had informed him about the Wai Wai a year earlier. But before he could come out with the name, the official he was dealing with assigned that very man, Andrew MacDonald, to the task. Before the trip ended their overseer would become a trophy of God's grace.

In January of 1949 contact was made with the Wai Wai. For the tribe, it was a frightening experience. Months before, word had circulated throughout British Guiana that white men planned to enter the forest. By the time the word had passed from village to village and up the forest-lined river to Wai Wai land, "white men" had become "white killers."

The Wai Wai once retaliated against their enemies by killing with clubs and arrows. Now, they relied on witchcraft which, any one of them could point out, was just as effective. By exercising the proper spell, a Wai Wai could cause an adversary or a rival in romance to fall from high in a tree or to burn from a fever. And if a relative died — death always resulted from someone's malevolence — there was resort to *farawa*, a sinister ritual that fingered the guilty party by causing his death within six days.

Babies the Wai Wai killed by a blow to the head. Babies were born on a banana leaf on the ground and until one was picked up it could be killed for any reason — perhaps it was not of the desired sex, or a parent wished not to have his sleep broken by an infant's crying. A child whose life was spared grew up in an atmosphere of despondency and fright. After all, every tree and rock and mountain and animal and bird had a spirit, and that spirit was dedicated to the destruction of the Wai Wai. They had no savior to help them. Generations ago their creator had stalked away in a huff, never to be seen again. Their only hope for a brief respite from trouble came from appeasement of the spirits. Desperately trying to escape their plight, they entered into drunken orgies that sometimes lasted for a full cycle of the moon.

It would take a while for Indians and missionaries to comfortably live together.

Neill and Bob, joined after some weeks by their brother Rader, found the Wai Wai to be lazy, selfish, thieving, whining, usually caked with mud, filthy-minded. Both men and women laughed when the lesson, taught in the simplest terms, spoke about a God who loved his creatures. Love? Love was exercised only when there was promise of something in return. And think about tomorrow? Why should they? Like their cousins, the

Taruma, they'd all be dead soon.

As the missionaries got to know the Wai Wai better, they learned that some of what appeared to be laziness was rather a resigned obedience to the taboos that governed their lives. And the mud came off with a dip in the river. But their inner lives — it would take a long time for the teaching to sink in. In fact, five seemingly fruitless years.

Early in the work, Neill went on to start a witness in other tribes and Rader returned to Georgetown. Florine and the children joined Bob, and over time other UFM missionaries arrived, chief among them Claude and Barbara Leavitt, nurse Florence Riedle and teachers Jean McCracken and Kathryn Pierce and later, Irene Benson. Bob and Claude traveled over the mountains and down into Brazil to other Wai Wai settlements. Having no reason to be rooted where they lived, and thinking possessions could be gained, families and even whole villages followed them back to the Essequibo. The original twenty-six swelled to two hundred or more.

Missionary work was slow and tedious — learning the language, gaining the people's confidence, translating the Scriptures, preaching, teaching, giving shots and pills, pulling teeth, battling isolation and frustration, overcoming crumpled hopes, praying earnestly when all that remained possible was prayer. A few eventually appeared interested in the Gospel, now and then. But none seemed able to exchange his fear of evil spirits for faith. Gradually, their primary language informant, a keen young man who they discovered was both tribal chief and witchdoctor, began to try the spirits to see whether they were of God. Elka had helped translate key passages of the New Testament into his people's tongue, and these, having introduced God to him, did not leave his mind. On some of the sick he performed his sorcerer's routine; for others, he prayed. He marveled that God had made the earth, the mountains, the trees; then, not having fixed in his mind the rule of Creator over creation, did obeisance to the spirits that dwelt in them. He wished to serve the God of Heaven, but still was a servant of the spirits.

A war raged in the pit of his stomach, the seat of the emotions for the Wai Wai. Elka honestly did not know whether God or *kworokyam*, the embodiment of all the spirits, would win. Then, one day while alone out in an old abandoned cassava field, he sent a simple message heavenward: "Father in the Sky, I want to know You. So make Yourself known to me forever. What do You think about that? Old Elka wants You to come into the pit of his stomach, Father, and make his spirit strong."

It was the beginning, not only of Elka's walk with Jesus Christ, but of his tribe's, and through them, a number of other tribes in the great surrounding forest.

For some months in 1954 Elka hung on to his witchcraft charms. He acknowledged they were not of God, yet all his life he'd known that a witchdoctor parted from his charms was sure to die. Everyone knew that; they'd all seen racking death pull a defiant witchdoctor to the bottom of the river or one careless enough to lose his charms fall prey to a big cat in the forest. Still, faith finally overcame fear. One day with everyone present under the big mango tree in the middle of the village, Elka handed over to Claude Leavitt his basket of smooth stones, feathers and tobacco-like leaves. In dread and fright, his people awaited sudden death for their chief and one-time emissary to the spirits, who now was the sole Companion of Jesus among them. When death did not strike that day, they were no less certain that it would claim their leader in a very short time. If not in the present phase of the moon, certainly in the next — or the one after that.

As a witchdoctor, Elka had given particular allegiance to the spirit of the wild pig. He was obliged to forgo eating this prime food from the forest. Some time after he had renounced *kworokyam* and had not died as expected, a large pack of sharp-toothed bush hogs was sighted heading toward the village. It had been a year since pigs had come around; no doubt, the people said, they had gone off angry because Elka turned his back on them. Surely, they now were coming to avenge their master's abandonment. Against the warnings of his people, Elka ran into the pack, chased the pigs and shot a pair. Much to their renewed fear, he brought the pigs back to the village, dressed them, boiled one and then, when it was done, ate chunks of meat from the animal forbidden to him. His moment of death, moaned the people, had surely come.

But Elka lived. He thrived. In a little while one, then another, in the tribe turned to the God who had given their chief victory over the spirits of evil. Men and women both asked *Chisusu*, Jesus, to take away their badness and to dwell in the pits of their stomach. Over the next two years, some ninety percent, or more, of the three hundred or so Indians then living on the Essequibo declared themselves to be Companions of Jesus. One church building after another was discarded as it failed to accommodate the growing congregation. Elders were chosen. They conducted the worship, preached and baptized. The Wai Wai church became thoroughly indigenous, and in later years when government pressure expelled the missionaries, preaching, teaching, singing, baptisms and prayer meetings continued. These once loathsome people had, indeed, become new creations in Christ, clean within as well as without.

Though still separated by hundreds of miles from the outside world, the Wai Wai had a world of their own for which they felt responsible.

"There are people in the forest who are just as fearful and dying as we once were," they said. In the years following their conversion, they sent teams into the jungle, dozens of teams over many years, to discover wandering tribes and bring them back so the people could learn about Jesus.

Finding them, they would say, "Now, while we are here visiting you in your village, we can tell you only a little bit about God. But you come home and live with us and you will learn all about what it means for Jesus to live in the pit of your stomach."

It was their method of evangelizing.

Mawayena, Tunayena, Shedeu, Katwena — these were some of the tribes that came to live with the Wai Wai, and finding their faith genuine, to accept the Wai Wai's God. Elka and other church leaders went with missionaries far from their forest to evangelize the Waica and Shirishana in Brazil and the Trio in Surinam. Building on this first contact, Claude and Barbara Leavitt moved to the Surinam jungle to work among the Trio as they and others had among the Wai Wai. They saw God transform this tribe as he did the tribes on the Essequibo. Translation, teaching, training leaders — every day was full. But there was satisfaction, especially in seeing their own children, raised on a mission field, accept the Lord's call upon their lives.

Bob and Florine Hawkins concentrated on translating the Bible into Wai Wai and in recording the scores of hymns the Wai Wai and Florine had composed. In later years they did this while caring for Bob's aging mother in Texas. They made periodic trips to the Wai Wai to check translation and to teach and counsel the elders. Florence Riedle stayed with the amalgamated tribes for thirty-four years, reproducing her medical skills in a cadre of clinic workers, but most of all, implanting her love in the Wai Wai who, in turn, learned how to love more deeply. Irene Benson in almost a like number of years developed a comprehensive school program and became a stalwart friend to both helpless children and tribal leaders. From time to time other missionaries, Brazilians among them, were a part of the Wai Wai ministry.

The Wai Wai grew to large numbers — they no longer killed babies, and disease was brought under control. Officials of the now independent Guyana began noticing them. Some in the bureaucracy wished to turn their villages into a tourist attraction. Others, sent in to govern them, seemed bent on erasing their Christian practices and returning them to their "pristine" state, which in reality had consisted of fear, fighting and early death. When an effort was made to get the children to rebel against their parents' faith, most of the Wai Wai, at least six hundred of them, did what was the Indian's privilege to do — they crossed the border into Brazil and again made their home there.

Avoiding unwanted interference was not the sole motive in the move across the border. Crossing into Brazil placed them closer to their prime target in evangelism. For some time the Wai Wai had been praying for — and planning strategy to reach — a killer tribe far down one of the tributaries of the Amazon, a barbarous people called the Atrowari. Speaking a different language, and certainly of radically different values and behavior, the Atrowari were their biggest challenge yet!

SOURCES, Chapter 9

Dowdy, Homer E., *Christ's Jungle*, 1995, Gresham, OR, Vision House
_____, *Christ's Witchdoctor*, 1963, New York, Harper & Row
Hawkins, Mary, Chronology, Missionary Roster, 1996
_____, Letters to author, 1995, 1996
_____, Telephone interview, 1996
_____, Notes on early draft
Hawkins, Neill, Prayer Letters, January, 1955 - November, 1981
Hawkins, Robert, Letter to author, 1995
_____, Notes on early draft
Leavitt, Claude and Barbara, 1996, Notes on early draft

10

Indians Confronting the World

N eill Hawkins believed that Christians bearing the message of Christ should effectively confront the world on every level at which it is met. That meant understanding the mentality of the savage Indian in the rain forest and standing ground with the professors of anthropology in the universities. He saw that before being allowed to take the Gospel to the Indians of the upper Amazon he would have to convince the erudite men who influenced government policy that an Indian with Christ in his heart was a better and happier Indian.

For this reason he enrolled in the University of São Paulo and studied further at the Ethnological Museum. Entering into the life of the huge metropolis, he was caught up by an idea that was sure to affect the evangelization of the Amazon. He saw southern Brazil as a country quite different from the backward north. He visited churches filled with capable and dedicated Christians and which had the potential to support a Gospel outreach beyond their own congregations. Why, he asked himself, was almost all the work among the Indians being done by North Americans and Europeans? Why shouldn't Brazilians step up to the task within their own land? Some day, he was convinced, they would.

In his year of study Neill made good contacts with government officials and men of influence, but as yet was unable to persuade them to permit a new work among the Indians. Two years before a coming furlough he and Mary were called to the Bible Institute in the State of Maranhão as interim successors to its founder, George Thomas, who had become ill and was forced to return to Canada. Accepting the call, the family moved to Barra do Corda. During his second year there the school moved to the more strategic coastal city of São Luis, Maranhão's capital.

Returning to the United States in 1954, Neill asked UFM to separate the Territory of Roraima in Northwest Brazil from the work centered in Belém fifteen hundred miles to the east. This was done. He then set about recruiting a band of prayer partners to deal with the major obstacle blocking a start there. These men and women prayed beyond generalities, asking specifically that either there would be a change of mind by the two high Brazilian officials who had denied permission, or that they would be replaced with more amenable men. Arriving back in Brazil in 1955, Neill discovered that the head of the Indian Protection Service, one of the two men prayed for, had been relieved of his post. The other, who now headed the agency, had had a change of mind. The new director suggested that the mission open work in the valley of the Uraricoera River, a center for the populous Yanomami tribe. The Yanomami were a coalition of many subgroups, each with its own dialect as different from the others as French is from Spanish. Waica, Shirishana, Parahuri, Maitas, Sanuma were among them. A census had never been taken, but the Waica alone were thought to number twenty thousand. Their sites bordered on the Uraricoera and other tributaries of the Rio Branco, reaching into the highlands that dominated the northwest portion of the Brazilian bump of land between Venezuela and what now is an independent Guyana, but then was the colony of British Guiana. A good many of the Yanomami spilled into Venezuela. Being somewhat sealed off from the rest of Brazil by numerous rapids and high water falls in these rivers, their area was little troubled by either visitors or settlers. Yet there was a convenient way to approach this land. Across the Tacutu River, in British Guiana, stood Lethem, that government's post for the whole southern region of the country. An easy crossing and a hike of two miles upstream put the missionary at his base on a ranch which Neill purchased as a training center for new missionaries and a launching pad to evangelize the Indians.

UFM asked Neill Hawkins to hold up in starting the ministry in this new region. Mission Aviation Fellowship, which following World War II had become an indispensable transportation and communication helper of missionaries world-wide, offered to extend its recently established service in Brazil to this field. Bonfim, the new UFM base, could be reached overland through British Guiana all right, but it was a base only. To penetrate the vast area where the Yanomami lived, up to a range of two hundred fifty miles from Bonfim, jungle aviation would be invaluable, cutting, for example, a three-month trip by forest trail to nine hours in the air. But, said the MAF pilots who flew Neill on an aerial survey of the area, twenty missionaries scattered over the territory would be required to keep a plane and pilot busy.

With all the linguists and teachers and health workers he'd need, it would take twenty missionaries. So for another year Neill put off beginning the work. The prayer partners asked God for the twenty, and Neill went around the States challenging young people to join in this crusade for the indigenous population.

The first of the twenty recruits arrived in early 1956, Kathryn Pierce and Rodney and Louise Lewis, who soon came to be known as Rod and Tommy. Rod set to work immediately to make habitable an old mud-and-stick building at Bonfim. Neill, eager to get contacts with the Indians underway, plotted strategy. He'd need more than the twenty prayed for. Besides all the Yanomami in Brazil, across the river in British Guiana lived the semi-civilized Wapishana tribe who lacked a witness, and also in that country there was a move to set up a new station among the Macushi. And in Georgetown, the capital on the coast, Neill's brother and his wife, Rader and Ann Hawkins, would soon require help at the rate the work was progressing, and in the opposite direction, in the southern jungle, younger brother Bob and his fellow missionaries had all they could do to take care of the burgeoning mission to the Wai Wai.

The arrival of an MAF plane and its pilot, Eldon Larsen, and his wife, Sylvia, in November, 1957, marked the start of the active phase of a Gospel thrust to the Yanomami. From the government airstrip at Lethem, across the river in British Guiana, MAF provided air support, mapping routes and dropping supplies, for the first exploratory trip up the Uraricoera River. Lasting four months, it was made by Rod Lewis, Bob Hawkins and two Christian Wai Wai, Elka, the chief, and Mawasha, one of four elders. Following up that venture, the Lewises and a more recent arrival, Frances Tracy, moved to Waica territory and began the first Indian station. The Waica had perhaps the most primitive culture of all the subtribes in the region.

After MAF moved over to Bonfim, further aerial reconnaissances of the Uraricoera and Mucajaí Rivers were made. Then came an exploratory trip up the Mucajaí by Neill, John Peters, who was a logger-turned-missionary from the Canadian northwest, and two Wai Wai. Aided by a small outboard motor, they pushed and tugged their canoe upstream and through enormous rapids and finally arrived at the spot where from the air weeks earlier Indians had been seen. But now none was about. The next day the question was answered as to whether the Yanomami of the Mucajaí were hostile, possibly killers, or friendly. A group descended on the visitors, ecstatic that traders had come. With this warm welcome, negotiations soon resulted in the Yanomami pitching in to help the missionaries and Wai Wai in the construction of an airstrip.

Peters was injured in the felling of a tree, but as a well-trained missionary he used his recovery time in the hammock to learn more of the Indian language. Axes and knives compensated for labor on the airstrip. Medicine was freely given. Men and women alike were amazed at the mystery of writing and the ability of one person to repeat the thoughts of another just by making a paper speak.

Mission Aviation Fellowship with its usual high degree of professionalism dropped supplies and lowered a bucket to collect mail. On completion of the strip, the plane landed, bringing Don Borgman as a replacement for Neill Hawkins, who was lifted out to Boa Vista, where leadership of the field demanded his presence. Borgman then worked with Peters, the Wai Wai and the Yanomami to build another airstrip since the first was dangerously short and could not be extended. That done, John Peters and the two Wai Wai men were flown out, with only Borgman remaining at the new station.

Far from this tiny opening in the jungle, in cities where to most Brazilians the Indians were only chimerical beings in a dark, unknown, impenetrable world, false accusations against the work by opponents of the Gospel first circulated in whispers then suddenly rang out clangorously in government offices and the press. Charges were answered and the clamor subsided. The work would go on. More of the twenty new missionaries arrived at Bonfim. More rivers were explored. Contacts were made with new groups of Indians. New missionary settlers built homes for themselves in the remote villages and with the help of their Indian neighbors carved airstrips out of the jungle.

For a new field, the North Amazon was going very well. The only real hindrance was absence of radio communication among the various stations, government permission to operate a transmitter having been denied. Then in mid-1959 a heavy blow fell. The government confiscated the MAF plane, severing the lifeline between the distant stations and Bonfim. Don Borgman, for one, was isolated on the Mucajaí.

What were these foreigners doing on Brazil's border? Were

they secretly stealing the nation's mineral and petroleum riches? Were they smuggling diamonds into British Guiana? People hostile to missionary work fed the suspicions of the fidgety bureaucrats with the aim of ending evangelism in Roraima.

Neill Hawkins went straight to Rio de Janeiro. There he found friends among the military, particularly the Brazilian Air Force, which had jurisdiction over a band of ninety-three miles inside the national borders. The crisis eased with the taking of several steps. MAF moved its operations to Roraima's capital, the small city of Boa Vista, about seventy miles inland from UFM's base at Bonfim. The Air Force announced it would put the mission's jungle airstrips under its authority. Neill took the first steps to set up a Brazilian organization to conduct the mission's North Amazon ministry. Satisfied, the officials in Rio cleared aerial operations. But, no authorization for radio transmissions.

Fernon Albert had come to Brazil, with his wife Athlea and two young sons, specifically to handle a network of UFM radios. With radio communication on hold, Fernon kept busy with other work—from repairing motors of many kinds to running the station in Neill Hawkins' absence. This was the pattern for all the arrivals. Do whatever needed to be done. It was what Rod and Tommy Lewis had done at Bonfim and what they continued to do when with Fran Tracy they began the station among the Waica.

The first contact of the Lewises with UFM came through Neill and Mary Hawkins when in 1954 the two couples lived in duplex housing in Dallas, Texas. The Hawkins family was home on furlough and Rod and Tommy were in their final year of study at Dallas Bible Institute. The Lewises applied for an appointment in Africa. While awaiting a reply, they caught from their missionary neighbors a vision for ministry among primitive Indians in a remote corner of Brazil. Neill and Mary asked the Lewises to pray that UFM would grant permission to start the work. UFM did, and the answer strengthened the younger couple's faith in prayer. Now they were asked to pray that twenty missionaries would be sent to flesh out this decision.

Receiving no acknowledgement of their application for missionary service in Africa, Rod and Tommy began praying about whether they should be two of the North Amazon twenty. They were host to Edwin Pudney during a visit he made to Dallas. Impressed with his warmth and leadership through servanthood, they wrote to withdraw their application for Africa. Still, they heard nothing. They then applied to UFM, which accepted them for pioneer work among the Yanomami.

Constructing buildings at Bonfim and later at the Waica station, clearing jungle for an airstrip at Waica, studying and using Portuguese and the Waica language, teaching the Bible, translating it, doctoring the sick, exploring new areas and making contact with heretofore unreached groups of Indians, every day doing the usual chores of living — these were the tasks that made up the ministry of Rod and Tommy Lewis and the others who followed them to the field.

By 1959, not just the twenty new missionaries originally prayed for, but three more than the twenty had arrived in North Amazon, to serve both in Brazil and British Guiana.

More missionaries on hand meant more stations could be opened. More stations meant more support work from the base, more trips to ferry people and goods in and out of the jungle, more possibilities of things somewhere going wrong. This once lonely spot on the Tacutu River was buzzing. At one point Neill wrote to his prayer partners in the U.S., "Did you ever feel like a babe before problems too hard for a strong man? That has been repeatedly our feeling as we face the problems of planting the Gospel in this part of Brazil's 93-mile-wide frontier zone. For almost fifteen months one crisis has followed another, some of them so serious that they threatened to put a full stop to the work. Yet time after time when an adverse decision would have stopped or seriously hindered the work, a hand of strength held back the enemy."

He enumerated some of the current troubles, including the fact that the MAF plane had made a forced landing upcountry and now a ruined engine kept it grounded. But optimist that he was, he closed his letter on a positive note:

"Pray that God will keep us faithfully living one day at a time, undiscouraged by frequent delays and even changes in plans that some may have set their hearts on, as long as God's plans go steadily forward. Then pray with us that when His plan and His work is threatened, the strength of God may be present to 'still the enemy and the avenger.' Pray too for us . . . that God's Spirit may find ready channels for His mighty working."

Charges against the missionaries resurfaced. The Brazilian press picked up wild stories that geologists and technicians of various stripes worked out of Bonfim, that the mission had completed full aerial photographing of the region and that Indians were hired to load their plane with diamonds and radioactive materials. Otherwise, it was asked, why would civilized people subject themselves to impossible living conditions in remote, primitive locations and make such effort to relate to savage Indians?

Protestant missions had their friends as well as detractors in high places, and their status was argued on the floor of the Chamber of Deputies in the Brazilian Congress at Rio. The charges were dismissed as absurd, then brought again, some thrown out, some continued. An order came down to evacuate all missionaries from Indian lands. Before the order could be carried out, however, the Brazilian Air Force began its long-awaited push into some of those lands and said UFM missionaries were needed to help them deal with the Indians they would meet up with during the operation. Radio would connect the stations — not the hoped-for mission network, but on the frequencies of the Air Force.

Two new airstrips were cut out of the jungle in the Parima region, far to the west near the Venezuela border. Because several of the prayed-for twenty (with twenty-three as the answer) were in training at Bonfim, waiting for the air to clear so they could be assigned, six were dispatched to the newly designated stations of Parima and Surucucu.

Yet, the trouble was not ended. Powerful forces were still to be dealt with. Neill Hawkins felt that as long as large numbers of foreign missionaries resided on an actual border of the country, Bonfim being a short rowboat ride from British Guiana, and they lived and moved about there without direct supervision of the government, this cauldron would never cease to boil. He approached the governor in Boa Vista, suggesting a police presence be established at Bonfim. Not that, the governor replied. But he did want the mission compound as an army post.

The governor said he would trade land in Boa Vista for Bonfim. The missionaries felt there would be advantages to resettling in the city, but were reluctant to leave all that had been built up at great personal effort. They'd leave the fruit trees that had begun to produce abundantly and the homes that, to construct them, had eaten into their minimal allowances. Easy access through Lethem to food and other essential purchases in Georgetown would be sacrificed for the near-empty shelves of Boa Vista. Most of all, the families in the area who had been won to Christ would be left on their own—their church, school and medical service facing an uncertain future.

In the end, to save the Indian work, there was no choice but to move headquarters and its personnel to Boa Vista.

The work in the outposts, among the tribes, continued unabated. At Waica, the first station, Fran Tracy and the Lewises and others who came from time to time kept at their tasks even though indifference seemed to be the main characteristic of the people. The Indians regularly went on fishing trips to avoid attending Sunday church services. Then, happily, they asked that the services be held later in the day so they could attend after fishing. Some Sundays attendance was good; on others, not a single person showed up.

The Shirishana on the Mucajaí River were more of an encouragement to the two couples living with them, Frank and Isobel Ebel and John and Lorraine Peters. There, Chief Iro had become a follower of Jesus. He stood firm when other tribes tempted his people with mind-altering narcotic binges. At Parima and Surucucu, the new stations, Don Borgman, who transferred from the Mucajaí, Russell and Pat Sasscer, Wayne and Bonnie Follmar, Sandy Cue, Sue Albright and Bob and Gay Cable all were making progress in learning the local languages and winning a hearing for the Gospel. Across in British Guiana, Kitty Pierce had done well in the Macushi language and Patrick and June Foster were settling into Nappi, looking forward to teaching and evangelizing one day throughout the savanna. Farther to the south, the Wai Wai continued sweeping their jungle to find people to bring to Christ.

The mission left Bonfim in mid-1961, regrouping in Boa Vista. The Brazilian woman who had conducted the school and a national pastor were allowed to remain on the Tacutu so as to disrupt the lives of the people there as little as possible. At the same time, and again largely for political reasons, the North Amazon field was divided between Brazil and British Guiana.

UFM's purpose for going into British Guiana had been to reach the Wai Wai deep in the jungle in the southernmost part of the country. For this target and for the work that developed in Brazil's Roraima Territory, a supply and service base was needed in Georgetown, the capital, seaport and largest city. Soon a corollary effort evolved.

A missionary in a support role doesn't merely buy and ship supplies and maintain liaison with government; he and his family have neighbors, and most likely these neighbors have as great a spiritual void as those at the end of the supply line. Hence, a witness grows up at the supply base and becomes a ministry in itself. This is what happened in Georgetown.

Rader and Ann Hawkins, he being the middle of the three missionary Hawkins men, started this witness by distributing

Bibles. On Tuesdays they gathered children under their house — typically, the Georgetown house sits on stilts — and there taught them God's Word. So many came that they split the group, about half the 300 youngsters meeting under their house and half under a neighboring house, which had become a boarding home for out-of-town children. This hostel resulted when Andrew MacDonald, who accompanied the Hawkins brothers on their first trip into Wai Wai country, sent two sons and a daughter to Rader and Ann to be cared for while attending school in the city. Others joined them, and the home was added to a number of varied endeavors.

Kitty Bible Church, which originally met at the Hawkins home, became a spiritual magnet in a poor section of Georgetown. A boys' club, a Bible study for young women, Christian instruction in the public schools and a Bible Lover's League were other early ministries. The latter, linked with an organization formed by the senior Hawkinses through their Dallas radio program, provided a library of Scripture portions for those seeking God's truth, and awarded a Bible to faithful readers of the Word. The church placed emphasis on youth, of which Georgetown had a disproportionate number. In a few years, a Bible Institute was in operation, a near essential on mission fields for assuring the work's continuance in future generations.

In Roraima and on British Guiana's far-spreading savanna, the Macushi Indians benefited from traveling medical-evangelistic teams. Working with Pat and June Foster and Daryl and Betty Teeter and other UFM missionaries, they helped the number of Macushi churches to grow. After several years with the Wai Wai, Claude and Barbara Leavitt moved eastward, into the jungles of southern Surinam, to do pioneer evangelizing among the Trio Indians. Some Wai Wai accompanied them, while others of this largely Christian tribe went south over the continental divide and, under the aegis of the Brazilian Air Force and the leadership of Bob and Florine Hawkins, set up a station at the foot of Anaua Mountain. From there, the Wai Wai made fairly frequent contact with the Atrowari, the arrogant and bloodthirsty people who sliced off heads as a measure of their anger.

"If God wants me to die in order to reach the Atrowari," one of the young men said as the Wai Wai contemplated another trip into hostile territory, "I'm ready to give my life."

Neill Hawkins looked forward to expansion of the work in Roraima. New surveys resulted in the opening of another station on the Parima, staffed by Bob and Gay Cable and Sue Albright, and later Wayne and Bonnie Follmar. Still, there were many tribes without the light of the Gospel. In the original push into this territory he had asked for twenty volunteers, and the Lord gave twenty-three. Now, he figured ten more were needed. Then he heard disheartening news from the United States. First word came about Fernon Albert, who with his family was in the States on furlough. Albert had intended to take care of the techniques of radio communications; but with that role denied him by the government, he became an all-around handyman and deputy field leader. This man would not be returning to Brazil. He suffered from a swift-enveloping, incurable cancer. Then, Isobel Ebel, who with her husband Frank had served at the Mucajaí station, was told by her doctor she could not return to the tropics. A second couple lost to the work. Others reported fevers, hepatitis and respiratory ailments that would delay their resumption of duties. After grieving for those afflicted, Neill did two things: He read the day's passage in *Daily Light* that restored his confidence, "Fear not, little flock; for it is your Father's good pleasure to give you the kingdom," and he turned toward São Paulo in the south of Brazil as his hope for replenishment of personnel.

Evangelist Joao Batista and nurse Julieta Souza became the first Brazilian missionaries to serve in the North Amazon force. Joao was responsible for starting five churches among the Macushi and Julieta saved lives during her internship at Auaris, a

Yanomami station opened by Don and Barbara Borgman during an epidemic of malaria. Soon after their arrival came Edith Moreira, a linguist who for many years worked on Bible translation. Many other Brazilians followed these, not a few coming from the Word of Life Bible Institute. UFM's Brazilian counterpart agency had been formed in 1959, the Cruzada de Evangelizacao Mundial. In 1970, the Cruzada underwent some changes, including its name. Missão Evangélica da Amazonia (MEVA) received governmental recognition and became the instrument through which UFM worked in that part of the country. Upon arrival in Roraima, all UFM missionaries became full members of MEVA and subordinated to the direction of the MEVA field council. Likely, it would be the coming pattern in missions.

SOURCES, Chapter 10

Albert, Athlea & Fernon, Personal and Prayer Letters, 1958-1963

Dowdy, Homer E., *Christ's Witchdoctor*, 1963, New York, Harper & Row

Hawkins, Mary, Chronology of North Amazon Field

_____, Letter to author

_____, A *Summary of the History of the Beginnings of the North American Branch — MEVA — of UFM*, 1996, Unpublished paper

_____, 1996, *Notes on early draft*

Hawkins, Neill, Prayer letters, 1955-1965

Hawkins, Robert, *Notes on UFM's Beginnings in British Guiana*, 1995, Unpublished paper

Lewis, Rodney, Letter to author, 1995

Lewis, Louise, *No. 2 and No. 3 of 20 Missionaries*, Unpublished paper, 1995

Light & Life, Bala-Cynwyd, UFM Periodical, 2nd Quarter, 1959; 3rd Quarter, 1963; 4th Quarter,   1963

Peters, John, 1996, Unpublished paper

Pudney, Lilian, *God Which Worketh*, Bala-Cynwyd, 1953, UFM

UFM Report, British Guiana Branch, September 1965

Waica Station Log, 1958-1961

11

"Over the Mountain"

"Over the mountain lies another mountain," goes an old Haitian proverb. If you repeat it often enough as you move eastward you run out of Haiti and find yourself in a different country — the Dominican Republic.

Another touch point on Columbus' voyages, the "DR" boasts several New World "firsts." The first town, La Isabella was established in 1493 on the north coast, but like La Navidad, the fort in Haiti, it did not survive. Santo Domingo, the capital, thus became the oldest enduring European settlement in the Western Hemisphere, founded in 1496 by Bartholomew Columbus, brother of Christopher. Its cathedral, begun in 1523, was the first in the New World; until the recent erection of the Columbus Lighthouse, a massive monument and depository, the church was said to contain the discoverer's remains, along with bells from his first three ships.

Haiti and the Dominican Republic occupy the island of Hispaniola. What looks like an arbitrary boundary on maps is in reality a natural barrier, a high range of mountains. The DR has many mountains, among them Pico Duarte, which rises to more than ten thousand feet. There are also lush-green, fertile valleys and broad plains near the coast, providing farm lands. Economically, the seven million Dominicans, most of whom are of Spanish-African descent, enjoy a better life than their neighbors the Haitians. But in no sense are they among the favored nations of the world. Until 1924 they lived under a succession of foreign powers — France, Haiti, Spain and United States Marines — followed by the tyranny of a dictator. Despite such a history, the people are hospitable, industrious and are fond of music, dancing and especially sports.

Spiritually, the DR is a needy land.

UFM entered the Dominican Republic in 1949 through the merger with the World Christian Crusade that extended its sphere in Haiti. At the time of joining, this Indiana-based agency sponsored nine missionaries in Port-au-Prince, the capital of Haiti, and two in the DR. Jack and Bessie Cook had worked under the Crusade in Haiti and entered the new field in 1944, establishing a work in El Seibo, then moving in 1948 to the larger community of San Pedro de Macoris. There, Gospel meetings started under a shelter in the backyard of the Cooks' home. E. J. and Lilian Pudney visited the field shortly after the merger, and that set in motion a moderate but steady inflow of missionaries.

Marion Young came in 1951, followed by a Cuban worker, Juanita Toirac, a sister of Florent Toirac, WCC's leader in Haiti. Before transferring to DR, she had served in Haiti. Larry and Donadene Dawson came soon after Miss Toirac, and Don and Audrey Wunker arrived in 1952.

Much of the evangelizing took place in the *bateys*, the settlements of sugar field workers. Jack Cook made good use of his knowledge of Creole, the language of the Haitians, in witnessing to the Haitian cane cutters. But the port city of San Pedro was not neglected. The mission rented an old bakery and remodeled it for services, which began with a preaching series by a West Indies Mission evangelist. During the campaign in this first UFM church the first three conversions were recorded. The work suffered a setback in the death of Donadene Dawson a month after she gave birth, but in a little while more missionaries arrived and the Gospel spread to a number of Dominican cities. The witness at first was usually intermittent, with the missionary itinerating among a number of locations. Churches in these communities started small, often in buildings abandoned by commercial firms or in unfinished houses. The Wunkers moved to La Romana, which in years to come would figure importantly in UFM's ministry and in the Domincan church's development. The Wunkers started from scratch. A later church leader once spoke of a similar beginning of evangelism in La Granchorra, his town:

"It was just an ordinary day in 1956 when for the first time the seed of the Word of God arrived at the picturesque community of La Granchorra. There is not the slightest doubt that God sent brother Donald Wunker in the most opportune moment because at that time La Granchorra as well as Algibe, La Cana and La Palmilla were all well populated communities. The brother made his entry to that needy area mounted on a donkey and bringing with him an arsenal of equipment such as an accordion, projector, etc. When he arrived, I would run around the neighborhood shouting, 'Mr. Wanke has come! Mr. Wanke has come!' And early in the evening, one by one, the people came to the house where the meeting was to be held."

Christians among the nationals held key positions in reaching the Dominicans for Jesus Christ. Silverio Martinez became the first pastor and evangelist and would be the first teacher when the Bible school got underway. Silito Caseres worked in Yuma, a center of religious fanaticism. Silito, whose livelihood was shoemaking, and his wife Minda were used by the Lord to win the confidence of the people and to plant several churches among them. Frequently, this couple encountered opposition; at times, rocks were thrown through the roof of their house. They kept the largest of these as "stones of remembrance." Several of their converts became pastors and leaders in the national church.

Meetings in the various locations were sometimes disturbed by hecklers, but proclamation of the Gospel went on. In one area a tent housed special campaigns — until it fell apart from usage and rot. Riding mules, rowing boats to cross rivers and hiking rocky trails in tropical downpours were common means to reach a location whose ground was previously softened by prayer. Sugar field workers, the madam of a house of prostitution, tough youths, spiritists, common folk — these came to Christ, and several of the new believers enrolled in the Bible School conducted by the West Indies Mission.

Len and Margaret Reinke, a rough-and-ready pair from Western Canada, joined in the effort in 1953. The work pushed out to new locations, and in several of them rustic chapels were built. The church at La Romana graduated to a second building, then a third, a solid, stone structure. A school and a bookstore opened in the new building. Moves were made into Santiago, the DR's second city, and another leading town, San Francisco de Macoris. The Lord raised up a group of believers in each place, and missionaries and nationals alike thrust into the outlying areas with their message.

Larry Dawson and his new wife, Marcellyn, formerly a UFM missionary in Congo, served the La Romana church, moving then to the capital city of Santo Domingo to hold services in the patio of the home of a well-known tailor, Carlos Dore. More than a hundred persons attended the first meeting, at which Felipe Alou, the ball player, gave a stirring testimony. The Dawsons moved to a large house and in it started Colegio Emmanuel, a Christian day school. The young church moved to a commercial center. Saturday night youth rallies were held there, and baptisms took place early on Sunday mornings at a cold stream just outside the city.

On May 30, 1961, an event occurred that changed life dramatically in the DR. Dictator Rafael Trujillo, who had ruled despotically for thirty-one years, was ambushed and assassinated. Months of great unrest followed, making it dangerous at times to be on the streets. To keep Colegio Emmanuel going, Larry Dawson had to continually change the bus routes to the school in order to avoid overturned vehicles and burning tires. One day shooting occurred all around and shots fell into the school yard.

But missionaries continued to arrive, and Dominicans continued to come to Christ and new preaching centers were established. Silverio Martinez took over the pastorate of the church in Santo Domingo. He inaugurated an intensive visitation program and soon the church could not fit into its building. Sunday School classes spilled onto the sidewalk and met in nearby homes. But that was not unusual where Silverio shepherded the flock. In one of his churches a group of regular members formed a club, "De los Parados" — *those who stand during the Sunday services so that visitors can be seated.*

In April, 1965, conflict between rebel forces and the army broke into serious fighting; once again United States Marines landed, this time to protect American citizens.

Roads were blocked. Tanks lined the highways. Cadres armed with Molotov cocktails patrolled the streets. A strict six o'clock curfew was imposed. Several missionaries were evacuated, but Don Wunker stayed on in La Romana, Larry Dawson in Santo Domingo and Len and Margaret Reinke in San Francisco de Macoris. Dawson spent much of his time carrying food to needy families. Because people dared not walk the streets, and only ten of his congregation showed up one Sunday, Silverio Martinez took church services to the homes of his members.

Three months later most of the evacuees returned, and though uncertain days still lay ahead — the rebels were not entirely subdued — the churches opened, stayed open, and the Christians even staged a big parade through the capital and held evangelistic meetings in the city stadium.

La Romana became the site of several new ministries. It was there that the churches held their first national conference, and out of it the Alianza Biblica Christiana was organized. Begun in 1960, the alliance was incorporated in 1967 and gained government recognition. The dedicated tailor, Carlos Dore, became its first president. For some time Don Wunker rolled out on an antiquated mimeograph machine an inter-church periodical that helped unify the churches. Christian camps were held at La Romana for both English-speaking and Spanish children. The first Youth Congress took place in nearby Higuey.

Colegio Emmanuel, the day school, lived an up-and-down history. Closed at times during the revolution and sometimes having no head, it nevertheless reached a peak enrollment of three hundred. Other schools opened, and week-end extension classes at various churches led to the founding of the Bible institute in La Romana.

The school began in 1971 with seven young men as students and very little in the way of funds. One day as the time to serve dinner neared there was nothing in the cupboards to serve. The cook begged Larry Dawson to go to the market. Dawson, however, had no cash. He put off going until he knew the mail had been sorted, then went to the market via the post office. The Lord had sent a gift of $5 in the mail. That paid for the school's dinner that night.

For several years after the overthrow of Trujillo, until democratic elections became the norm, jittery nights could be expected. Dawson experienced one such night during the attempt by rebels to overthrow the government in 1973. Having departed a successful evangelistic meeting in the town of Azua about eleven o'clock, he and his fellow missionaries, Bob and Anna Atwood, drove through the dark until they came upon an armed man whose threatening rifle forced them to pull up and stop. The man climbed in the car, placed the end of the barrel of his rifle in Dawson's back and ordered him to drive to Santo Domingo. He was a part of a small group bent on a Castro-like revolution in DR. His co-conspirators had gone to the mountains; his assignment was to take a message to allies in the capital city.

Mrs. Atwood started to speak to him about the Lord.

"This is my god," he said, slapping his rifle. He ordered quiet.

In the city, the three were taken from one house to another and held captive while the revolutionary drove about town in Dawson's car. On promise not to tell anyone about the abduction, they were released. A month afterward, they read of it in the newspaper. Their captor was the source of the story.

In 1974, the initial class of seven men was graduated from the school and their wives were trained in the Ladies Bible Institute. Several of the Dominicans took the initiative to open new centers, pushing out from one village to another; Christian day schools often accompanied the establishment of churches. The staging of the Pan American Games in Santo Domingo in 1974 gave opportunity for a massive tract distribution. Bible correspondence courses followed, with several thousand being completed over a number of years.

Teacher training classes started in the 1960s. On week ends Larry and Marcellyn Dawson traveled with their family to a different church every month to conduct these sessions. Patio classes for young children had originated in the early days with Bessie Cook and Juanita Toirac. Inheriting these activities at a later date, Mary Wyllys and Darlene Rimer teamed with national workers to make the round of the churches, giving courses and supervising the children's work.

In 1977 land became available near Maimon de Bonao and this was purchased for Alianza's conference center and camp ground. Volunteer work groups built facilities, with particular help from Teen Missions, a US ministry. After moving from site to site in and near Santo Domingo, the Bible institute, Seminario Biblico Cristiano del Caribe, settled in Maimon in 1985. It trained most of the Alianza pastors. The school also sent its graduates to Bonaire and Curacao and even to work among DR emigrés in Brooklyn, New York, and one for radio work directed at Cubans and other Latin Americans in Miami.

Another educational undertaking was INPEC, a Christian pedagogy institute set up by the Dawsons' daughter, Margaret, to give teachers, especially those of church-operated schools, a Biblical foundation and world view. Volleyball and basketball camps and tournaments were conducted in city housing projects; to participate, players first attended Bible studies. Missionaries and nationals joined together in numerous excursions to points of interest in the DR, and this helped cement good relations between them.

Six day schools, a Bible Institute, book stores, teacher training, the annual conference, Gospel films, youth camping, children's classes, sports evangelism — UFM fostered a wide-ranging program in the Dominican Republic. But no ministry eclipsed the primary goal — to win the people to Christ and gather them into Bible-believing churches. Never an easy work, winning them came one-by-one. In 1995, the Alianza Biblica Christiana numbered eighteen full-fledged churches and twenty-one outreach stations. The ABC goal for Year 2000: Twelve new churches.

SOURCES, Chapter 11

Dawson, Lawrence, Undated, *Addendum to History of the UFM and the ABC in the Dominican Republic*

_____, 1996, Notes on early draft

Lifeline, 3rd Quarter, 1965; 2nd Quarter, 1967

Pudney, Edwin J. and Lilian G., *Miracles Multiplied*, Undated, Unpublished manuscript

Wunker, Donald W., Undated, *History of the UFM and the ABC in the Dominican Republic*

_____, 1996, Notes on early draft

12

After the War

The advance on New Guinea by the Japanese army in World War II caused the withdrawal of all missionaries from the island. Sixteen members of the Australian Unevangelized Fields Mission were forced to bid good-bye to the Papuan tribesmen to whom they had ministered, and to commit them to God's protection and merciful care. What might happen to these babes in Christ, they hardly dared think about.

At war's end the missionaries returned. They discovered the number of believers in Papua had doubled!

Though not a project of the North American UFM, Papua nevertheless caused rejoicing in the Philadelphia headquarters and the stations in Africa and South America. There was gladness, too, for the release that the war's end gave those fields – release from travel restrictions, from tight money and sometimes the absence of support, from the inability of the home offices to supply additional missionaries or replacements.

The war had sent young Americans and Canadians to battlefields and occupation zones around the world. Many who were Christians returned home with a vision for world evangelism. They were determined to serve in God's army and battle the forces of darkness they had seen enveloping the people in the South Pacific, Burma, Libya, France, Japan and a hundred other places. UFM was one of the agencies in which they enlisted.

The men and women who made up the new missionary corps replenished the on-going fields of Brazil, Congo and Haiti and made possible the advance into British Guiana, Brazil's Roraima Territory, the Dominican Republic and Dutch New Guinea, which later became Irian Jaya.

In many instances, they brought new skills to a field. But whether new or old and whether performed by old-hands or neophytes, the tasks of a missionary seemed unending. Charles Piepgrass, who served in Haiti before he was called to headquarters in the United States, compiled a list of jobs he and his fellow missionaries had been obliged to do within the past month.

"My list may be incomplete," he said, then presented it: Pastor, translator, musician, evangelist, nurse, teacher, electrician, salesman, parent, preacher, counsellor, writer, artist, printer, secretary, carpenter, engineer, mason, chauffeur, redcap, hostess, administrator, mechanic. At his station, he and others also paved the road up their steep hill, administered exams to Bible Institute students, gave guidance to baptismal candidates, taught illiterates to read and spent much time in praying for the young men entering the Christian ministry at a time, humanly speaking, when it was certainly not propitious in Haiti to commit themselves, neither financially nor socially, to such a calling.

Besides their daily obligations, almost all new missionaries had to spend hours every day in learning a language, either a national tongue, a trade lingo or a local dialect, and often all three. And then, most of these new missionaries were newly married, some of them parents of very young children. They bore all the pressures one would in raising a family at home and, in addition, had to cope, and had to help their families cope, with a strange and sometimes almost inexplicable environment and culture.

Standing behind them were the faithful loved ones, local churches and mission officials who had sent them out. Whether passing through headquarters en route to a field or returning from one, newly appointed and veteran missionaries alike were struck by the prayerful atmosphere of UFM's Philadelphia and Toronto offices. It was the greatest impression left on Robert and Nona Bitner as they attended candidate school in 1955 prior to going to Haiti. Interestingly, forty years later they went to their first retirees' conference, and though the leadership of the mission had changed three times in those decades in between, the emphasis on prayer was still the same.

Bob Bitner also took note that the mission's general director sincerely looked to his Council members for the contribution to the operation that each man could make. Edwin Pudney had drawn a number of skilled and experienced men of God to be his administration's advisers and policy makers. Pastors of strong, independent churches in the Philadelphia area, businessmen and professionals in various callings made up the Council. One of those men, a practical individual, provided a new automobile to the mission every other year. He also gave specifically to a fund that allowed Mr. and Mrs. Pudney to travel to the various fields and become missionaries to their missionaries.

For many years George C. Patton and F. W. W. Small gave their talent and time freely as treasurers of the Philadelphia and Toronto operations, respectively. Another Council member, Dr. Henry Brandt provided professional services at each Candidate Orientation. A clinical psychologist, he pioneered in basing professional counseling of troubled people strictly on what the Bible says; year in and year out he took time from his practice and heavy speaking schedule to visit UFM's fields and there to help missionaries with a myriad of personal, family and ministry problems. Other Council members made pastoral calls and preached at the far-away stations.

The Pudneys felt it essential to maintain a first-hand knowledge of all the activities of the mission. This was especially important to an organization that looked to its front-line workers for major decisions. But more than seeking better professional ties, the Pudneys kept in touch with their missionaries, face-to-face when possible, because they felt they were all of one family. After a trip Mrs. Pudney often wrote of their experiences and impressions, and this helped to clarify issues and encourage constituents.

By 1953 the mission had outgrown its two houses on 63rd Street in Philadelphia. There was no room large enough for the expanded public meetings, the short-term accommodation for missionary families was inadequate and the noise of traffic both day and night made work and sleep almost impossible. The Pudneys placed the need of larger, quieter quarters in the hands of a Christian real-estate agent, Alex Dunlap, who was a good friend of the mission and an elder of Grace Chapel. Within three days Dunlap phoned, saying he had looked at a dozen places and the last one proved to be just what was needed. Two members of the Council joined the Pudneys as they accompanied the agent to a large, imposing dwelling on three and a half acres in the quiet western suburb of Bala-Cynwyd.

"Do not tempt us," exclaimed Pudney as they drove into the manicured grounds. "This is far beyond anything we have contemplated."

"Let's look it over and believe God if He wants you to have it," came Dunlap's reply.

The interior excelled the outside. The main house had fourteen rooms and five baths. An annex consisted of six rooms, and a gate house of seven. A one-time conservatory had been converted into a five-room apartment, which, it could be easily seen, would make a fine office. The property appeared to be a perfect match for UFM's requirements.

The price was double what the mission could pay.

Alex Dunlap dealt with the owners, a Christian couple, Frank and Gladys Baker. He was a stockbroker. The couple attended the nearby Methodist Church. Dunlap felt she was particularly warm toward his clients and their need. He told the Bakers what they could pay. Two weeks of silence followed. Then as others stayed behind at 63rd Street to pray, the Pudneys again visited the Bala property. They would like nothing better, the Bakers said, than that their home of thirty years should become a missionary society's headquarters. On the other hand, the mission's offer was less than what it would take for them to purchase another, considerably smaller home. If one party could go up in price, they suggested, the other perhaps could come down and the two would meet half way. Reluctantly, Pudney was forced to admit that without a miracle of God even that arrangement, though fair, was impossible.

Mission personnel began looking at other properties, but none was suitable. They decided to stop looking until word came that 306 Bala Avenue was sold. For a month they prayed daily about the matter. At the end of the month, during the last week, Mr. and Mrs. Pudney decided to take their evening walk in Bala-Cynwyd. They walked around the block where the 306 Bala Avenue estate stood, and paused each time to pray at the gate of the property. On the seventh evening, like Joshua and the armies of Israel, they walked around the block seven times, praying at the gate each time around. God answered their prayers. Then their agent approached the owners once more, the mission all the time in prayer that God's will be done. Dunlap returned, saying the Bakers had found the right home for them and that if UFM covered certain expenses the original offer might possibly be accepted. An emergency meeting of the Council was called and this proposition approved. The price was accepted, the sales agreement drawn up and a deposit paid.

Still, there was the matter of proper zoning. At a meeting of the zoning board, some forty of the near-by neighbors appeared, demanding to know just who were these people who wanted to insert a mission into their reposeful residential neighborhood. Would the community be sharing this block with a rescue mission, with all sorts of very doubtful characters wandering up and down their streets night and day? Would the mansion's lovely grounds turn into a center for boisterous picnics and bazaars with loud speakers and ice-cream sales? Was it a school the new owners would be conducting, with the student body made up of converts from questionable countries abroad?

For forty-five minutes the Pudneys answered rather pointed questions. They spoke to the people of the work UFM did, the world-wide scope of their witness and the success God had graciously given. Entirely new to the audience was the fact that the mission could receive adequate finance without being part of a religious denomination. The questioning continued, and to permit other items on the agenda to come to the floor, both questioners and those questioned were moved to an adjacent room to continue the discussions.

Prior to their dismissal, the chairman of the zoning board thanked the Pudneys, their real-estate agent and their attorney for the testimony concerning the Bible and missionary work. A few days later the necessary approval was granted, and the property became UFM's new, commodious, efficient and comfortable headquarters.

One evening after moving in, those present in the house read the text of the day's *Daily Light* devotional, Haggai 2:9. They decided the passage, speaking of "this latter house," applied to the mission. A few days later the same verse came up in morning devotions. On the day of dedication, cables arrived from abroad. The one from the Haiti team quoted Haggai: *The glory of this latter house shall be greater than of the former, saith the Lord of hosts: and in this place will I give peace, saith the Lord of hosts.*

It seemed a stamp of God's blessing for the days ahead.

Prayer and praise services were held morning, afternoon and evening on Dedication Day. Messages were brought by three of the mission's warmest friends, Dr. Edwin Johnson, pastor of Grace Chapel, Havertown; Dr. Frank Torrey, Calvary Independent Church, Lancaster, and Dr. William Allan Dean, Aldan Union Church, Aldan, all in Pennsylvania. The property was yielded to the Lord's hand. "Bala" soon became a fixed entry in UFM's lexicon.

Growth of an agency doing God's work cannot with any degree of accuracy be measured by its income. Yet, finances, when achieved in God's way, are an indication of His blessing. In 1931, the first year in Toronto, UFM received $2,000 in North American contributions. For the first ten years, total income was $96,794.56. In the next ten years, the aggregate exceeded a million dollars. Through the 1950s, annual income increased gradually from a quarter to well over a third of a million. From one missionary when the Pudneys first moved to Canada from England, to a dispatch of two hundred sixty by 1960, the fields and income expanded in parallel. This was due to Pudney's philosophy of individual missionary support, which was contrary to UFM's predecessor agency when he and Lilian went for their first term to Congo. At that time, each new missionary who was added to the mission's roster meant a tightening of the belt by all others. Pudney introduced the principle that a person's call to the mission field was sealed by the pledge of adequate support by churches and individual donors.

By 1961 Edwin and Lilian Pudney had been in mission work for thirty-eight years. He was sixty-five years of age, and they felt the time had come for younger soldiers in God's army to replace them. They had led the North American branch of UFM through its uncertain beginning and had guided its growth under God to a status that in later years had achieved a humble but honorable place among mission societies. That the United States and Canada had contributed importantly to UFM's global service was evident in a report carried by the organization's news magazine, *Light & Life*. In the third quarter of 1961, the report said, in paraphrased summary, the following:

UFM today has a total of 366 missionaries in eight separate fields on four continents, preaching the Gospel in 16 distinct languages. The Mission has a total of 61 main stations. Brazil with 14 stations and 88 workers is the largest of the eight fields. The United Kingdom has 89 missionaries in Brazil and Congo. Australia has 66 workers in New Guinea. North America is the largest with 211 missionaries in Brazil, British Guiana, Congo, New Guinea, Haiti and Dominican Republic.

That UFM is building for the future on a solid foundation can be seen from the institutions it has established in the educational and medical fields. The Mission has 14 Bible Institutes, two each in Brazil and New Guinea, four in Congo, four in Australian New Guinea, and one each in Haiti and British Guiana. The total enrolled in 1960-61 is 347.

Elementary education for the children of converts is provided in 135 elementary and six secondary and professional schools. Total enrollment is 13,439 scholars. The professional school gives training in the fields of teaching, nursing and home economics.

The medical work is progressing with gratifying results. Two hospitals in Congo and one in Haiti minister to the bodies and souls of thousands of patients each year, many of whom find the Lord during their stay in the hospital. Outpatients are treated at the mission's 56 dispensaries, 38 of these being in the Australian half of New Guinea.

Two orphanages in Haiti and three boarding schools in Brazil care for and educate hundreds of children.

Twenty-three qualified nurses and medical technicians conduct the clinics and dispensaries. In Congo, 18 national workers carry on the bulk of the medical work. Seven Haitian girls have been trained and graduated from the La Pointe medical school and a Haitian doctor works in that field's hospital.

UFM missionaries have engaged extensively in translation work. Languages reduced to writing include Kayapo, Tupi, Ge, Wai Wai, Macushi, Waica and Shirishana in Brazil; Gogodala, Foe, Zimakani and Aekyom as well as the Motu trade language and the Tari tribal tongue in Australian New Guinea. Dani and Galum are being worked with at present in Dutch New Guinea. In Africa, missionaries have contributed to the improvement of two widely used trade languages, Bangala and Kingwana. Other missionaries working on their own, in Africa, have reduced Babali, Basali and Bangelema tribal tongues to writing, mainly for their own personal use in order to reach those who have little or no knowledge of the trade tongue.

The mission in Brazil and British Guiana has sought to evangelize some 19 Indian tribes throughout the years: Guajajara, Kayapo, Kuben-Kran-Ken, Chee-Kree, Kokraimoro, Guaja, Wapishana, Shedeu, Shirishana, Waica, Maiongongs, Wai Wai, Macushi, Mawayana, Gorotire, Urubu, Canela, Tembe and Tembira.

In Congo, two ordained pastors, 162 evangelists, 64 teachers and 18 medical workers of the Congolese themselves are largely responsible for the work. The national churches of Brazil publish *Luz Evangelica* and the Bible Institute in Haiti publishes the monthly *Parole de Vie*. The mission presses in Haiti and Australian New Guinea are ever busy with new publications and helps.

Sales of the bookstore in Haiti, have reached $1,000 monthly. Brazil, Dominican Republic and Congo each has two bookstores. There is a substantial increase in the sale of Christian literature on all the fields.

Launch evangelism is carried on in the lower Amazon River region. Three Gospel launches are now in operation. The mission has three weekly radio broadcasts in the West Indies, two in Haiti and one in the Dominican Republic.

When it became evident in 1958 that the workload would some day have to be shifted to younger leaders, calls for nomination as general director were dispatched to the fields. Brazil put forth their field leader, the Rev. Charles Sarginson, and the Haiti field theirs, the Rev. Ralph B. Odman. The Council chose both men, Odman as general director and Sarginson as associate director. Odman and his wife, Majil, returned from Haiti and began assisting in the Bala office in order to become fully acquainted with every detail of administration. Sarginson was assigned to direct the affairs of the Toronto office.

Retirement for the Pudneys came in 1961. The mission entered upon a new era, and even in it, the Pudneys, from their retirement home in Florida, would have a role to play.

SOURCES, Chapter 12

Bitner, Robert O., 1996, Letter to author

Harris, Leonard F., *Our Days in His Hands*, London, UFM, undated

Larson, Alfred, 1996, Telephone interview

Light & Life, Bala-Cynwyd, UFM periodical, 2nd Quarter, 1959; 3rd Quarter, 1961

Nesbitt, James H., 1996, Letter to author

Pudney, Edwin and Lilian, *Miracles Multiplied*, undated, unpublished manuscript

_____, *Sacrifice of Praise*, undated, Bala-Cynwyd, UFM

13

From the Pudneys to the Odmans

Edwin and Lilian Pudney moved to South Florida. They had been acclimated to tropical temperatures in Congo, and felt at home in the warmer weather during their visits to Haiti, Brazil and Africa. They chose to live in Boca Raton, where they could be active in the Bibletown Community Church.

The couple continued to serve UFM by representing the mission in their section of the country and by much prayer. They also shared the Gospel with Florida's migrant workers, who as unevangelized people fell within the sphere of UFM's mandate. In a short time Pudney was asked to chair the Bibletown missions committee. But was the appointment in deference to his distinguished career as a missions executive? For its size, the church had done rather little in the support of missionaries.

E. J. Pudney did not wear ceremonial hats, however. He set about organizing a week-long missions conference. At its conclusion, a faith-promise offering was taken. For it, individuals or families pledged a certain amount "above and beyond" their usual budgets, trusting the Lord to provide it. Great was the astonishment of church officers and members when $91,000 was raised. That sum grew, and fifteen years later under Pudney's continued leadership the church was giving $208,000 annually to support one hundred fifty-six missionaries and twenty projects.

In Bala, the transition went smoothly. Ralph Odman shifted quietly over to the general director's desk, his apprentice years having prepared him for a multitude of tasks in this expanding organization. Perhaps as vital to his training as the three years spent in understudy to Pudney was his service in Haiti, beginning in 1947 and all but six months as that field's elected leader.

During his ten years in Haiti, Odman envisioned many advancements, and time after time they became reality: expanded Bible teaching; education for young people, pastors and lay leaders; greater opportunity for fellowship among the believers; adequate facilities for all activities; rest and renewal for tired missionaries.

Chosen field leader by his peers, he did not slacken the hands-on approach that had defined him from his first day in Haiti. If he were not to be found at his desk, he might be discovered under a truck adjusting its brakes, or in the attic of a building clearing out a worthless accumulation. If a call came from the printing department for help in hand-collating the pages of a new hymnal, Odman would be there, spending the evening walking around the table gathering up the sheets with other volunteers.

As field leader and responsible for UFM's missionaries and their work there, he served simultaneously as church pastor, circuit rider, school director and teacher, course writer, house builder, counselor, conference organizer and speaker, purchasing agent, liaison to government, problem solver, father and husband.

A graduate of Seattle Pacific College (now University) and Dallas Theological Seminary, he was a student of the Bible, and for a while served a Seattle church as its assistant pastor. Having been on the mission field and then as a mission executive keeping in touch with global developments and trends, Odman became greatly concerned about the ecumenicity that was starting to engulf missions and national Christian entities in many parts of the world. Christians working together and the promotion of harmony among believers drew his hearty involvement. But much of what was going on in the name of spiritual unity lacked, as he saw it, the centrality of Jesus Christ as the world's only Savior and Lord. The message of humanistic religion was propagated by the World Council of Churches and there was danger that some of the churches in lands where UFM had pioneered, and even their national organizations, would be swept together with nonbelievers into organisms that denied the deity of Christ and the inerrancy of the Bible.

He wrote a significant paper titled, "Where Stands the Unevangelized Fields Mission in the Present Theological and Ecclesiastical World Scene."

In it, he expressed gratitude that in the spread of the Gospel there was the use of radio, literature, Bible institutes, youth camps, hospitals and clinics, orphanages, educational institutions, linguistics, launch evangelism, church planting and supervision. "But in all such ministries," he cautioned, "the acid test is, 'What place is given to the Word of God? What place is given to the Person of Christ?'" He went on to say, "We realize that in the accomplishment of our God-given task there is the relating of man to man and also man to organization and organization to organization. The guiding principle for the UFM and its members is: We shall only relate organically to those individuals or groups who will meet us on the basis of our doctrinal statement . . . and demonstrate Christian conduct."

As a warning to his fellow missioners, he concluded the document thus:

"At this moment, the prime mover in the 'Ecumenical Movement' is the World Council of Churches and we recognize its efforts to engulf 'faith missions' and churches we have established. Although our declarations have been made of desiring not to affiliate with this movement or any of its extended service organizations, i.e., literacy, relief, etc., it seems that the WCC maintains a paternal attitude toward us in extending good wishes and favors and courting young churches with financial help, etc., hoping to establish the relationship that [the] church at home directly helps [the] church abroad, and thus remove the need for the 'faith missionary' and his program.

"We are instructing our national brethren in the Word of God and the dangers of the World Council of Churches. We are initiating evangelical fellowships which will unite the young churches locally and nationally in order that they may encourage one another to steadfastness to the faith.

"We therefore continue our ministry, seeking to minister to the whole man — body, soul and spirit on the basis of the Word of God. Our greatest objective is to preach the Gospel, thus bringing souls into glory by the blood of the Cross and making possible the establishing of indigenous local churches which are and shall be encouraged to join in fellowship with those of like mind and purpose."

The form of fellowship differed from country to country. The usual overarching pattern, however, was for the churches on each field to tie to each other through their own non-denominational organization. In Haiti, the churches born of UFM's ministry became Baptist because that group was UFM's partner there.

The work in this Caribbean nation of African culture took on a new dimension in 1949 when the World Christian Crusade merged its missionaries and Bible school in Port-au-Prince into UFM. To negotiate an agreement combining the two missions, Lehman Keener was sent by his WCC colleagues to the United States, and that task accomplished there, it fell to Ralph Odman to put the merger into effect in Haiti. Mission headquarters moved to the capital city, and the Bible school at La Pointe joined with the former WCC school in the partly completed building in suburban Bolosse. Because the mission was now in the environs of the capital did not mean the atmosphere had cleared of the daunting witchery that characterized the country. Luella Keener reminisced one day over the early experiences of Lehman and herself:

On the mountain above Port-au-Prince, behind the mission station, lived many Haitians in villages of mud and wattle huts. They did not comprehend why the missionaries had come. 'They have no right to be here; no right to live on our land; no right to eat our food,' were their thoughts.

Curses from the witchdoctors were pronounced upon the strangers. Voodoo priests performed rites against them. Voodoo drums beat loudly and wildly the throbbing dance rhythms and the eerie ceremonial music of the spirits.

Nights were often pierced with chilling, high-pitched wails of those experiencing death in their family. Utter hopelessness! It was frustrating and saddening to the missionaries that these people would not listen to the message of salvation and hope.

But listen they did eventually, and the presence of a Bible school on the hill overlooking the villages provided evidence that many people had accepted the message and some now were preparing themselves to better deliver it to others.

Combining the institutions gave the Evangelical School of the Bible more students and a strengthened faculty. The building was soon completed. The gleaming white structure on the hill highlighted the mission's presence in the city, and gradually homes at the foot of the hill were bought and others erected on the campus. UFM became as recognized an institution in Port-au-Prince as it was in the north of the country.

Lehman and Luella Keener were a couple who came with the merger. Originally an independent missionary, his intention for service in Haiti was youth work, and anticipating a retreat facility some day he personally bought land in Pétionville, a desirable location west of the city where many of the well-to-do citizens lived. He redirected his effort when Florent Toirac started the Bible school at Bolosse. Joining the faculty in 1947, he stayed with the school until 1953; his wife's life-threatening illness forced the couple to leave. For the next eighteen years he was a member of the UFM home staff, assisting with Candidate Orientation and conducting deputational meetings for the mission. He traveled to all the fields to minister to missionaries and to gather visual aids for presenting the mission's work at home.

Luella Keener left a legacy among the Haitian children. She introduced Child Evangelism to the churches. Assisted by Arlene Piepgrass, whose husband, Charles, taught at the Bible school, and an all-Haitian staff, Luella Keener supervised CE classes, drawing a thousand children a week, 5-Day summer clubs, with up to eight thousand attending, and training sessions for the teachers.

Removal of the Bible school from La Pointe to Port-au-Prince prompted the initiation of extension classes for pastors and church lay leaders. In later years the program became known as TEE — Theological Education by Extension. It was just one of the programs Ralph Odman began for the growing clergy of Haiti. Pastoral seminars were held the week before the Bible school dismissed for the summer, and in that vacation period a Summer Institute presented shortened versions of the regular school curriculum to the wives and intended brides of the men students.

As a further attempt to fit the program to the needs of those in it, the Bible school hours were changed. To benefit working students, classes were held between 3 and 7 P.M. Continuing education seminars from one to four days in length were offered in four regions, contributing to the spiritual development of pastors and lay leaders.

As its first president, the Bible school chose a Haitian of both spiritual and intellectual stature. Edner Jeanty graduated from Grace College and Seminary in Indiana. He became an authority on the Creole language, which he once said was forty per cent French, forty percent African dialects and a twenty percent mixture of English, Spanish and Arawak. He changed the teaching of Creole from a base of English phonetics to French. He worked with others in translating the Bible into Creole and authored a number of books, including a collection of Haitian proverbs.

Field Leader Odman carefully tended to the Bible school, teaching classes, writing courses, scheduling programs. He took a direct interest in projects throughout the country, and regularly visited the various villages to encourage and minister. He was mindful, too, of the missionaries. In 1954 he called the first Spiritual Life Conference for representatives of all missions in Haiti. He was responsible for the building of a rest home in Pétionville where missionaries could enjoy a brief respite from their labors. The vacation house was built on land the Keeners donated to the mission before leaving for the States.

Several of the UFM staff were troubled that the education offered by the churches stopped short of secondary school. To some, in a land that was only twenty-three per cent literate, elementary schooling might have seemed sufficient. The Bible school, for example, required the equivalent of an eighth-grade diploma, though that was waived if the applicant lacking the credentials showed promise. But leaders among the people needed more. Vance and Joy Brown opened a secondary school, Bethel College, in Jean Rabel, the first on Haiti's arid Northwest Peninsula. Mme. Paultre extended the school at La Pointe to include higher grades, and later added a trade school that taught tailoring, shoemaking, typing, woodworking and other practical subjects.

Dick Wilkinson and Ralph Odman each longed for an outstanding school that would take church-school graduates up through the level of the American junior college. Its students would be spared the indifference to their faith or an attack on it by the secular and religious secondary schools in Haiti. And they would be well prepared for university or professional studies. Now and then one or the other mentioned the dream, finding an ally in Dr. Orius Paultre, now president of the national church. But elsewhere they encountered doubt. Again, was the undertaking too big for a mission organization in Haiti?

Persistence opened Maranatha College in 1956 with twelve

boarding students and one girl commuter, meeting in a rented building in Bolosse. Among the early faculty were Edner Jeanty, the first director, and Claude Noel, a member of the Bible school's first class and later a graduate of Providence Barrington Bible College in Rhode Island. When Jeanty went to the United States for further education, Noel succeeded him as the school's director, and at the same time pastored a growing church in Bolosse. Maranatha College expanded by a grade each year, so Dick Wilkinson was called to Port-au-Prince to build a campus for the school and to lend it his enthusiasm and experience.

The U. S. radio ministry, Back to the Bible, helped financially in the construction of two buildings on a hill next to that of the Bible school.

From the days when the north was UFM's only area in Haiti, much of the activity now occurred in and around Port-au-Prince. The medical ministry still centered at La Pointe, and the day came when limited surgeries were accomplished there, in a storage area converted to an operating room. But come July, there was no doubt where the focus of the mission and the churches lay. Once another vision of Ralph Odman, the Béraca Convention at La Pointe became the red-letter week of the MEBH calendar.

Begun in 1948, the convention drew bigger crowds each year. It was not unusual for five thousand men, women and children to attend. Many churches hired buses for their delegations. Families also arrived on horseback, mule, donkey or on foot. Years that the rains were heavy meant crossing unbridged, overflowing rivers and wading through knee-deep mud. Still, they marched joyfully toward La Pointe singing and quoting Scripture. They brought their own food, cooking pots and charcoal burners and mats for sleeping. Men slept in a wooden tabernacle where the meetings were held, women and small children in a large extra-seating tent next to it.

From Thursday through Sunday three conferences went on

— for adults, youth and children. An old train bell mounted on a post outside the tabernacle rang early each morning, calling the people to prayer. Throughout the day there were periods of worship and prayer, preaching and teaching, and much singing. In between, fellowship filled every moment. Many a church sent its choir. Each was given time to sing. In the early days at the closing meeting on Sunday after the final message and communion were ended, Grace Gulick massed the many choirs into a huge chorale for the *Hallelujah Chorus*. The Béraca Convention, reflecting the Biblical Valley of Blessing, energized the church as few other ministries could.

SOURCES, Chapter 13

Annual Reports, 1990 and 1995, Bala-Cynwyd, PA, Unevangelized Fields Mission

Annual Report, Haiti Field, 1995

Beerley, John A., 1995, 1996, Letters to Author

Bitner, Robert O., 1996, Letters to Author

Boggs, Boxley, 1996, Notes on draft

Brazil Field Council Meeting Minutes, 1964

Brown, Joy, 1996, Letters to Author

Conference, Retired Haiti missionaries with author, May, 1996, Lancaster, PA

Larson, Alfred and Jean, 1996, Interview

Lifeline, 1st Quarter, 1966; 2nd Quarter, 1966; 2nd Quarter, 1967; Summer, 1968; February, 1981; April, 1991

Light & Life, Bala-Cynwyd, Unevangelized Fields Mission, 1st Quarter, 1952; 4th Quarter, 1958; 1st Quarter, 1959; 2nd Quarter, 1959

Pearl of the Antilles, Audio-tape script, Undated, Bala-Cynwyd, Unevangelized Fields Mission

Pudney, Lilian G., *God Which Worketh*, 1953, Philadelphia, Unevangelized Fields Mission

Wilkinson, Richard, Audio-tape, 1996

Wilson, Majil Odman, 1996, Letter to author

_____, *Ralph and Majil in Bala*

14
On the Amazon

In Brazil, the prohibition of work among Amazon Indians was ended by the government in 1955. Aside from visits by Horace Banner, the officials had permitted only occasional contacts by missionaries from the time of World War II. During these years of restriction the Indian work held its own surprisingly well. The witness among the Brazilians expanded dramatically.

River work intensified. Boarding schools for Brazilian children were started. The Bible Institute serving the State of Maranhão moved to São Luis and a second school opened in Abaetetuba. The churches were organized into a fellowship alliance.

Their peers had called Charles and Effie Sarginson in 1947 from river work to Belém to lead the field. In this period of growth theirs was a busy but happy life. Administration, purchasing, dealing with government, teaching Portuguese to new missionaries, overseeing and supporting the work scattered over a vast area — all fell on Charles. Often he did administrative chores for other missions. Effie's load, too, was heavy — office duties, management of a ten-bedroom house and caring for the missionaries who constantly came and went, with as many as twenty in the house at one time. They were also responsible for a church in the suburbs of Belém. He led the young people in Saturday night street meetings and she organized the women in a study and service circle and began children's clubs. Each activity drew people into the church.

The Sarginsons had no opportunity to return to the launch work they loved, but were thrilled years later when on a visit to the river they found alive and thriving three churches started by their ministry. Each had progressed without a missionary pastor, though their successors had managed to visit them regularly and study the Bible with them. In their visit, one elderly man held up a Bible for them to see. It was the one they had given him nearly thirty years before, one of the thousand or so they distributed on the river each year.

Angus and Rosemary Cunningham were typical of those who before World War II had labored among the Indians but who had to leave that field and begin anew in areas more closely guarded by the government. They joined the growing fleet of river evangelists. During the war and in the years following, the mission operated three launches, then a fourth, to carry the Gospel up and down the lower Amazon and its tributaries. Douglas and Mary McAllister, Charles and Effie Sarginson, Les and Anita Jantz, Delbert and Marguerite Harrell, Ted and Janet Laskowski and the Cunninghams — these were the pilots, navigators, map makers, engineers, stewards, cooks, colporteurs, preachers, teachers and medical personnel who steered their craft into the tiny ports along the route and there among fifteen people or five hundred planted the seed. Nurturing came as follow-up visits were made. In many places the Lord transformed these little clusters of believers into churches. Some — Portel, Cameta, Igarape Mirim and São Sebastião de Boa Vista among them — became large and strong and akin to tall spiritual lighthouses in their regions.

In the early days of the launch ministry, the town of Abaetetuba, near Belém and the wide mouth of the Amazon, served as the base. The first vessel, the *Colaborador,* had been bought from the British and Foreign Bible Society, whose sellers of Bibles and Scripture portions had plied these waters in it for twenty-five years. Doug McAllister built the second UFM launch, the *Araúto*, or Herald. The Harrells joined the team in 1952. They built a larger boat and extended the limits further westward, anchoring the *Aurora* in Porto de Moz at the mouth of the Xingu. The fourth launch in the mission's service was the *Maranatha*. It was started by Cecil McMullen, but was finished by others because during its construction this Irish missionary died of a heart attack.

Before choosing the small settlement of Porto de Moz as their home port, the Harrells cruised up the Amazon as far as Santarem. They returned to Porto, choosing it for its safe haven from the brutal tide action and turbulence of the Amazon. The people welcomed them "with open arms," to quote the mayor. Negotiations for buying water-front land were completed, and Delbert built a dock for the *Aurora*, then started a house for the family.

After their intention to preach Christ became known, it was not long until the town split, a few willing, some even eager, to hear their message, the larger number indifferent or hostile. The open arms of the mayor now thrashed against them. The established church authority became a bitter enemy, its loudspeaker blasting them as the Devil.

The mayor ordered construction on the house halted until, he said, title to the land was cleared. This meant the Harrells would continue living on the launch for a while. For five months the town council divided on whether to approve the purchase, but then a majority decided it was legal, the title valid. The mayor was furious. Ordered out, the Harrells decided to go on a trip, hoping that by the time they returned the tempest would have calmed. Their plans made none too soon, they heard there was a plot to kill Delbert and sink the launch. The town's policeman warned him to leave immediately.

Before they left, the town lawyer, one of their friends, said he would draw up a telegram addressed to state and national officials asking for governmental protection for their rights as lawful residents. On their way downstream the couple would dispatch the message at the overnight port of Gurupa, where there was telegraph service, an intention that became known around the town.

The night they were to cast off was terribly stormy. Delbert walked into town to pick up the title and the telegram composed by the lawyer. As the darkness gathered, Marguerite, at home on their boat, peered through the slashing rain and saw a large party of men making their way to another vessel at the river's edge. Thirty-one men. She made out that each was armed. Their leader wore a long, dark robe. They shoved off from shore and headed downstream.

It was true, she said to herself, while eyeing with fear their two young children. The rumor of a plot to kill Delbert was true.

Del knew it was true. He had walked from the home of the council president with legal papers and title in his pocket, followed by seventeen men, each of them armed. Coming abreast of the church, he turned into the path toward home. As his stalkers continued on to the town's port, their numbers increased. Not daring to kill him in town with its many witnesses, they would intercept the *Aurora* in a lonely stretch downstream, and under cover of the tumultuous thunder riddle his body with bullets and throw it to the piranhas and alligators and anacondas. Or they would sink the *Aurora* with the family aboard, and the raging surf of the Amazon would obliterate their murderous deed.

Delbert returned to the *Aurora*, the title safely tucked inside his shirt. There was one change in their plans, he said to Marguerite. The lawyer's message was too long for a telegram — they wouldn't have money enough to pay for it. Instead, the lawyer had substituted a letter that they would send by airmail. That meant going up the Xingu to Altamira, where this service was available, not down the Amazon.

Hurrying to shove off, they began their journey up the river and despite the raging rainfall outside, stayed dry and comfortable. They spent the night under the solid cover of a friend's house. Downstream, thirty armed men and their robed leader waited all night, packed as a sodden, sorry mass in an open boat, looking through the darkness and slow-arriving dawn for a familiar launch that never came.

Rejection and persecution became routine for all the couples in UFM's launch ministry. But there were successes, too. Often crowds of a hundred or more, the entire population of some towns, gathered whenever the Gospel was preached. Churches were born, including one at Porto de Moz, and most of these grew to be solid, enduring witnesses. Instruction in the Word of God became the prime need of the leaders of those congregations. Ted Laskowski envisioned a Bible school for the river dwellers. He figured Abaetetuba, the original base for the launch work, would be an appropriate location. Douglas McAllister had bought at a cheap price some land for raising pineapples as a needed diet supplement. This land was used, instead, for the new school.

After eighteen years on the river, Doug and Mary McAllister were called to Belém to start a home for newly arrived missionaries and a school to teach them Portuguese. They visited extensively in the homes of city residents and from these contacts started a church in the Marco district. It grew to become the largest congregation in the UFM-affiliated association.

John and Bonnie Canfield were assigned to head the new Bible Institute in Belém. This was but one of many assignments in a missionary career that originally was predicted to last one year. He was crippled by polio at age three, she at age seven. John became interested in Brazil and UFM through George Thomas, a fellow Canadian. Thomas was UFM's first North American missionary. On his first furlough he spoke many places of his vision to start a Bible school to train teachers for an outreach to the Guajajara Indians of the State of Maranhão. John Canfield's heart was touched. Bonnie heard John's testimony that despite his twisted leg and cane, he was going to Brazil as a missionary. She became interested not only in Brazil, but in the young man who was going there. After graduating from Prairie Bible Institute, John went to the field in 1934 and accepted George Thomas' invitation to teach music in the new Bible school. Bonnie was unsure of the future. She wanted to be a missionary, and even preached on Sundays at the neighborhood school. But she had no money and little assurance that John or anyone else in Brazil needed her.

One day late in 1938 she received a letter from him. He asked, "Are you ever coming?" That was all she needed. She prayed in the money for getting there. She sailed with two other young women, Florence Hough and Rosemary Anderson, later Cunningham. After she and John were married, he took her to Barra do Corda, where the school was located, using coastal ship, train, truck and river barge to get there. They worked in the Bible Institute until 1953, when they were asked to move to Abaetetuba to begin the new Bible school.

Ted and Janet Laskowski were chosen to assist at Abaetetuba. Then in 1954 the Canfields were transferred to lead the older, larger Bible Institute — the school had been moved from Barra do Corda to São Luis on the coast. Leslie and Anita Jantz were pulled in from river work to join the Laskowskis. Another change came when Laskowski was elected field leader. The Jantzes took over headship of the school and William and Dahna Regier moved in to help. Bill Regier was a popular musician, entrancing audiences with his skill on the musical saw, and after a while he directed the school.

But because the number of students never reached a practical minimum for a year-around Bible institute, the school was changed to a rainy-season operation. Each February church leaders came for a month's study. São Luis gave academic credit, and those completing the course qualified for ordination.

Even with this shortening of the school year, the site still had more use than merely growing pineapples, for which it had been bought. It became a much-used camp and conference center. After serving at Abaetetuba for fifteen years and at headquarters in Belém for twenty, the Jantzes went back to this spot to host the camps and conferences, and continued to do so following retirement, even returning from Canada for periods of up to one year through the mid-1990s.

John Canfield had not only a Bible Institute to direct, but a building program as well. He and the family lived two miles from the school, so every day John walked — with assistance of his trusty cane — two miles. In 1967 the Canfields moved to Brasilia, the new capital city of Brazil, where in four years they organized four churches. Four graduates of the Bible Institute in São Luis filled the pulpits of the four churches. Other former students of the Canfields became members of the congregations. When they left the mission field, the Canfields could look back on a long and varied career — thirty -seven years for Bonnie, forty for John. Quite a difference from the expectation of a single year's service.

Even as early as the war years, another need in the Amazon region showed clearly. The children in the river villages were unable to read. They were ignorant about many things. All of them desperately poor, they lived in pain and filth, and their homes were filled with superstition and error, cruelty, fear, evil practices and bondage.

Angus and Rosemary Cunningham settled in Breves, a town on the south shore of Marajô Island, which sits in the mouth of the Amazon and is larger than the combined states of Massachusetts, Connecticut and Delaware. When traveling on river steamers or in making a run up the river in the *Colaborador* with Charles and Effie Sarginson they saw children in squalid conditions, little ones suffering from malaria, tropical ulcers and intestinal parasites. On one trip out of Breves Rosemary complained to her husband, "One would think that some — some — well, some missionary or *someone* would start a home and school to teach those who want to know of the Lord and make it possible for some of these little ones to have a better life than their forefathers have had."

She kept repeating, "Why doesn't someone do something about it?" until she discovered the answer in her life's Scripture verse, "Whatsoever thy hand findeth to do, do it with thy might."

Thus was born the Amazon Children's Home and School.

Two other similar schools were opened, at Barra do Corda, where once the Bible Institute had been conducted, and at Cururupu, both in the State of Maranhão.

The New Tribes Mission ceded an off-and-on work in the town of Cameta on the lower Tocantins River to UFM. The going there had been tough; only one believer could be counted on as faithful. David Ross and his family, from Britain, went to revive the work. Ron and Lois Combs worked from a cabin cruiser and this they took to Cameta, which they made their base. Their ministry showed good progress. They ranged up and down the river and into tributary streams, founding churches in several communities.

The day after Christmas one year they loaded up their boat with presents for children in the river ports, gifts from Christians in America. As was their custom on these water treks, they stopped along the way for lunch. While Lois prepared the meal, Ron and their two sons, aged six and eight, went for a swim. The tide, however was high and the current swift. The boys drifted out of the reach of their father. He swam toward them and from the boat Lois threw a rope, but it was too short. She called for help, and immediately Brazilians on shore answered, quickly paddling their canoes to where Ron and the boys battled the river.

The rescuers snatched Mark, the older boy, and lifted him

into the boat, then headed for Ron and Steve. The boy they rescued. Ron dropped beneath the water. His body was found the following day.

At the hour a little Brazilian boy discovered the body in shallow water near a sand bar, Lois sat at their kitchen table in Cameta, head bowed in a prayer of acceptance. Mark said to his mother, "Mommy, Daddy's with the Lord, isn't he?"

"Yes, honey, he is," she replied.

"Then, don't you think he got the best Christmas present of all?"

Lois, Mark and Steve continued on in Brazil for eight more years, then Lois became a member of the home staff at Bala-Cynwyd.

The Sam Backmans and the Martin Joses were others who labored daily in this area to plant the Gospel seed, nurture it and to thankfully participate in the harvest. They helped establish numerous churches on the big island of Marajô. Several single women had much to do with spreading the Gospel on the Lower Amazon.

Phyllis McLean, a teacher, and Jean Bradshaw, a nurse, worked as hard as anyone. They had no real home, but lived in small shacks that congregations would build for their stay, which usually was six months in any one place. They enjoyed no conveniences, neither kitchen nor toilet, but their contentment came in conducting clinics for the sick, day schools for the children, Gospel meetings at night. Their aim was to teach the Word of God and live the life of Christ before people.

Jean Bradshaw returned to England to care for her ailing mother. In the mid-1990s Phyllis McLean still made her headquarters at Abaetetuba, where she opened a new testimony in the midst of a heavy witchcraft area.

Fifteen years after the end of World War II, workers from Germany became part of the mission team. They were followed by those of the Swiss Alliance Mission. The Europeans led in extending the network of new church plantings into the states of Piaui and Bahia. Others penetrated the Japanese colony in Northeast Brazil. Japanese had lived in Brazil since the 1930s and made up the largest concentration of Japanese people outside Japan. For the most part they were involved in farming or some other phase of agribusiness. Industrious people, they were successful. Having lived in the country over a span of two or three generations, they were becoming increasingly submerged in Brazilian culture, but still retained customs that were distinctively Japanese. Could Christianity break through this double shield? It could, and did.

Some of those bearing the news of salvation were second-generation Japanese from North America. Anne Uchida was the first. She was introduced to a Japanese couple whose home was in the outskirts of Belém, and there she began living and started Gospel meetings. English classes, home Bible studies, children's clubs, camps and a tape ministry became effective tools to win converts among this ethnic group. Within a few years three churches were established. Anne kept with the work for many years. Eventually she went to Japan, on loan to TEAM, to extend her ministry to Brazilian Japanese who, for whatever reason, went to Japan to live.

Evangelizing and discipling through literature was as old as the Protestant ministry in Brazil. The colporteurs with their Bibles, New Testaments and tracts had paved the way for the first evangelists. Following World War II, Harry and Lily Heath started a book store in Belém, expanding it from sales on a table in the town market. Stella Tofflemire, transferring from the Bible Institute at Abaetetuba, stepped in when poor health forced the Heaths to return to England. Jessie Foulds succeeded her. Through the years the store gained an important role. Another missionary from England, Gwen Harper, opened a second book store, this one in São Luis. Marylin Woodworth, then

Jessie Foulds, managed it in later years. Additional stores offered Bibles and Christian books in Teresina, the capital of Piaui, and in Imperatriz and Altamira. Moody Press and Evangelical Literature Overseas contributed significantly to the success of the stores.

A ministry began among adolescents, Jet Cadets, with emphasis on weekly meetings, Scripture memorization, participation in projects and vacation-time camping. Started by Joan Hunsberger, it spread to some one hundred churches. Numerous pastors were to testify that this program kept them in the faith during difficult teen years.

Florence Hough shifted from the Bethany Boarding School in Cururupu to an itinerant ministry with the National Women's Union, organizing and supervising women's groups in churches in a five-state region.

Radio came into use in the 1960s, with programs beamed into the area from the Trans World Radio station on the island of Bonaire in the Netherlands Antilles. Dan Canfield, son of veterans John and Bonnie Canfield, and Connie, his wife, were loaned to the station by UFM to produce Portuguese-language programs. For decades, this ministry's impact was felt wherever church planting took place. John prepared some of the messages, and he and Bonnie spent their last three years of active service on Bonaire. While teaching at the seminary in São Luis, Ted Laskowski prepared tapes for a layman's training program, "Good News Radio School." He continued this for fifteen years, eventually moving to São Paulo in the south to work more closely with TWR. On his retirement the program passed to the Brazilians.

The needs of MKs — the children of missionaries — were recognized in the launching of a school for them in Fortaleza, but which eventually moved to Belém and onto its own campus three kilometers outside the city. It later opened to children of other missions. For the students, the Amazon Valley Academy was a family. One of the duties of the faculty was to visit the homes of students in vacation time, whether in a coastal city or in a jungle village, thus giving the teacher a better understanding of the members of his or her class and creating a closer tie between school and home.

Language specialists Earl and Ivy Trapp joined those who continued the evangelization of the Kayapo Indians. Translation of the Bible was sorely needed, for a church without the Scriptures in the native tongue of its people was in danger of growing tares among the wheat. The ability of people to read was a twin requirement for a stable church. Among impediments that had to be overcome, Trapp cited confusing generalities in the Kayapo language. The word for sin, for example, also meant sickness. People expressing a wish for deliverance — was it from the sin that they hardly recognized, or from the sickness that sent them reeling into their hammocks?

The cultural pressures remained great, even on the professing Christians. Many of these were exerted by the witchdoctor who, naturally, was loath to give way before the life-changing Gospel. Trapp counted about two thousand Kayapo members in four main groups in which UFM worked, plus another five hundred to the north where no contact had yet been made. Winning the Kayapo would be a long, tedious process.

Back in the U.S., Ralph Odman, UFM's new general director for North America, aggressively recruited new missionaries. A good many of them landed in Brazil. New personnel also came from the British UFM, the German Missionary Fellowship and the Swiss Alliance Mission. Richard Roche from Great Britain and his Canadian wife, Dorothy, played an important role in the early days, working first in Breves and later among the Kayapo. Richard died of cancer, and Dorothy then taught many years at Amazon Valley Academy. In 1968, another significant source came on line, the vision of Karl Berger, a UFM missionary before he was sponsored by the German Fellowship.

Missão Evangélica aos Indios do Brasil (MEIB), known in English as the Evangelical Mission to the Indians of Brazil, was formed in Belém as a joint effort of the missionaries and the Brazilian churches. It became an independent but cooperating agency for sending national Brazilian workers to the Indians. Through MEIB, Bible institute graduates helped man stations among the Kayapo, and working with experienced missionaries they had a hand in establishing churches in the Kuben Kran Ken, Gorotire and Kokraymoro clans of the Kayapo. The testimony advanced among the Guajajara Indians and opened in another tribe, the Canela.

A vital service to the ministry scattered widely among the Indians was the air transport and radio contact of Mission Aviation Fellowship. Wycliffe Bible Translators aided in reducing tribal languages to writing and in translating the Bible into local tongues.

In March of 1964 the Brazilian Army revolted against the national government, deposing the president whom some said was leading the country into communism. After this near-bloodless revolution, policy changes affected large segments of national life, particularly the economy. Felt by UFM in the far northeast, regulations were issued from the new capital of Brasilia regarding boat traffic on the Amazon. No longer would fuel be subsidized, raising the price significantly, and the government demanded that more men be employed on every launch. Running vessels up and down the Amazon and its feeder rivers became too expensive for the mission. Other means of evangelizing would have to be found. The changes he saw coming weighed heavily on Ted Laskowski, who was elected field chairman when Charles Sarginson was called back to help in UFM's North American administration. During his twelve-year tenure, he was to learn the truth of a remark made to him by Sarginson in the transfer of responsibilities, "I think you'll find this much more work than position." Laskowski likened the Belém office to the hub of a wheel — the connecting spokes conveyed pressure from the whole rim to the axle.

In the mid-1960s the field council examined all operations in their region and made some hard decisions concerning Missao Crista Evangelica do Brasil, which under this name now grouped UFM of North America and its fellow missions from Europe. MICEB was getting too institutionalized. The three boarding schools were closed. The bookstores were given over to the national church. The Bible Institute at Sâo Luis, which became a seminary, passed majority control to Brazilian Christians. Church planting and leadership training was to become once more the main thrust of the mission. Every church established by missionary activity was to be organized as a church of the Aliança, AICEB.

This fellowship of UFM-related congregations was led by a very capable man, Abdoral F. da Silva. He graduated from the Bible Institute in 1945, when it was at Barra do Corda, then taught there. When it moved to the coast, he moved with it, and later became its director, from 1970 to 1981. For twenty-two years he led AICEB, the alliance of evangelical churches related to UFM. In that period the association grew from a handful of churches to ninety, the result of wise leadership and continuous evangelism by both missionaries and Brazilian believers. He himself pastored churches, along with duties at the seminary and alliance. He described AICEB's development in a book, *Nossas Raizes* — Our Roots.

Pastor da Silva was known for his humility. As a young man he did chores that most Brazilian men refused to do. While gaining a high school certificate in the city of Fortaleza, he helped in the running of the home for missionary children. He did much of the home's shopping and often returned from the market in a manner men thought embarrassing — one arm wrapped around a bag of groceries and the other steadying a sack of charcoal on his back.

Prior to his election as president of AICEB, Pastor da Silva demonstrated his skills of peacemaking. Sports for Christian young people had become an issue; two influential pastors spoke out strongly against any participation. Most of the missionaries disagreed. There was danger of a split. But da Silva stepped in, calling the differences a matter of conscience. He said the pastors were wrong to condemn those they opposed, and for his stand received much criticism. However, he contained the argument and eventually it ceased. Through the reconciliation he achieved, Pastor da Silva gained widespread respect. .

Nationalism in Brazil was on the rise. To some extent it affected the Christian community, though minimal was the animosity toward foreigners that some countries experienced. The mission suggested that whatever authority it held be given over to the church fellowship. The offer was refused.

"Were we to swallow the mission," Pastor da Silva said, "it would be like a snake trying to swallow a large animal of the forest."

The good relationship between mission and church continued, in large measure due to a coordinating committee made up of an equal number of missionaries and national leaders. There was much to foster encouragement. Accompanying a film maker, Ted Laskowski one day flew from Altamira on the Xingu River back to Belém. En route he pointed out the communities on the lower Amazon where churches had been planted and now were steadily growing. In the State of Para, all the main rivers in the vast network south of the Amazon had a church, along with numerous locations beyond sight in Maranhão, Piaui and Bahia. His mind went back to when he and Janet lived in Breves on the huge island of Marajô and he then thought that "some day" the Gospel would reach into these many places, but had no idea how it would. Seeing this land out the plane window caused him to humbly praise God for what He had accomplished in a few short years.

But there was so much more to do!

SOURCES, Chapter 14

Brazil Field Council Meeting Minutes, 1964

Cunningham, Rosemary, *There Is Singing in the Rain Forest*, Manuscript in preparation

_____, 1996, Notes on early draft

Harrell, Delbert and Marguerite, 1995, Letter to author

_____, 1996, Notes on early draft

Harrell, Marguerite, 1979, *Open Door on the Amazon*, Book published by author

Hough, Florence, 1996, Letter to author

_____, 1996, Telephone interview

Jantz, Les and Anita, 1995, Letter to author

_____, Notes on early draft

Larson, Alfred and Jean, 1995, Interview

Laskowski, W. T., 1996, Letter to author

_____, 1996, Audiotape

_____, Notes on early draft

Lifeline, 1st Quarter, 1964; 1st Quarter, 1966; 2nd Quarter, 1967; February, 1981, Bala-Cynwyd,   Unevangelized Fields Mission

Light & Life, 4th Quarter, 1963, Bala-Cynwyd

McAllister, Mary, 1995, 1996, Letters to author

_____, 1996, Notes on early draft

Pudney, E.J. and Lilian, undated, *Miracles Multiplied*, unpublished manuscript

Pudney, E.J., 1961, Audiotape

Sarginson, Effie, 1995, 1996, Letters to author,

_____, 1996, Notes on early draft

Sharp, Larry, 1996, Notes on early draft

Stoner, Charles, 1987, *Indians, Institutions and Churches*, Unpublished manuscript

15

What Happened in the Valleys?

The swift, massive sweep of conversions through the deep valleys of Dutch New Guinea, in which thousands of "stone-age" people burned their fetishes and voiced allegiance to Jesus Christ, posed a problem. In this almost impenetrable land, which after cession to Indonesia was called West Irian then Irian Jaya, peace had replaced nearly constant warfare. Old animosities were buried, fear and dread of evil spirits gave way to a trust that God was now their shield. Disease was being conquered by medicine and hygienic practices.

The cause of these cataclysmic changes was an espousal of Christianity by a very large number of people in a very short time. Promising as this phenomenon was, it became a matter of something good that was sure to turn bad unless handled right.

There was very little question that following the "burning and turning" thousands of the Dani tribe had truly become believers in Jesus Christ as Savior and Lord. But in many instances faith was fragile, and ties to the old animistic culture had not been cut. Or if severance was started, the old beliefs still hung by a rather stout thread.

Not yet knowing the guidance of the Holy Spirit, the Dani reacted to situations by employing the rituals that in other dress had worked for them for centuries. A good result depended on strict conformity to the rules. The insignificant took on importance, even to the obscuring of what was truly important. They imitated the missionary because they believed that some day they would be his image, in race, speech and possessions. To drop a single movement or phrase in the act of worship would bring retaliation from God.

Prayer became a "taboo talk," recalled Shirley Horne, who with her husband, Charles, served at Bokondini. Failure to shut one's eyes during prayer would cause blindness. Sitting in church, on the other hand, ensured immunity from sickness. Stealing and lying plummeted for fear that God would sting in retribution. It became a rite to memorize Scripture and to recite it rapid-fire, and the built-in competitiveness of the Dani caused one to pride himself should he outquote another and, of course, to expect a greater reward.

In the old days the Dani gathered around a fire at night while someone told an ancient legend. Then, at the story's end, all would shout a special code word as a proper finish to the tale and spit into the fire so as not to awaken in the morning with a crooked back. Nowadays, the missionary told his story and at the end of his closing prayer his hearers joined in a great chorus of "Amen!" which they believed was the current code that assured no crooked backs in the morning. As for the concept of immortality, some read into the message they heard that death was banished and even their dead ancestors would be restored to life.

Not all those professing conversion held these beliefs, and outstanding examples existed of new believers grasping the Biblical truths that the missionaries taught them. Those with especially hungry hearts responded to the teaching immediately after burning their fetishes, now that "the veil over the eyes of their heart" was lifted. Typically, these earnest learners went on to be spiritual leaders in their communities.

But errors of various kinds were becoming common enough, affecting far too many of the fetish burners, that the missionaries worried lest false beliefs crystallize before the bulk of the people had opportunity to learn God's truth. A meeting of the various mission societies working in Irian Jaya was called to deal with this rising problem. Everyone at the conference agreed that Biblical teaching was paramount. The issue of baptism was not so unanimously settled.

One agency regarded baptism as the singling out of the genuine believer from the nominal adherents, and this process ought to be done sooner than later. Four of the missions, including UFM, agreed with the sifting, but reaffirmed their policy of requiring a long period of instruction prior to baptism.

An argument was made that incarnating Christ into the existing culture, albeit appropriately, can change lives and thereby transform, rather than destroy, culture. There seemed to be sound reasoning in this, because in family structure and community loyalty the Dani had some admirable traits. In the specific of baptism, however, certain distinctions had to be made. In some instances, the Dani looked on baptism as an initiation ceremony, now substituting for the rite in the old Dani experience which each person had to go through to be authorized and able to handle the secrets of the spirit world. The difference in gaining access to the old spirit world by a traditional performance and entry into God's realm had to be made clear. Contrary to expectations of those who saw magic in this new rite, some who were baptized fell sick, others lost their pigs or their gardens failed or they themselves died.

It was agreed by all the missions that a man having more than one wife should not be denied baptism, providing he had taken his wives before conversion. Not in any way an endorsement of polygamy, the decision merely recognized that God receives people in whatever situation they are and that baptizing them is an act of accepting those whom Christ has already accepted.

The first baptisms on UFM stations occurred at Ilu in May of 1963, thirty months after the burning there of the fetishes. Six weeks later five thousand persons gathered on the banks of a small stream at Mulia to witness the first baptism there. This followed months of Bible teaching and the thirteen men and women who were considered spiritually mature enough for this step gave personal witness to their fellow tribesmen that they were forsaking all for Christ.

Because Biblical teaching was of such prime importance, the UFM missionaries inaugurated Witness Schools, which had already been successfully conducted at Ilaga, the Christian and Missionary Alliance station where the wildfire of fetish burning began. Village chiefs in the UFM areas of Bokondini, Kelila and Mulia were each asked to pick out a promising couple for this training. They were to be married and monogamous (usually limiting the choice to younger people, who also were more apt to learn), living in no known sin and having a desire for Bible learning. Dwellings for the schools were built at the three stations. Interestingly, the missionaries proposed the traditional layout of a men's house, surrounded by huts for the wives; the students, however, preferred a small house for each couple. Hygiene was stressed, with the students' pigs corralled rather than given the usual free range in streets and houses, latrines were dug and paths were lined with flowers.

During the week the representatives of each village were taught the Old Testament as a foundation for Christian faith and the New Testament for the life, work and teachings of Jesus Christ as the ethic of living. On week ends the students went back to their villages, and there in conversations around community night fires taught their people what they themselves had learned.

The schools also taught reading and writing, but in the first schools the students continued to learn by rote. Almost as a fetish in itself, they recited exactly what had been said to them. Though not yet achieving all that their mentors had hoped for, this method nevertheless ensured against propagating error.

The purpose of the Witness Schools was to quickly spread basic knowledge of the Christian faith among the Dani villages already opened to the Gospel. Schools teaching the basic skills of reading and writing were set up at several sites. David Scovill developed a literacy program that won the acclaim of educators throughout Irian Jaya. A member of another mission with a college major in literacy journeyed to Mulia to see the program in operation. After observing it he exclaimed, "Why this works at all, let alone so profoundly, I'll never know. You violate everything I was taught, and yet you've got the greatest literacy program going!"

Scovill wasn't always sure about the theoretical. The workable he knew and practiced.

To prepare for church leadership and for invading the many valleys of yet unreached Dani as well as other tribes, something more was needed. In 1964, Leon and Lorraine Dillinger began the Dani Bible Institute, a resident school at Ilu that later moved to Mulia. Twelve couples made up the first class of a three-year study of the Bible and related subjects. For these classes, the teaching was in Dani. But since the Indonesian language was to become the national medium, it, too, was a required subject. Lest the Institute be thought of as an elemental exercise for scarcely-taught people, the curriculum included such courses as Harmony of the Gospels, Doctrine, Christian Ethics and Geography.

Priority was also given to translation. More and more as issues of belief and conduct arose, the Dani turned to the Bible for an answer. The book of Genesis and a few parts of the Bible were available when the Bible Institute began. By the end of 1965 the literate could read for themselves what Matthew, Luke, Paul in his Epistles to the Corinthians and Daniel had to say, as translated by David Scovill and Menno Heyblom, and by mid-1969, added to them were the Gospel of John, Acts, most of the Pauline epistles, Hebrews and the Epistles of John.

A Christian atmosphere clearly dominated the UFM stations of Bokondini, Kelila, Ilu, Mulia and Wolo. How far the people had moved from their old superstitions could be measured in a small citrus orchard at Kelila. At the time the airstrip there was under construction the Dillingers planted some trees obtained from the Dutch government. The villagers kept an eye on a particular tree in the yard of the missionaries. Years later Leon and Lorraine learned that the Dani had determined that if this tree lived, the missionaries would be allowed to live; if the tree died, they, too, must die. It was an old Dani test for truth. The citrus flourished, and so did the Gospel!

At Mulia the changes were even more evident. Mulia once had been contained in a small world of its own, its entire range only about 10 miles. Enemies in every direction hemmed the people in. Theirs was an area devoid of natural iodine, giving rise to huge, repulsive goiters in half the population. Cretinism accompanied this malady. Nine of ten babies died. Those that lived most likely were retarded. The people of Mulia were said to live in the Valley of the Castoff, and thus were shunned by other Dani.

With the missionaries came medicine. Doctors sent in by the government and philanthropic agencies cured the goiters with injections of iodine. Normal children were born and lived. Fruit trees were planted, peanuts and soy beans introduced as crops, rabbits, chickens and goats became sources of protein. A clinic, slowly evolving into a hospital, served the people. Mulia became a different place, its spiritual and physical development occurring hand in hand.

The local churches springing up around the various UFM stations banded together to form the Evangelical Church of Irian Jaya. Later, as it joined with congregations in Java, another part of the country, the name was changed to the Evangelical Church of Indonesia. The maturing of the Dani believers was also shown in the conferences that brought together delegates from the several valleys. The first occurred in 1963 and represented Dani Christian leaders from 13 areas. Stanley Sadlier, who attended that conference, wrote that it was thrilling to see them "peel away the externals and make a clear statement of the nature of salvation.

"It was a real source of encouragement for them to see the essential oneness that there is among believers. Can you imagine the joy of seeing two men, formerly mortal enemies, sitting together talking about their oneness in Christ?"

After two days of fellowship and discussion, the delegates took to the trails again to return home to reproduce there what they had experienced while together.

Village upon village made spiritual progress. In great measure due to the Witness Schools, in which Biblical truth was committed to faithful men and women who thereby were enabled to teach others also, vibrant churches produced believers with solid faith. Error began to melt away. That the people possessed hearts of compassion was proven by their sending choice ones of their own as missionaries to tribes who as yet had not heard of God's salvation. By the mid-70s, more than a score of Dani missionaries, many of them Bible Institute graduates, had invaded the valleys and the Eastern Highlands and even the swampy coastal lowlands to take the Gospel to still warring tribes. One of these tribes lived in a valley whose confluence of rivers looked from the air to be a "T." Isolated from the Dani and all other tribes, these people had never been visited by outsiders. But now on their way to them over seventy miles of mountain range were David Scovill and Stanley Sadlier, accompanied by ten Dani Christians. This Gospel-bearing party did not know what to expect, but was fully aware that language differences would heighten whatever problems they encountered.

"T" Valley had been sighted and surveyed from the air two and a half years previously. It appeared below one day as missionaries flew a new route to Kiwi, a recently opened work among a particularly primitive, heathen, warring tribe. From the day of discovery, the "T" and its people loomed large in the evangelizing strategies of UFM personnel. Now that the imperative for entering it was about to be fulfilled, what would their entry bring?

The villages in the 50-mile-long valley had been the objects of much prayer. With radio communication flowing between the investigative party and the outside world, thousands of people prayed concurrently with their approach to the first village. Would Sadlier and Scovill and their Dani partners be received peacefully? Would they be driven out? Would they all be killed?

It was nearly dark when the group huddled against a wall of earth and committed their lives afresh to the Lord. Then they ventured into the open and in single file walked the last hundred yards to the settlement. As they neared the village fence, two old men and two boys emerged from a house and shouted happily, gesturing for the strangers to step inside.

Little surprise that in gaining such a welcome, relief and joy flooded over them!

The next day the party walked nearly eleven hours through the valley to a second village, and were welcomed by the people as they went. Once descending fifteen hundred feet down a frighteningly sheer rock face, they discovered more people. After five hours of walking on this day, November 1, 1963, they arrived at the site chosen in the air survey for an airstrip. The promise to Joshua came to them as they stood on the spot and looked at the villages on the surrounding hillsides: *Every place that the sole of your foot shall tread upon, that have I given unto you.*"

These pilgrims claimed "T" Valley for the Lord.

The Sadliers opened a station in the Naltja Valley, the real name for "T," and were assisted by a number of rotating missionaries as well as Dani couples. Mission Aviation Fellowship once more provided the essential link with their fellow missionaries outside and their sources of supply.

Until 1959, all of UFM's work in Irian Jaya was under the direction of the Australian branch. Then a North American field council was formed and was given the administration of the station at Mulia, and as they opened, Ilu, Kiwi and Naltja. Americans, Canadians, Australians, every available missionary, Western, Dani or others, needed to extend the Gospel to the people of Irian Jaya. The task still ahead was formidable.

Over the next several years UFM and the Dani would evangelize a dozen tribes. The Ketengmban, the Iao, the Kimyal in the Naltja Valley, the Duvle were some of them. The Nggalum at Kiwi, once coming to know the Lord, carried on their own evangelism and Bible Institute. More translation was completed, including books especially helpful in the Bible schools. Dani Christians served as missionaries, pastors and teachers, not a few of them in tribes whose languages they had to learn.

As UFM's general director, Ralph Odman visited Irian Jaya. He was greatly interested in each of the mission's fields. The entire world fell within his vision of evangelization. He suggested to other mission executives that they meet together and plan a strategy for preaching Christ to all the nations. It would be a Congress of the Church's Worldwide Mission, and he would be one of its prime activists.

SOURCES, Chapter 15

Dillinger, Leon and Lorraine, Undated, *Experiences of Leon and Lorraine Dillinger in Dutch New Guinea / Irian Jay*, Unpublished paper

_____, 1996, Notes on early draft

Hayward, Douglas, Letter to author, 1995

_____, *The Dani of Irian Jaya Before and After Conversion*, 1980, Sentani, Irian   Jaya, Indonesia, Regions Press

_____, Dissertation, Draft for publication, 1996

_____, 1996, Notes on early draft

Hively, James, 1996, Audio tapes

_____, 1996, Notes on early draft

Horne, Shirley, *An Hour to the Stone Age*, 1973, Chicago, Moody Press

Larson, Alfred and Jean, 1995, Interview

Lifeline, 1st Quarter, 1964; 1st Quarter, 1966; 2nd Quarter, 1967; February, 1981, Bala-Cynwyd, Unevangelized Fields Mission

Light & Life, 4th Quarter, 1963, Bala-Cynwyd

Pudney, E.J. and Lilian, undated, *Miracles Multiplied*, unpublished manuscript

Pudney, E.J., 1961, Audiotape

Scovill, David L., Thesis, *The Dani World View*, 1984, Columbia, South Carolina, Columbia Graduate School of Bible and Missions

_____. 1996, Notes on early draft

16

Uhuru in Congo

Congolese soldiers in the service of Belgium returned home at the end of World War II with new concepts of the world. They had been places and seen things that before this exposure they had never imagined. Some arrived back in their villages in the Ituri Forest with a new notion of their personal importance.

"The Belgians were losing the war," more than one explained to Kinso, "and that's when they sent us out to fight."

Convinced they achieved victory where their colonial masters could not, and with views of duty and obeisance altered by their brush with people of other lands, some among them began thinking about independence. But it was not to come for several years. First, there was much catching up to do in a country that for half the decade had in many ways stood still.

There were roads to be constructed, health improvements to be made, schools to be built. In Congo's post-war surge of growth and development, Protestant missions kept pace. UFM missionaries who had been isolated regained freedom to circulate and some who had been long without furloughs went home for much-needed rest. New missionaries arrived in record numbers.

The handful of UFM main stations increased and in a few years would number twelve. During their more than twenty years at Maganga, which they had opened as the mission's second station, George and Dora Kerrigan explored a completely unevangelized area called Wanie Rukula and in 1954 moved to it. This neglected region appeared backward and undoubtedly would be difficult to infuse with the Gospel, but the Kerrigans had yet to flinch in their work for the Lord. Faithful preaching, insightful teaching and consistent living would penetrate unregenerate hearts, and all this the Kerrigans did. They also made time and found the energy to explore another untapped area, this one around Ponthierville, on the extreme southern edge of UFM's allocated sector.

In 1955, the Baptist Missionary Society turned over to UFM a station they had neither personnel nor financial resources to properly operate. Banjwadi was considered an ideal site for a Bible school to serve all the churches in UFM's territory. Under Kinso's enthusiastic leadership, land for the school was cleared and grubbed of its stumps, foundation stones were collected and hauled to the site — many of them by canoe. Bricks were made. The chief builder came from Haiti by way of the United States. Missionary Glenn See was home in Michigan enjoying a furlough when he heard Congo needed a builder. Having put up many rammed-earth structures in Haiti, he easily adapted to African materials and methods and worked well with his Congolese crew. Missionaries Herbert Boyes and David Grant contributed their skills, as did a visiting staffer from Bala headquarters in America, Lehman Keener, who, it was discovered, was an expert welder.

Marshall Southard became director of the Central Bible School. This epitome of UFM's educational effort in Congo quickly registered success, though political upheaval was to delay the graduation of its initial class. The new school crowned the system of education that the mission and the local churches had produced over the years.

At base, individual churches operated primary schools. The stronger churches sponsored more advanced boarding schools, their students coming from a rather large area. On the secondary level, a teacher training institute was set up at Ekoko. Bible schools were conducted at Bongondza, Boyulu and Maganga, each in the trade language of its region, and it was these three schools that provided the church's leadership for the nation's turbulent 1960s.

Buildings to house the schools were minimal and teachers were most often poorly paid. But government inspectors declared their scholastic content excellent and praised the mission's system for accomplishing much with little.

After World War II, the liberals rose to power in Belgium. The change which that brought to the political climate in Brussels was felt in the village schools of Northeast Congo. Unlike prior to the war, the government now opened its purse to the Protestant primary schools, putting them on a par with the Catholic institutions. As long as standards were maintained, public funds paid teachers, even missionary teachers, who turned their stipends over to a fund set up to hire more national teachers. For teacher support, the Congolese government reserved the right to approve the curriculum, but kept hands off its religious content.

The churches benefitted greatly by the system of schools, which by 1962 was run by Congolese. Training of pastors and lay teachers was in reality the original motivation in the mission's educational effort, although the need for an informed laity, taught both by teachers and pastors, spread the base throughout UFM's sector. And the dividends were plenteous. Scarcely a church existed without a strong emphasis on evangelism. Gospel teams from the boys' school at Bongondza fanned throughout their area, giving training to future pastors and evangelists while introducing new villages to the message of Christ.

In this era of growth, new missionaries came from England, Ireland, Belgium, Canada and the United States. Among them was a couple who once scarcely imagined they'd serve the Lord as missionaries to Africa and some day direct the affairs of a wide-spread mission endeavor.

Alfred and Jean Larson met at Shelton College, which then was a Christian school in New York City. Al was set on becoming an electrical engineer. Jean was open to the Lord's leading for the future — as long as it did not involve missions, especially in Africa. One evening at a missions conference Al stepped forward at the closing invitation and said he was willing to trade his chosen field for whatever the Lord had for him. He became involved in a youth ministry. After he and Jean were married, a call came from a church in New Hampshire. But at the same time, God had been speaking to them both about missions — particularly Africa. In the crisis of decision, they opted for Africa, joining UFM in 1952 and, after several months of studying French in Belgium, arrived in Congo the following year.

New missionaries were placed on stations with experienced missionaries who could oversee their language learning and guide their orientation to African ways. The Larsons went to Ekoko. They soon fell in love with Africa. For the days ahead, any newcomer to Congo had to love it, or he'd leave it, if he could.

Herbert and Alice Jenkinson returned to Congo from Europe in late 1958. But it was a different Congo from the one they had come to know intimately and love intensely. Everywhere the cry was for independence. Resentment of white people — not only of Belgians but of all whites — and Belgian control of the country boiled, rather furiously in some quarters. Kinso was not surprised. He had seen these times coming.

While on furlough he had gone across the English Channel to Brussels to help operate the Protestant mission pavilion at the Brussels International Exhibition. A small segment of the acclaimed show opened the eyes of the world to what Belgium was producing in her valued African colony. The full exhibition proved to be even more of an eye-opener for the hundreds of Congolese who attended it, either as staff or visitors. Congolese troops in World War II had returned home with broadened horizons; the nationals coming back from Brussels had gained an even wider outlook. There were things out there — tools, conveniences, gadgets — and ease of life, security, freedom. Congo, Kinso was convinced, would never be the same again. Neither would it be the old Belgian Congo after a visit by General Charles de Gaulle to neighboring French Congo in August of 1958. In Brazzaville, the capital, he offered either autonomy within the French community or outright independence.

Across the Congo River in Leopoldville, the demands for independence from Belgium mounted. Soon the shouts of *"Independance!"* changed to *"Independance Immediately!"*

Several years earlier UFM missionaries had told their Congolese church leaders that the day was coming when the people of Congo would want to take over the administration of their land and would ask, or compel, the Belgian authorities to leave — and possibly the missionaries, too. The missionaries urged their national colleagues to assume control of all church affairs. This the church leaders refused to do; they said never would the white man leave their country. But near the end of 1959 a conference of pastors and missionaries was called. Those attending drew up a constitution for the Eglise Evangélique du Haut Congo (Evangelical Church of Upper Congo) and a Mission-Church agreement for working cooperatively.

More quickly than anticipated, Belgium granted independence on June 30, 1960. Independence held many meanings for those who owned it now. The dead would be raised to life, the poorest villager would drive his own car, no longer would a cyclist have to keep to the right of the road but could travel where he pleased, money — lots of money — would be printed for everyone, there would be no need to work any more. The white man, who had withheld these good things, was all the more the enemy.

Despised, too, were the children of Belgian men — never mind that their mothers were Congolese. There were many of these mixed-race youngsters in the country and Mabel Wenger was determined to save as many as she could. As a UFM missionary, Mabel had started a school for girls at Maganga. She knew that among many non-Christians the value of a girl was not much. If one wasn't fully an African — and hated Belgian blood ran through her veins — there was little hope ahead for her. Ready for furlough, Mabel proposed taking four teen-agers, three girls and a boy, home with her to Pennsylvania.

"Impossible!" said some officials.

"A missionary adopting native children? It just isn't done!" This sentiment among the missionaries was not uncommon.

She persisted. Kinso and Ralph Odman supported her. Mabel flew home with her new family. As menacing clouds lowered over Congo, she was glad she had done what she could. With all the rancor in the country, it was certain that children of mixed races would likely be among the first to fall victims of uncontrolled hate.

Disturbances spread from Leopoldville to many parts of the country. Chaos threatened. To protest an incident occurring near UFM's headquarters in Banjwadi, Kinso went to see Patrice Lumumba, the new premier. This key figure in the move for independence and now the nation's governing head proclaimed respect for Protestant missions and forswore further trouble. But more disorder arose, some of it violently fatal.

The Christians remained steadfastly loyal to the missionaries, and frequently protected them from the dangers to which their race had exposed them. Yet, the evangelicals were a minority among the Congolese. In some areas the agitation directed toward all whites further threatened life. Kinso, as field chairman, left to the missionaries at each UFM station the decision whether to evacuate or stay. Most of the women and children left the country. So did several among the men. Some protested that leaving in the midst of trouble would violate their testimony. Others felt that to defy common sense by standing pat only tempted God, disobeyed British and American authorities who said to leave and perhaps jeopardized their Congolese brothers.

Mary Baker was short and stout, talkative, vivacious and filled with humor, a determined single woman from Virginia whose only motive for living was to lovingly serve those the Lord had given her in the village of Bopepe. Before he could climb the steps to her home and inform her of a forthcoming flight out from Stanleyville, she halted her mission leader in his tracks.

"Kinso, I'm *not* going home!"

The turmoil surrounding independence and the first months of the new national government reduced UFM's presence from sixty-nine missionaries to fifteen.

The sudden self-sufficiency forced on the Congolese Church thrust into leadership a man whose schooling had been limited to one of the regional Bible institutes but who through the experiences of a pastor and his innate abilities had become a voice for the Congolese believers. Assani Benedict and Bo Martin were twin brothers living at Bopepe, an all-Christian village. Bo possessed the gifts of an evangelist; Assani was an organizer, an administrator, a planner, a persuader. Assani became the spiritual head of the Eglise Evangélique and the legal representative of the UFM section of a larger body of Christians, the Church of Christ in Congo. Whether missionaries dwelt in the country or were forced out, he would shepherd the church for years to come.

Within a year of independence most of those who had left the field returned, each of them invited back by the now indigenous church. Still, there were pockets of trouble, and differing factions gained then lost control of the government and splinter groups warred on each other. It was possible that communists would take over the country, and the threat was nowhere more evident than in UFM's sector in the northeast. But peace and happiness prevailed as the missionaries gathered for their first post-independence conference at Banjwadi. A primary item of business was Kinso's retirement as field leader. For the last twenty-five of his forty-one years as a Congo missionary, he had loved and prodded and encouraged and challenged his corps of God's workers and he and Ma Kinso had lived before them as missionary models. But the years of harsh tropical life had taken their toll and they were aging. He felt it was the right time to hand over his responsibilities to a younger man, Alfred Larson. But Kinso wasn't through yet. He had known how to lead up front, and now he would demonstrate how to sit circumspectly in the back pew.

Scarcely had Al Larson received the mantle than heavily armed soldiers moved into the meeting and placed the entire conference under house arrest, which lasted ten days. Kinso and Larson were hustled off to Stanleyville. The charge: Distribution of anti-government literature.

Prior to Independence, the mission had distributed a tract of spiritual content titled *Uhuru*, Freedom. In his meeting with Lumumba, Kinso had given one to the prime minister, who was pleased with it. With political freedom on everyone's mind, the tract was well received, so much so that another organization produced a similar one, but titled *Uhuru — Siku Ngapi?* Translated, it meant, Freedom — For How Long?

Its intent was spiritual, but the provocative title caused a furious reaction among officials. Because of the mix-up of the two tracts, Larson and Kinso were prosecuted, but released with a warning not to "publish, sell, circulate or distribute or introduce into the Republic of Congo writings, brochures or tracts dealing with any foreign political ideology or of a political character."

Before independence troubles began, many Congolese looked on Christianity as purely a white-man's religion. But during the absence of missionaries, the faith of the Christians in one community proved that God was not bound by color. With no outside help or encouragement, the believers at Bongondza not only carried on their church but the Bible school as well. The tithes from their meager economy supported both. The school director served without salary. How he and his wife had lived was a matter between them and God.

In all but a few communities the churches were on their own, and during this missionary hiatus the sifting their members went through authenticated their faith. As he had bade good-bye to the missionaries as they left, Pastor Assani predicted a period of trial lay ahead, but believed that those who trusted Christ would remain true to Him. When the Belgians were no longer there to subsidize local schools, he said, "We will now see who among the school teachers are serving God and who were simply working for a pay check."

There were some ten thousand church members in UFM's sector, and many times that who took part in what the churches had to offer. The churches, united in their organization, had assumed responsibilities once shouldered by the mission. It was good that they had reached this maturity because they and the missionaries were about to be severely tested once again.

Mutinies by the army, riots and mob violence, tribal conflicts, attempts by the mine-rich province of Katanga to secede — all these had been endured and the new nation of Congo held together, barely. The United Nations dispatched a peace-keeping force to assist, and conditions did improve. Then shortly after 1964 began, troubling rumors, then eye-witness accounts, circulated that from clandestine jungle hideouts wild bands of young men were striking out to terrorize villages, government posts, monasteries and mission stations. Two Baptist missionaries in an isolated station in Kwilu Province were menaced to within an inch of their lives and soon afterward in the same area three Belgian priests were beaten and slashed to death. From various locations came accounts of village burnings and long nights of terror. Two women missionaries were attacked, one of them dying from an arrow in her neck.

The violence began to fall into a pattern — idle young men, disillusioned that independence made them neither wise nor wealthy, were banding into units of a loose-knit organization called the *Jeunesse*. Robbing, pillaging, threatening, torturing, killing, destroying, they aimed their attacks at Africans and foreigners alike. It became apparent they were the makings of a growing army. The communist-trained Pierre Mulele was their inspiration, and much they did was done in the name of the assassinated Patrice Lumumba. By mid-year, incidents had turned into premeditated rebellion, supercharged by the taste of blood.

Unable to persuade dissenting members that its presence in Congo was necessary, the United Nations pulled out its peace-keeping force at the end of June. It was up to the Congo government now to maintain order. But because it was weak, this it could not do beyond Leopoldville. Thus, the way opened for opposition leaders to return from exile, to emerge from the camps Red China had set up to indoctrinate in the communist technique of subversion. The plunderings in Kwilu evolved into full-fledged revolts in all of East Congo. The target, however, was to the west — Stanleyville. This principal city was to be the capital of the new People's Republic. Stanleyville stood in the midst of UFM's sector.

UFM missionaries lived on a dozen or more stations throughout the northeast. Word of trouble in one area filtered through to all other locations. Again, the missionaries had to decide whether to evacuate or stay. Some who had left their posts at the time of independence believed in hindsight that they could have stayed and weathered the storm. They were now inclined to remain where they were. Feeding this conviction, statements by various rebel leaders assured that (1) Americans and Europeans were not their targets, and (2) missionary work, particularly Protestant work, could continue without hindrance. But could such pronouncements be trusted?

As field leader, Al Larson contacted the stations on the mission's radio network. Several missionaries spoke up quickly. They were all for sticking to their posts.

"Are we or are we not a part of the African Church?" one

asked.

"We are!" cut in another. "By their invitation we are. And if by staying we can help the Congolese stiffen their backs against the wrong, shouldn't we stay, even if possibly it means we lay down our lives alongside them?"

After several such exchanges, each supporting the position to stay, Larson summed up for those on the network what they had said:

"God called us to Congo. I think we're willing to pay the price of serving as long as He allows us to serve. I can't order you to stay, but I'll ask you all to stay. If any one of you feels he ought to leave, feel free to do so."

No one left.

The push by the rebels continued. Assuming the name Simbas, they acted like angry, arrogant, powerful, vicious lions, all of which was conveyed in the Swahili term.

The *Jeunesse* members and others who joined and now led them believed themselves to possess mystical properties that set them apart from ordinary humans. While loyal to the cause and obedient to the rules and clothed in specified regalia, they were invincible. If one was shot at, the bullet, on touching his skin, would turn to water. Abetting this defiant spirit was the free use of hemp, a narcotic that infused its users with an abandon to kill when normally they would not. It became the Simbas' aim to destroy all vestiges of Western heritage. Teachers; postal workers; anyone able to speak French; shopkeepers; government employees, no matter how lowly — all were enemies who must be killed.

Planes swooped into Stanleyville to take out European women and children. That same day gunfire resounded in the streets of "Stan," the familiar name for this riverport city. The Simbas had entered the city, led by four hideously costumed witchdoctors. They overran the pitifully faint defense of government troops, captured the mayor, marched him to the public market and there disemboweled him and as he was dying feasted on his vitals. Mercenary soldiers hired to act in behalf of Leopoldville were many miles away to the south. Even so, what could one column of a hired army do when raging lions now infested all the Ituri forest and the open fringes beyond it?

UFM's people lived throughout this area. Large stations might have a half-dozen missionaries in residence, smaller ones only a man and wife. Ekoko was the site of a church, a dispensary, a maternity hospital, a primary school of more than four hundred children, a secondary school, a Bible institute and a teacher-training school. After others had left on furlough or vacation, William and Dorothy Scholten and two single women, Pearl Hiles and Betty O'Neill, continued to serve there, and fairly close by, Charles and Stephanie Mann at Aketi. Far away, forty miles southeast of Stanleyville, Elsi and Volker Gscheidle, a German couple, had joined George and Dora Kerrigan, originators of the work there. In returning from vacation in Uganda, the Kerrigans got only as far as the eastern tin-mining town of Bunia because Simba occupation blocked them from going farther. Laurel McCallum was another living at Wanie Rukula; she was drawn to the numerous orphans in that village, always lightly sleeping with two or three dangerously ill infants by her side, and with the love of a devoted mother had gathered more than eighty children into her kindergarten.

In the vast area between these points, the blithesome but indomitable Mary Baker had been joined at Bopepe by Margaret Hayes, a nurse, though Margaret was temporarily at Banjwadi. Dr. Ian Sharpe and his nurse wife Audrey operated the hospital at Bongondza; Robina Gray, better known as Ruby, was in charge of the government-sponsored maternity unit at the station. David Grant was a builder and maintenance worker at the Bible Institute at Banjwadi and his wife Sonia a nurse. John and Elizabeth Arton, Chester and Dolena Burk, Olive McCarten and Louie Rimmer, the latter a woman who at age sixty-five had been a missionary for thirty-six years, served as evangelists, builders, nurse, mechanic and in various other capacities at Boyulu, UFM's first station. A newcomer, Jean Sweet, taught at the teacher-training school there. Heather Arton, out from England, was spending her school holidays with her parents. Dennis and Nora Parry, a quiet couple, worked steadily at Bodela, preaching, teaching and healing. A number of children were scattered over the various stations. In the middle of Stanleyville, Kinso, Ma Kinso and Mary Rutt worked at a bookstore and literacy center and lived over it. The mission's headquarters by this time had moved to a large house just north of Stan, a place called Kilometer 8. In their trips to the city, all the missionaries had stayed for varying periods at Kilometer 8. It was home to Al and Jean Larson and their two-year-old daughter. Trapped there at this time by the sudden advance of the Simbas from the south were Robert and Alma McAllister, Hector and Ione McMillan, Delbert and Lois Carper, Charles and Muriel Davis, Thelma Southard and three single women, Viola Walker, Olive Bjerkseth and Mina Erskine. These folk would have been at their home locations but for the variety of circumstances that had brought them, with thirteen children among them, to headquarters.

Until their radios were confiscated by the Simbas, the missionaries in the outlying areas heard daily the awful news coming out of Stan. Raucous public trials, with rumor the only testimony required, condemned hundreds to death, and the sentences were carried out promptly in front of a monument to the slain Lumumba. The square in front ran deep with blood. Some of the slaughter could be considered sacrifices, the killings dedicated to advancing the gory code of the People's Republic. To stimulate greater participation by the citizenry, which by wild promises and threats the Simbas had won over, the trials were moved to the soccer stadium. Claps or boos sealed the fate of an accused. The crowds entered the stadium in holiday mood, but often emerged with their faces drawn in dreadful fear.

Then when the Simbas seized all radios and threw up roadblocks every few kilometers on the roads, each region, each village, became engulfed in absolute isolation.

The congregations of the Eglise Evangélique suffered greatly. Pastors and teachers were harassed, often taken prisoner, tied up and tortured. After their churches and homes were burned, their crops destroyed and family members carried off, thousands of believers fled to the forest. Bo Martin stood staunchly by Mary Baker in the attacks at Bopepe, and when she and Margaret Hayes were marched fourteen miles from their home to a jail at Banalia, he went with them. He might have gained freedom, but instead chose to intercede with their captors and for it was himself imprisoned and cudgeled severely. The Bongondza pastor, Masini Philippe, and his son Mbongo Samuele defended the Sharpe family when Simbas imprisoned them and carted them off to Banalia. A man who had worked for Bob McAllister at Ponthierville walked the seventy-five miles or so to Stanleyville to bring a suitcase of food and clothing for the McAllisters' little daughter "because I thought you would need these things." Other Congolese believers endangered their lives by standing with the missionaries, thinking it nothing strange since the missionaries had remained and stood by them.

The Simba regime in Stan was not anything if not inconsistent. Kinso kept open the bookstore, and was permitted to take food into the prison across the street to the staff of the American consulate. From Kilometer 8 Al Larson, Del Carper and the other men entered the city on business and even argued for their rights before Simba officers. Yet, cars were commandeered and some people, such as David and Sonia Grant, were held at a Catholic administrative center under house arrest. Hatred built up against the Americans. The ordinary Simba believed the Americans were the enemy of his cause. Weren't the mercenary soldiers driving up from the south Americans? They were not, but the apprehensive Simbas did not know they were, in fact, largely South Africans. Didn't the Americans fly overhead and once in a while drop a bomb on the city? Not Americans, but Cuban exiles hired by the Congolese government did.

Then one day the order was broadcast to seize all Americans.

Taken at Kilometer 8 were Larson, Carper and Charles Davis, a new missionary from another society who had come to Africa to teach at the Banjwadi Bible school. They were confined in the Hotel des Chutes, along with a number of Europeans. After some days, all the hostages were moved to the Hotel Victoria. They joined one already held prisoner there, Dr. Paul Carlson, a missionary of the Evangelical Covenant Church.

Unpleasant visits by Simbas became an almost daily feature of life at Kilometer 8, now housing women and children and two men missionaries, Bob McAllister, an Irishman, and Hector McMillan, a Canadian. The adults tried to maintain as normal a life for the children as possible, conducting school and Sunday school and playing games and making mealtimes pleasant. Life was no picnic at either the Chutes or the Victoria. Once the prisoners were hauled off on trucks, unquestionably to be taken to some obscure spot to be executed. But along the way one of the trucks broke down, and in being ordered to fix it, one of the prisoners made sure it would never run again. So back to the hotel for the captives.

Bill Scholten was the first of the UFM missionaries to die. He suffered from filaria, malaria and diarrhea, and though it might be said he was the victim of natural causes, the long night drives the Simbas forced him to make for them and the harsh treatment he received after being thrown into jail at Aketi made his death certain.

It would be months before many heard of Bill Scholten's death. Day after day, the world was kept informed that Paul Carlson stayed a prisoner of the Simbas, a condemned man. He had been taken captive at his hospital at Wasolo. Accused as a spy for possessing a radio, he was sentenced to die. Several times the Simbas marched him out to be executed, but each time yanked him back. A yo-yo on the string of Simba intentions, he drew world headlines. His desperate plight focused widening attention on all the missionary prisoners. Had the glare of the world press not focused on him, stirring the ire of nations around the globe, it is thought likely that no missionary and few non-Africans would have escaped death at the hands of the rebel army.

One morning airplanes buzzed overhead. Word flashed through the Victoria that Belgian paratroopers were landing at the airport, their sole purpose to rush into the city and snatch the hostages to safety. The Simbas heard the planes, too. They ordered the two hundred fifty Europeans and Americans, including the doctor, out of their rooms and hurried them along to a city square.

"Sit down!" they commanded.

The hostages did, on the ground and in the direct aim of rebel guns. It was most likely that rescue was at the airport, but would the Simbas kill them before it reached here in the center of town? They knew it was to be rescue or slaughter today. There was nothing to do but wait — and pray. A shot was fired, perhaps by some Simba's nervous finger, and then bullets whizzed across the square and into the seated prisoners.

Those fortunate enough to not be hit sprang up and ran for cover. For Al Larson, Paul Carlson and Chuck Davis, a house across the street from the square became their target. Carlson was the last to scale a wall that projected from the house. He hoisted himself up and was about to climb over. A Simba dashed around a corner, saw one of the prisoners escaping and opened fire, killing him instantly.

Only inches from safety, Dr. Carlson was shot in the back and the head. After months of tortuous ambiguity, so close to freedom! Yet just short of it!

The mercenaries in the employ of the government were supposed to have reached Stan simultaneously with the paratroopers. Running Simba gunfire on the way into town had held them up for several minutes. When they did arrive, those they came to rescue were scattered, as were the Simbas. The city center was the safest place to be now. But not much beyond the square. The farther from the center and out into the countryside, the more likely that Simbas could kill at will.

Larson persuaded a mercenary patrol to run the deadly gauntlet to Kilometer 8 and rescue the group there, which now numbered more than two dozen. Coming across David Grant in the streets, he pulled him into the cortege, consisting of a jeep and trailer, loaded with ammunition and gasoline, and a small truck. With mercenary guns at times answering rebel fire and splattering through roadblocks, they ran the course, picked up the people there and sped them to the airport and escape. All but one at Kilometer 8. Earlier that morning, a group of Simbas stopping by had shot Hector McMillan to death in the driveway.

The hope was that the mercenary columns would proceed immediately to Banalia and Bafwasende, locations where it was known that missionaries were held hostage. But the battle for control of Stanleyville detained them. When the city fell to the government the entire region was placed in danger. As the defeated rebels fled the city, they spread through the region with renewed hate and determination to gain vengeance. They became a tonic for Simbas in remote areas who had become somewhat lethargic.

It was three weeks before a volunteer troop of liberators reached the ferry crossing over the Aruwimi River some eighty miles north of Stan. There at the blood-stained Banalia slip the shocking truth hit the would-be rescuers. They were too late. The prisoners were dead. They had been shot or sliced with machetes, their bodies dumped into the river to feed the crocodiles. Bloody clothing and identification papers were found.

From Banalia the squad turned eastward to Bafwasende. Only three remained alive there, Dolena Burk, Olive McCarten and the venerable Louie Rimmer.

Eleven died at Banalia — Mary Baker; Ian and Audrey Sharpe and their three children, Jillian, Alison and Andrew; Ruby Gray, and Dennis and Nora Parry and two of their children, Andrew and Grace. Six were killed at Bafwasende — Chester Burk, John and Elizabeth Arton and their daughter Heather, Laurel McCallum and Jean Sweet.

Stanleyville continued to be a city of the dead. Where enemies of the Simbas once had been piled in bloody stacks, the lion men, who learned that bullets did not turn to water, lay in heaps in the streets where government and mercenary forces had killed them. Dogs without masters roamed the city, tearing flesh from bones. All shops and offices and many homes were sacked, every safe was blown. Looting was the paymaster for a hired army.

Those liberated from Kilometer 8 and Stanleyville gathered each morning after breakfast on the upper veranda of the Union Mission House in the capital city of Leopoldville. After such chilling experiences, sitting there was peaceful and secure. But there was sadness and uncertainty. The fate of their colleagues at Banalia and Bafwasende and even Aketi and Ekoko was as yet unknown. Prayers were poured out each morning.

Newsmen from the world's press dropped in at all hours to interview the refugees.

"How did people react to rebel pressure?" a correspondent asked one of the missionaries.

"Do you want to meet a brave man?" the missionary replied. The reporter nodded. "Do you see that man over there?" The missionary pointed to Al Larson at the far end of the veranda; Larson was helping his little daughter color a picture book. "There sits the bravest man in Congo."

He then related how Larson had exposed himself to Simba wrath time after time to safeguard the missionaries under his leadership, capping his account by telling how Larson had organized and led the rescue team to Kilometer 8.

The field leader was at his best as in these tense days he gathered the people to pray and himself attended to the dozen matters a day that fell to him. The day after the Stanleyville massacre and rescue he gained a valued helper. Ralph Odman, UFM's general director, had realized that a rescue attempt was soon to be made so rushed from headquarters at Bala-Cynwyd to Congo; he wanted to be present to greet all who emerged from captivity — and to weep with the ones whom the day would leave weeping.

Odman, Larson, Del Carper and Dick Sigg, who had flown in

from Uganda, made frequent trips to the airport. Once in a while a misisonary or two would emerge with other rescued hostages from a flight from the interior. But none of UFM's folk, until one day the prisoners of Aketi and Ekoko, who had been gathered in one place, walked down the steps of a plane.

In the prayer sessions there was praise as well as petition. No one seemed more at ease than Ione McMillan, who, now that Hector was gone, had six sons to raise alone. How she missed her dear husband, but with him absent the presence of Christ expanded to fill the void. Back at Kilometer 8, the morning Hector was killed and two of the boys were injured, one whose wound bled rather freely, she met despair and conquered it. After Hector's body was brought into the house and laid in a bedroom, she called to her sons.

"Come in here, boys," she said. "I want you to see your father." The boys ranged in age from teens to ten. One of the younger ones cried, but seeing his mother's soft smile wiped his tears away.

"You can cry if you want," she said. "I don't think I will. After all, we know Daddy lived in the will of God, and God doesn't make any mistakes . . . You can be proud that your Daddy was counted worthy to give his life in the service of Jesus."

Later in the morning shots were heard, so most of the adults took the children and ran to hiding places in the nearby forest. Only Bob McAllister, who was constructing a coffin for Hector, and Ione and her sons remained in the house. Kenneth, who could not escape because of his wound, lay on pillows from a davenport in the hallway. His mother sat on the floor beside him.

"Mother," Kenneth said.

"Yes, Kenny?"

"Mother, if somehow we escape, will you come back?"

"Yes, son, I'll come back.

"Mother."

"What is it, Kenny?"

"Mother, I think that Jesus someday may call me to be a missionary to Congo. Maybe I'll get the chance to tell the love of Jesus to the men who shot Daddy."

Ione returned and in years to come so did Kenneth — as a missionary doctor. And Steven, one of the brothers, returned, too, to tell the love of Jesus.

One day at the Union Mission House a newsman interviewing Ione McMillan asked if such events as had happened weren't irregular for people who believed in God.

"No," Ione replied, "I don't think it strange — not strange at all — what we have had to go through. When we give our lives to Christ, we say that He knows best — and we mean it. He doesn't expect us to be foolhardy, but hardy; and if we suffer in serving, well, others before us have suffered."

In these gatherings on the veranda, experiences were shared and concern was expressed for those still held captive — or dead. No one knew which, until news came of the killings at Banalia and Bafwasende. Anxiety was expressed for Bo Martin. It was known he had stayed with Mary Baker and Margaret Hayes. Whatever happened to them would undoubtedly be his fate.

"At least Assani and Yokana Jean escaped," someone remarked. Assani, the president of Eglise Evangélique, had taken his wife for medical treatment to Uganda before the Simbas' descent on Stanleyville. Yokana Jean, the director of the Church's schools, had accompanied them.

"Assani will have to take the lead in putting things back together," someone observed.

"He's capable," said another.

George and Dora Kerrigan had flown in from Bunia, and now sat on the veranda with the others. They spoke of their time of waiting for the scene to clear so they could get back to Wanie Rukula after a holiday in Uganda. At Bunia, they lived in a house belonging to missionaries who for the time were away. Next door to them was a houseful of Simbas.

"Did they give you much trouble?" someone asked.

"Good Simbas and bad Simbas often visited us," Ma Kerri replied. "When the good ones came, I let them in because making inspections was a part of their job."

"What did you do when bad ones showed up and demanded to get in?"

"Humph!" she snapped. "I put my foot down and said, 'You can't come in. Not talking that vile talk and waving that gun around, you can't.'"

And none of her hearers doubted that in the four months they lived among the rebels Mrs. Kerrigan ever met up with more than she could conveniently handle.

In all, thirty missionaries, including six children, perished at the hands of the Simbas. The Catholics had suffered terribly, scores of their priests and nuns sacrificed to Simba fury. Other missions besides UFM enumerated their casualties — Worldwide Evangelization Crusade, the Methodists, African Christian Mission, Assemblies of God and, of course, Paul Carlson's agency. But in numbers, none approached UFM's loss — thirteen adults and six children.

Yet, what the missionaries suffered was overwhelmed by the affliction of the Congolese Church. Its effect was to be felt for years to come.

Sources — Chapter 16

A *Congo Miracle*, undated pamphlet, Unevangelized Fields Mission, Bala-Cynwyd

Dowdy, Homer E., *Out of the Jaws of the Lion*, 1965, New York, Harper & Row

Jenkinson, Herbert, Undated, unpublished manuscript

Larson, Alfred and Jean, 1995, Interview with author

Lifeline, 1965, Memorial issue; 2nd Quarter, 1967; Bala-Cynwyd; Unevangelized Fields Mission

Light & Life, 3rd Quarter, 1960, Unevangelized Fields Mission

Pudney, E. J. and Lilian, *Miracles Multiplied*, undated, unpublished manuscript

Truby, David W., *Congo Saga*, 1965, Unevangelized Fields Mission, London

Wenger, Mabel, 1996, Interview

17

On to Savoy

The evacuation of families during the upheavals that accompanied Congo's independence sent a signal to Bala-Cynwyd that it was time to develop an alternate field for some of UFM's French-speaking missionaries. Ralph Odman pondered this obvious need.

What could be a more direct answer than France?

France? UFM's name began with the word *Unevangelized.* This had always implied a primitive culture where the name of Christ had not been heard. Northeast Congo fitted the image well, as did the interior of New Guinea. Even in Brazil the emphasis was on the jungle Indians and the only partly acculturated river villages and trading centers. Haiti was a transplanted section of Africa. Could France fit within the term *Unevangelized?*

What did it mean to evangelize? To transform a rudimentary community into one of more or less refined civilization? In that case France, with its great history of language, art, literature and other elements of culture, would need no attention. But in France, less than two per cent of the people were Protestant, and only about a third of that number evangelical. Among the Roman Catholic majority, few attended church except for baptism as a new-born and burial when death came. France had bred a nation of free-thinkers, and this meant that millions had shaken off the influence of the priest and, indeed, of any semblance of religion. If to evangelize was to persuade men and women of the truth of God's word and to offer them His salvation, was there any land on earth more in need of a Gospel witness?

Before he went to Congo and there in the Simba uprising died as the first of the UFM martyrs, William Scholten recognized the need to evangelize France. For three years he served God in Belgium, designing and distributing tracts and other publications while he studied the French language. In 1960, he carried out a methodical survey of France and sought a small mission with which UFM might work for an outreach there. One day while canvassing the Alpine region not far from the Swiss border he casually walked into the garden of a home and there met Donald Orr, an Irishman who headed the Alpine Mission to France. As the two strangers talked, they discovered a mutuality of interests.

The Alpine Mission worked in the valleys of Savoy and Ain Provinces. Four couples and two single women conducted Bible studies, classes for children, holiday youth camps, did literature distribution,and went door-to-door seeking opportunities to share their faith. They had difficulty, however, maintaining adequate resources, and desperately needed a more solid home base. Prior to this seemingly chance meeting with Orr, Scholten had no knowledge of this problem, nor were UFM's intentions known to Orr. As they talked further, a merger of the Alpine Mission and UFM made sense, actually, as Orr later said, it was God's answer to the need. Alpine would gain home support and UFM a start in France as a field. Merger had worked well in Haiti and the Dominican Republic. It held promise in this situation.

The five existing stations were scattered throughout the two provinces. The mountains of the region were high and majestic, topped in the distance by snow-clad Mont Blanc, the highest peak totally within Europe. The valleys were richly green.

Tourists flocked to the ski and hiking trails and filled the inns of the numerous villages. Industry, too, had been attracted by the abundant water power of the mountain streams. The people were of the working class and more likely than the proud sophisticates of Paris and Lyon to give the Gospel a hearing.

Adjacent to Switzerland, the Alpine region of France had come under the influence of John Calvin in the Sixteenth Century, and the Huguenots gained a rather solid foothold. But Louis XIV's edict in 1685 drove the Protestant believers across Lac Léman, the French name for Lake Geneva, and the evangelical position was dimmed to the point of darkness. Occasional revivals broke out in the French-speaking section of Switzerland, the most memorable being one led by Robert Haldane from Scotland. He influenced theological students such as Adolphe Monod, who became France's foremost Reformed pulpit orator in the nineteeenth century. Adolphe and his brother Frederic were used by God to spark revival here and there throughout France. However, in the latter half of the century, after their deaths, the evangelical position weakened to a sputtering flame. In 1889, two English women went on holiday to Lausanne, Switzerland, and after attending a conference of Christians in nearby Morges, took an interest in Thonon, a town in France almost directly across Lac Léman. Miss Larritt and Miss Wilson (no first names from that period are recorded) had aimed to go as missionaries to China, but that door closed. Instead, they went to Thonon.

They began a Gospel witness in Concise, a hamlet on the outskirts of Thonon. From time to time other women who had private means of support joined them. A London committee was formed in 1908, and after nineteen years of endeavor, the Misses Larritt and Wilson retired and a Mr. Pinkerton was named the work's superintendent.

Miss Forrester and Miss Wood joined in the effort in 1921, and five years later another Irishman, Mr. Purdon, journeyed to Thonon for his health and stayed to become the new superintendent. This small band of determined Christians pedalled their bicycles to the villages around Thonon and gradually enlarged their sphere to include towns farther away like Annemasse, practically a suburb of Geneva, Switzerland, and Cluses. A young man converted at Annemasse later became the founding pastor of a Baptist church there.

In 1932 Purdon went to Chamonix to settle on arrangements for Miss Forrester and Miss Wood to open a work in this town at the foot of Mont Blanc. After writing his approval to the London Committee he suddenly died. His replacement was to shape the mission for many years.

Donald Orr had been headed for Brazil for mission work when on board ship he was stricken with a mysterious ailment. After battling the illness for several months, he went to Upper Savoy to recuperate. The spiritual needs he observed there challenged him. For some months he helped part-time with the work the women had started, and in 1936 devoted his full time to it, settling with his wife Olive in Sallanches, a village in the valley of the Arve River. One of the main efforts of the Orrs and British and French Christians who aided them intermittently was the distribution of Bibles and tracts.

World War II brought the Nazis bounding headlong into the beautiful, peaceful valleys and mountain towns. The Orrs were forced to flee with their two children; in a hair-raising trip they drove across France to Bordeaux and boarded a ship back to England, from where he saw service in Lebanon with the British Army. The two women in Chamonix somehow managed to keep open their little chapel, and two or three others kept to the tiniest of villages and survived German occupation.

At the end of the war the Orrs returned to Sallanches. They and their co-workers branched out into new communities, pushing over the line from Upper Savoy into the Province of Savoy. A new volunteer wishing to join them was a single young man

217

who, in 1948, was fresh out of Bible school in England, Donald Knight. As a prerequisite to membership in the mission, he was placed on a farm. Over the next year he was to learn to speak French. Like members of the farm family, he looked after the cows and tilled the fields, and from them learned *je suis, tu es, il est*... His hosts were believers; they introduced him to an evangelist from the city of Annecy, a few kilometers to the south. That summer Knight assisted in the man's tent campaigns, mostly by guarding the tent at night. At the end of his learning period Orr invited him to start a work at Chambéry. He stayed there for four years.

Orr traveled to the United States in 1951 to raise up workers and financial support. At the Baptist Church in Quidnessett, Rhode Island, he met a young woman by the name of Jane Bernardo. She was to be the first American to join the mission. On this trip Orr put together a loose-knit committee as an auxiliary of the Thonon Evangelistic Mission. It was under their auspices that Miss Bernardo left for France in 1952. Three years later she was joined by two other Americans, Juanita Elwood and Frances Meekem, and then by Naomi Umenhofer and Enid Skuce, a Canadian.

The Orrs moved to the town of Albertville and there developed the work along several lines — children's meetings, youth activities, Bible stands in markets, evangelistic services. They opened a home for the elderly. Their own home became a haven for missionaries to Europe regardless of affiliation. Olive and Donald Orr possessed the gift of encouragement, inviting half-defeated Christian workers to their home for a week end. Their home became a counseling center before counseling was widely practiced in Christian circles.

The time came that it seemed appropriate to split the work between Upper Savoy, nearer Lac Léman and containing Thonon, and Savoy, south of that region and in which stood Albertville. The American Auxiliary became independent of the British organization, the latter holding to the area around Thonon, and the new Alpine Mission to France, the American entity, sponsoring the work to the south. Donald Knight left Chambéry; he had the choice of going to the established mission in Upper Savoy or to pioneer a work under the Alpine Mission in the Albarine Valley, which, geographically, was the less desirable of the two. At Argis, in the valley, he rented a building with meeting room on the ground floor and living quarters above and pitched in. In 1957 he and Frances Meekem were married.

The Orrs, Jane Bernardo, Juanita Elwood and their colleagues labored untiringly. In the Department of Ain, next to Savoy, Donald and Frances Knight saw hopeful signs of progress. The town of Ambérieu lay at the northern end of the Albarine Valley. Among its six thousand inhabitants was a handful of Protestants who were under the care of a pastor of the Reformed Church of Bourg, some twenty kilometers away. Knight organized a tent evangelistic campaign, but did more than guard the tent. Donald Orr and a Plymouth Brethren evangelist, Abel Félix, preached. Two conversions that week made the beginning of a church. Follow-up meetings were held each week for four years, and response was sufficient to buy land and erect on it a hall and auxiliary rooms below and a pastor's apartment above. Enid Skuce assisted a French pastor and later joined with Jane Bernardo to serve in this town.

James Nesbitt first met the Orrs while he was a graduate student at the University of Paris. On his spring break in the resort town of Albertville, he visited in the Orr home. It was at the time the merger of the Alpine Mission and UFM was in discussion. Nesbitt was impressed by the spiritual maturity he encountered in Orr, which was marked by an evident love for evangelizing the insignificant, out-of-the-way places. On several occasions the missionary took the student up to the higher valleys, and there in the villages they knocked on doors and canvassed the market centers and stopped at scattered farms, everywhere meeting people, giving them Scriptures and explaining the Gospel to them.

Nesbitt had applied to another mission whose focus was Paris, but Orr's bent for quiet evangelism caused him to contrast the Paris work that had many recruits with the Alpine Mission with just Orr, the Knights and four single women for the entire area.

In the summer of 1964, he and his wife Nancy joined the Alpine Mission workers, Enid Skuce in Ambérieu and the Knights and Naomi Umenhofer further up the valley in Argis. The day following their arrival at Ambérieu, their assigned place, he preached and assumed the responsibilities of a pastor. It helped that he was already fluent in French and Nancy was well along in her learning. Door-to-door evangelism, such as he had done with Orr, marked their ministry, following up contacts from summer meetings, preaching services and village visitations. Children's work was a big part of what they did. Schools dismissed early on Thursdays, so that was when Bible clubs met. Parents were happy for someone to care for their children that day, perhaps explaining why attendance was good.

The young teen-agers who came, however, were totally without discipline. The Nesbitts did much to win them over by making trips to the chateau at Saint-Albain, which had been purchased by the Grace Brethren for a Christian program center. Another draw for the youth was music imported from England.

Drums, bass guitars and singing in English — Beatles style — was neither understood nor appreciated by the adults among the French nor by most of the missionaries. But concerts of the Peacemakers attracted crowds of young people, sometimes four hundred or more. The words of their rock music were Biblical and the "Jesus talk" between numbers was pointed, though at times little but the loud sound came across and Nesbitt worried whether the message was often lost. Enough came through, however, to keep young minds tuned to the Gospel, and, for good or ill, these UFM concerts reflected a new musical taste that was descending on France.

Juanita Elwood helped Phil and Nancy Gegner and later Henry and Alice Bryant start their first missionary terms in the little village of Géovresset, west of Oyonnax, a center for the French plastics industry. After beginning in Argis with the Knights, Carol Rumpf joined the Bryants to work with university students in Grenoble. Sutherland and Rodina MacLean joined the campus team and effectively reached many students through visitation and a book-table ministry. The campus workers linked their activities with the dynamic church planting ministry of Marcel Tabailloux, a Plymouth Brethren evangelist. Carol Rumpf was encouraged to develop a center for student outreach, so adjacent to the Grenoble campus organized the Foyer Evangélique Universitaire, or FEU (meaning "fire"). Hank Bryant started training new believers in discipleship. Classes were held at convenient hours at the church, and the effort to build church leaders eventually became a year-long program.

Marcel Tabailloux and his brother André led the Grenoble team with boundless energy. Marcel in particular was gifted with the ability to come up with new projects and innovative methods. Door-to-door witnessing, Boys' Brigade and Pioneer Girls, youth retreats, music groups, tracts, handbooks for the children's clubs, Bible correspondence courses, Christian magazines — there seemed no legitimate avenue that could not be used to bring the Gospel home to the French people.

The 1968 Winter Olympics in Grenoble presented an opportunity to evangelize not only the French but people of nearly all of earth's nations.

Bright blue ski jackets were their identification. Some two hundred members of Christian organizations, including UFM missionaries and church members, scattered over the Olympic sites, met trains at the railroad station, manned the skating rinks and ski slopes, covered the restaurants, walked the streets — everywhere crowds gathered, the Blue Jackets were there. They gave out an "Olympique" issue of the Gospel of John and an attractive brochure titled *Sécurité*. Then they invited people to viewings of

Billy Graham films in a theater, presented folk concerts and stayed afterward to engage in conversations regarding the Lord. They found that in the midst of the excitement of an Olympiad and an intent to push away all care there were many people who under it all were seeking something that would last beyond two and a half weeks of games. And they were happy to report that for some the search ended in a new faith in Jesus Christ.

The Winter Olympics in Grenoble gave momentum to the church-planting effort in that city and its suburbs and outlying towns. By the mid-1990s, six churches had been established, all the way to Gap, the hometown of William Farel, the Reformer.

Following Ambérieu in 1967, then Oyonnax and Bourg-en-Bresse, the emphasis in church-planting by UFM personnel shifted from villages and small towns to larger population centers. In this, the mission worked with local churches or French pastors where possible, but if no evangelical witness existed endeavored to start a church. A team approach was employed. Men and women with varying gifts worked together, each contributing his or her particular skill, whether in preaching, teaching, counseling, music or in ministering to children and youth.

UFM's method in France was to plant churches and as soon as possible turn them over to French pastors and the people in the churches who had been won to Christ. This generally required six years, as was the case for Ambérieu. If a church had not taken hold in six years, experience indicated that an effective ministry there was unlikely. The work in Oyonnax never grew and in time flickered out. The ministry in Bourg was cut from a different pattern — the use of public meeting rooms. The team there built up a group of believers into an assembly that met regularly. But lacking their own land and and structure, and with the frequency and time of meeting governed by others, the Christians found it difficult to grow numerically.

In Valence, however, it took only four years to go from the

beginning Bible studies to an independent, self-governing and self-financing congregation. The church in Valence, on the Rhone River south of Lyon, grew to be one of the larger evangelical churches in France. Eighteen workers from several organizations dovetailed their labor, all serving together, to record this success.

In each city and town evangelized by UFM, local conditions presented a unique timetable. Given the words of Jesus about the types of soil into which seed falls, it is not surprising that spiritual fruit also varied from place to place.

No interconnecting association was set up; rather, congregations were encouraged to link with a denomination of their choice. Several joined with the Plymouth Brethren, some with the Baptists, others the Evangelical Free Church. Thus, as missionaries came and went, the autonomy permitted each congregation to stand on its own.

Inter-church activities brought French Christians together in conferences, retreats and training seminars. The one-year Bible institute in the central Grenoble church equipped about eighty part-time students for evangelism. The churches grew in number of members, but by the 1990s generally stabilized, with attendance on a Sunday morning running from seventy at Saint Egrève to two hundred at Montpellier.

Printing became a major thrust of UFM's mission in France. It had a humble start in the basement of the Grace Brethren Chateau de Saint-Albain, west of Ambérieu, the effort of John and Jan Miesel, who had taught in the North Congo Seminary in Banjwadi. In the formative years, other transplants from Congo, Richard and Mimi Sigg, joined the Miesels in the printing of tracts and other Christian literature. The press was given land by a Christian farmer near La Bégude de Mazenc, south of Valence. Led by Hank Bryant, the mission force built a new print shop in the middle of peach orchards and next to the office of Christian Literature Crusade. French tradesmen joined the staff, and direction of the work started by the Miesels and Siggs eventually passed to other missionaries. Darold and Barbara Driscoll supervised a great increase in production. Color presses turned out millions of copies of the Gospels, some in the languages of Central and Eastern Europe. Also printed were New Testaments, Christian books, tracts, children's books and posters. In 1990, a total of 538 titles came off the presses, amounting to nearly nine million pieces of literature. Joining with the Grace Brethren, the press published commentaries and other Bible study books under the imprint of Editions Clé.

Government architects and planners created the new urban centers of Villefontaine and Isle d'Abeau east of Lyon. UFM linked with French evangelist Gerard Peilhon for church planting there. Eventually, this gave rise to a radio ministry, Radio Colombe, a small station that carried the message of Jesus Christ into the homes of the Lyon area.

A large team started a church in Bourgoin and then worked between it and Lyon, covering the eastern suburbs. In four years a dynamic young church was going in Saint-Priest, under the leadership of Tom Walsh and Jacques Iosti, from Ambérieu.

France has long been a melting pot for many ethnic groups. The churches in Ambérieu and Argis involved Italian and Spanish families, as well as French. At the other end of the Albarine Valley, in Belley, missionaries worked for a time with refugees from Albania. Lou Felo, based at the Black Forest Academy in Germany, became a leading consultant for evangelism in Bosnia and with Muslims, and contacts with this religious group became the norm throughout the work in France.

Because France opened its doors to citizens of North Africa when granting independence to its former departments lining the Mediterranean, a large number of Muslims moved to France. The Tabailloux brothers and Eli Chouakry, a Kabyle, all of them Christians, came from Algeria, where they were discipled by Ralph Shallis, a Brethren evangelist. Shallis worked with Andrew Orr,

Donald Orr's son, in the summer evangelism of the Alpine Mission's youth teams. Chouakry, who later became Alain Choiquier, worked with Jim Nesbitt in university evangelsim in Paris in the 1960s and went on to be a noted evangelist. Cahed Rachid, from Tunisia, was a charter member of the Valence church. These men filled leading roles in evangelizing the Muslim in France. But every UFM worker sooner or later found opportunities to witness to Muslims. As Muslims accepted Christ, they were integrated into the French churches.

For several years, UFM conducted a specialized Muslim ministry. Richard and Ruth Heldenbrand successfully contacted a number of Muslims over five years in Lyon's predominately Muslim suburb of Vaulx-en-Velin. They discipled the new Christians among them, though no church was established. The Heldenbrands transferred to Biblical Ministries Worldwide in 1996 to help that group launch Muslim ministries.

Donald Orr retired in 1969, only to return to his native Ireland with a burden for sharing the Gospel with his people. Though he did not initiate the evangelizing of Southeast France and in time turned it over to younger people, his stamp on the work appeared indelible. Undoubtedly the patient, unassuming character that attracted Christians to work alongside him also brought people to Christ. He was remembered as a great story teller. At a conference, his brief remarks were often sandwiched between hour-long sermons. He would use his fifteen minutes to tell a story, wrapping it in a Scriptural principle. Long after the sermons were forgotten, people recalled Orr's stories and why they had meant so much to them.

Some thought he was too frugal, but he led the mission during periods of very little money. Others felt his selflessness allowed less principled people to take advantage of him. That is why, they said, the mission lost its valuable Albertville center, so strategically located for evangelism, church planting and camping ministries, to a group of evangelicals who gained control of it and turned it into a language school for new missionaries.

Orr felt that if God had directed these brethren — and who was he to judge? —then they should be allowed to move ahead, and he graciously and quietly stepped aside. His concern was for the Church as a whole, not just for one particular part of it that involved him.

Both foreign missionaries and French believers stepped in to carry on where Donald Orr and his contemporaries left off. From a modest witness in tiny villages of the Alps, the UFM ministry had in thirty years touched a half-dozen provinces in one of Europe's most important countries. Still, the number of born-again believers among fifty-five million Frenchmen suggested that the work had only begun.

SOURCES - Chapter 17

Annual Report, 1981, Bala-Cynwyd, Unevangelized Fields Mission

Annual Report, 1995, Bala-Cynwyd, UFM International

Bernardo, Jane, *Beginnings,* undated, unpublished paper

_____, *Origins of the Alpine Mission,* Undated paper

Larson, Alfred and Jean, 1995, Interview

Lifeline, 2nd Quarter, 1967; Summer, 1968; April, 1991

Light & Life, 1st Quarter, 1962

Nesbitt, James H. *UFM's Beginning in Europe,* 1996, unpublished paper

_____, 1996, Remarks to author

_____, 1996, notes on draft

Manual, 1967, Bala-Cynwyd, Unevangelized Fields Mission

Pudney, Edwin J. and Lilian, *Miracles Multiplied,* undated, unpublished manuscript

Sécurité, brochure, 1968, Ambérieu-en-Bugey, France, Mission Evangélique des Alpes Francaises

18

The Simbas

Kinso and Al Larson returned to Congo in April of 1965. The government had wrested control of the main towns and roads in the northeast from the Simbas, though hundreds, perhaps a few thousand, of the lion men were thought to roam the deeper caches of the Ituri forest. The two UFM leaders were dispatched to the site of UFM's greatest loss of missionary life, and perhaps the greatest in modern missions, to check on the conditions of the Congolese church and to learn the whereabouts of Margaret Hayes.

It had been supposed that Margaret died with Mary Baker, her partner at the Bopepe station. The two were marched to Banalia, and Bo Martin, the gifted evangelist and twin brother of Assani, the president of the church association, walked alongside the two women, choosing to suffer imprisonment himself rather than let the Simbas have their way with the women on that long, wearying hike. In the wake of the rescue of hostages at Stanleyville, the rebels slaughtered all the missionaries held in the Banalia prison. Bo, everyone said, probably died in the massacre.

But recently Margaret had been sighted, as had Bo, so the two, though still held captive, might yet escape the fate of those who had given their lives in their service to God. Kinso and Larson tracked down leads, but it was not until they had returned home, Kinso to England and Larson to America, that Margaret Hayes and Bo Martin were found alive and rescued.

Four years after the Simba uprising Kinso went back to Congo again, this time with Ma Kinso. Robert and Alma McAllister, Betty O'Neill, Volker and Elsi Gscheidle, Olive McCarten, Ione McMillan and others who had suffered during that tragic time were on the field once more, and other missionaries had scheduled their return, including Margaret Hayes, if it was determined the people wished them to come. This in a six-month visit the Kinsos would find out.

The veteran couple who had seen Congo develop its foot trails into fairly good roads and move from only mud-wattle buildings to hospitals and schools of glass windows and brick now sadly observed its recent but extensive deterioration. Many roads were one continuous pothole, often laced with three-foot trenches cutting the route. They had been dug by the Simbas to delay the progress of the mercenary army racing toward Stanleyville, and were still just as deep and wide as when they were dug. Buildings were pockmarked by bullets, porch roofs left to sag when their posts were blown away by bazooka fire, whether Simba or mercenary it was anyone's guess. Many roofs were gone; some structures were now merely shells. At one point of his inspection Kinso figured this region of Congo had been set back twenty-five years.

Stanleyville was no longer called by the name of the famed explorer. It was now Kisangani. The capital, Leopoldville, had been renamed Kinshasha. In a few years the old name of Congo would be traded in for Zaire, to designate both the country and the river. A change in names did not bother Kinso. Old African names replacing those of European origin made sense, he thought. African names had meaning. He recalled a name Pastor Masini and his wife had given their son, whose birth followed the births of four girls. Translated, the name meant, "What held you up?"

Boyulu, Maganga, Ekoko, Bongondza, Banjwadi — these

and other places, including countless small villages, all so familiar to the Kinsos, were visited. At times the two were accompanied by the McAllisters, and after her return, Margaret Hayes joined their party. The reception given them was overwhelming. Cries of utter surprise and joy greeted Margaret. As the group neared the Christian village of Bopepe two men jumped out into the road, stopped them, lifted Margaret out of the Land Rover and toted her in a decorated carrying chair, with an accompanying crowd singing and dancing, all the way into town. That evening all sat long at the village campfire as Margaret and the Bopepe people exchanged stories of what had happened since last they were together.

During the rebellion a man had been told by boasting Simbas that they had killed Kinso, his old friend, and all the missionaries. The heads of Kinso and Volker Gscheidle, they said, were displayed in the bookstore window in Stanleyville. Now, after years of mourning his friend, he heard Kinso had come to his village. He sought him out, sat for a long time and stared intently at the missionary, then spoke up in awe:

"Yes, it's really him."

At every stop people, though very poor and sometimes reduced to wearing coverings of bark cloth, brought gifts of eggs, chickens, sweet potatoes, sugar cane and paw-paw. Some of the eggs were of the crocodile. One fellow rushed up with a small tree branch, stripped off its leaves and threw them at the feet of the Kinsos, an old welcoming custom of his tribe.

But there was sadness and on occasion sadness mixed with joy. At Aketi the travelers visited the grave of Bill Scholten, the first of their number to die in the rebellion. On the ferry slip at Banalia it was a moving experience to read a plaque commemorating the killing of six adults and five children, and to be told that at a memorial service there on Christmas day, thirteen months after the gruesome murders, eleven Simbas gave their hearts to Christ.

Heaviness came from the tales told them by the Congolese.

At Maganga, casualties exceeded thirteen hundred, forty-nine of them known to have died, the others presumed dead because they never emerged from the forest where they had fled for refuge. At Boyulu the death count was one hundred fifteen; at Wanie Rukula, forty-five. Every community had its list. One ran to seven hundred names. Skeletons of victims were still turning up here and there. At one of the hospitals there was good news to report, though the buildings were in great disrepair and the beds and mattresses had been destroyed. One of the staffers, hearing that Simbas were about to attack, had buried the hospital's microscope and other valuable instruments. At the end of the "troubles," he dug up his precious tools, and when Kinso saw them they had been polished to a brilliant luster.

As people had fled to the forest to escape the Simbas, jungle animals moved into some of the settlements. Many old houses around Maganga were still empty. The population there had clearly been decimated. It was there that the Simbas had been the thickest, and the leader of the local band of rebels was caught only during Kinso's stay in the region.

In contrast to the people's material poverty, Kinso happily discovered widespread spiritual prosperity. Everywhere the churches bulged. The roll of drums announced a service, and in a few minutes it was packed out, whether the building held a hundred or nearly a thousand. Choirs were accompanied by drums and rattles, giving a lift to the worship. Prayer meetings drew full crowds. Prayers proceeded with no pauses between. At one church the pastor exhorted his people:

"Don't pray long and don't teach when you pray."

In some areas new villages had sprung up, and in almost all of them a church had been built. On the road from Banalia to Bodela, not a very long distance, Kinso counted twenty-six village churches.

Schools also were filled, four hundred fifty students at Banjwadi, five hundred at Bafwasende. But none had books.

Everywhere, government officials, pastors, the people in the pews, pleaded for missionaries. In a visit to the bookstore in Kisangani, Kinso longed to be back there as a worker. In bitter-sweet memory, he recalled that every business day of the one hundred eleven days the Simbas occupied Stanleyville, the bookstore had stayed open, a record to be claimed by no other business in town. The garbage cart rolled by the store every day, filled with corpses, and Simba leaders boasted they would stamp out Christianity, but the store sold more than a thousand Bibles and New Testaments. One sale was to the wife of the rebels' General Olinga. After the government regained Stanleyville, Olinga fled to Uganda, where he was arrested. While in prison, he became a Christian, the faithful witness of his Bible-reading wife the critical factor in his conversion.

Kinso desperately wanted to be one of the missionaries who would be returning on a permanent basis. But climbing into a canoe one day, and finding it extremely difficult, he admitted he was too old. The joy of serving God among these people would have to be surrendered to younger folk.

Following his six-week trip back to Congo in the spring of 1965, Al Larson toured churches in the United States, accompanied by Assani Benedict, who added a national's perspective to the missionary's view of the tumult in Congo and its effect on the church there. The Larsons were expecting to return to the field, as were the Del Carpers and the Marshall Southards. But at that date it would be two years yet before the Simbas were cleared out of the jungle, and as Kinso would discover in his visit in 1968, that time-table was in some areas an underestimation. But on the assumption there were places that could be entered, a team of men was assembled to go back for preliminary set-up work. Larson, expecting to be one of them, was asked not to leave home.

Ralph Odman was ill. The mission's general director had

worked unceasingly since called from Haiti to Bala-Cynwyd to succeed E. J. Pudney. With Henry Brandt, the Christian psychologist who was on the UFM Council, he traveled around the world in 1962, visiting mission work. Political turmoil brought problems to Haiti and the Dominican Republic the next year. Opening France as a UFM field was high on his agenda. So were Quebec, Egypt and New Mexico. UFM missionaries numbered more than three hundred, and two candidate schools were needed each year to screen and orient prospective new members. Combatting heresy in the move toward mission ecumenicity was another concern. Of great interest was a forthcoming congress of evangelical missions at which strategies for future evangelization would be explored. The recent tragedy of Congo hung heavily over him.

There had been a shepherd-like quality in Odman's decision to fly to Congo to be there when UFM missionaries emerged from detention in the northeast. Those who were evacuated would have come out whether he was there or not. The speed of their liberation had nothing to do with a mission executive lodged in the Union Mission House in Leopoldville. But Ralph Odman determined to be there when Dorothy Scholten and Ione McMillan and Dolena Burk and others stepped off the planes that carried them to safety. He was ready to weep with them, to comfort, to encourage, to let them know that a mission agency was no corporate entity but a family, and when one member of the family suffered, so did all the others.

He was at the airport to meet every plane from the interior, not knowing who would emerge, or, indeed, if any of his people would. After breakfast every day he prayed with those who gathered on the old home's veranda. He listened to stories of great sadness, near-despair, courage and steadfast faith. Not for a report to the Home Council or to the mission's constituents, though they were eager to hear, but because he loved his colleagues in Christ, and. for them, he just wanted to be there.

Returning home, he spoke to churches and groups around

the country on UFM's dark days in Congo. But he saw in the tragedy a breakthrough of God's love for both the martyrs and those they left behind. He titled his address, "The Congo Coronation." It evoked much response, including conversions and greater awareness of missions.

But now he was very ill. Al Larson noticed on return from his effort to locate Margaret Hayes that Ralph spoke with difficulty and his answers were not always coherent. In the hospital a brain tumor was discovered. Doctors operated, but though he rallied remarkably, the prognosis was not promising. Charles Sarginson, who had been recalled from Brazil to supervise the Canadian office and later was moved to Bala, became acting director, but he also was felled by illness. Severe arthritis disabled him. The Council sent him to Florida, where the sunshine did effect great improvement in due time.

Friends of the mission held a memorial service for the Congo martyrs in December, 1965, at the Aldan Union Church. Dr. Richard Seume, Mary Baker's pastor in Richmond, Virginia, brought the main message. The hundreds gathered for the service sang with great triumph the majestic hymn, adopted by the mission as its own, *Great Is Thy Faithfulness*. Dr. William Allan Dean, a member of the Home Council who was like a pastor to the mission, pronounced the benediction. Only then was it learned that during the service Ralph Odman, who had suffered with those who were suffering, would feel his pain no more. At age 44, he had gone to be with the Lord.

Tributes poured in from over the world. His own missionaries and executives of other mission societies recalled his touch on their lives. " . . . devotion, humility and yet real statesmanship . . . his gift of clear expression and an ability to reach young people with the challenge of missions . . . he put everyone at ease . . . he did not tell us of the faults of others, but of their strong points . . . that personal touch . . . he met us at the airport in the middle of the night as we flew in from Haiti . . . "

Resolutions of appreciation came from the Congress of the

Church's Worldwide Mission, which he had initiated and gave leadership to its formation, and from the Interdenominational Foreign Mission Association, of which he had been secretary.

Al Larson, "the bravest man in Congo," was asked to assist Charles Sarginson. When it became clear that Sarginson would not be able to assume the executive's duties, Larson was chosen by the Council to become, in May of 1966, UFM's third general director.

With the burden of leadership for the entire mission on his shoulders, he realized he needed help, a lot of help. Edwin Pudney had conducted UFM's affairs from his personal knowledge of nearly every detail. But the mission had grown and Odman brought in an associate. Under still-developing plans from Odman's watch, it was in the process of expanding further. Unlike some organizations that outgrow the span of single leadership but are not aware they have, UFM was in process of making the transition from the my-hat-is-my-office method of administration to a more organized set-up. Yet, what Larson had in mind was not a top-down flow of authority.

UFM, he reminded himself, was a field-run mission. The Bala office was there to set general policy, to establish broad guidelines and to assist the field councils in executing their missions within those policies and guidelines.

John and Helen Beerley were on furlough from Haiti, and for the next year he served as Larson's associate director and she was placed in charge of the mission's finances. Later they were assigned to the Canadian office. Charles Piepgrass, who had just completed a doctoral study, was asked to work in Bala rather than start another term in Haiti. Larson felt he needed good men to assist him, and looked on these two as among the best. He sent for another man, John Miesel, who had seventeen years of mission experience in Congo and France. Charles Sarginson, Charles Piepgrass, John Miesel and John Beerley in Canada, these were the men who worked closely with Larson for most of the twenty-five years that he headed UFM. Each had a specific responsibility — personnel, candidate orientation, summer interns, pastoral counseling and the like — and was the director, not an assistant, for his homeside job. Each also was liaison with a geographic grouping of fields — Latin America, Asia/Pacific, Africa and Europe. If a matter arose on a field for which Bala's help was needed, the leader on that field contacted his Bala liaison. Bala also had on staff a finance officer and business/office manager.

At a meeting of mission executives Larson was asked one day how he could be subordinate to one of his associate directors in the matter of orientation.

"Orientation of candidates is his job," Larson replied. "He's the expert. I'm just a teacher in the program."

"But if there's a problem with another department?"

"He'll call me in."

"Hmmm."

"It's not the boxes and lines drawn on a paper," Larson said. "It's the spirit in which an organization operates that counts. We men understand each other, we respect each other, and we recognize each man's talents. We meet together regularly and maintain good communication."

The associate director for Canada was included in all U.S. Council meetings, and the general director attended all meetings of the Canadian Council. The Councils in both Canada and the United States would be reconstituted as Boards of Directors in 1980, a designation more in keeping with their legal responsibilities.

Over the years, Larson cultivated this same cooperative independence with the fields. He took the mission's bent toward field-centered administration a step beyond where it had been. He held himself open to problems occurring on the fields, not to dictate solutions but to listen and understand and to offer the counsel of his experience. Like his predecessors, he traveled to the widely scattered mission stations. As a first, at the time of his installation as UFM director, he gathered all the field leaders to Bala for sharing of experiences and practices and for mutual encouragement. At that session, Ted Laskowski, leader of the Belém field in Brazil, received Larson's guidance for which he was grateful. The new general director helped him think through, step by step, the purposes of UFM in Brazil. Laskowski returned to Belém with the assurance that church planting and leadership training were the prime reasons missionaries were there, and what they did should reflect this.

UFM's field procedures had a practical application. A missionary departing Britain and one leaving the United States were, in effect, neither British nor American once they arrived on a field. They dropped their jurisdictional ties to the homeland office and came under the field set-up. If a national church association was in charge of a field, such as the two fields in Brazil were, the missionary was assigned and supervised by the association's mission arm and answered to it. If no church association existed, the employer, so to speak, was the field council, made up of all the missionaries. That body might have members from two or more of the UFM national entities — such as North America and Great Britain —the host country and people who had been sent from other organizations. The system worked very well on the fields.

There were problems, however, at the national level of the three UFM sending agencies, British, Australian and North American. Financial and legal regulations and certain practices in the homelands were among the difficulties encountered. For years the heads of the three entities had met triennially and constant correspondence among them was maintained. Frequently officers of the three divisions met at annual council sessions of the fields. Larson and his people felt, however, that more autonomy for each was needed. Britain wasn't so sure. Australia found no reason not to separate; its interest had focused on Asia and the Pacific.

Talks were held. They were warm and friendly. There were differences of viewpoints, but each conferee treated the others with respect and mutuality was achieved. It helped that there was no property to divide.

In 1975 the separation was made. Not a split, as Larson described it, but an amicable separation. No longer would the agencies be hampered by differences in traditional thought patterns and national obligations. The three directors and their councils or boards mutually agreed to continue cooperating in their outreach ministries, with nothing changing on the fields, but to conduct their own independent administrations. Each could do its job better, and the glue that held them together was the spirit in which they all worked, realizing the attitude toward God and man was what governed both individuals and organizations.

In North America, Unevangelized Fields Mission became UFM International; in Britain, UFM Worldwide; in Australia, Asia Pacific Christian Mission.

SOURCES, Chapter 18

A *Congo Miracle*, Pamphlet, Undated, Bala-Cynwyd, Unevangelized Fields Mission

Annual Reports, 1967, 1980, 1990, 1991, 1994, 1995, Bala-Cynwyd, Unevangelized Fields   Mission, UFM International

Jenkinson, Herbert, Prayer Letters, 1965 - 1988

————————————————, Trip Diary, 1968 - 1969

Larson, Alfred and Jean, Interview by author, 1995

Lifeline, Special edition, 1965; 4th Quarter, 1965; 2nd Quarter, 1967; Summer, 1968; Fall, 1969; September, 1972;

Pudney, Edwin and Lilian, *Miracles Multiplied*,

19

New Fields

ew nations of the world had the Gospel before Egypt. Athanasius, Clemens and Origen, all Egyptian, were some of the early fathers of the Church. As a center of Christianity, Alexandria was equal to Jerusalem, Rome and Constantinople. But in 640 A. D. the conquering Arabs ended the Christian era in the land of the Nile; to plant the seed of the Gospel thereafter, hard work was required, as were patience and much faith to plow even a few small furrows.

Seven young men of Dublin, Ireland, strove valiantly to sow the seed among the Muslims, beginning in 1887 in the Nile delta. By the start of World War II, sixty missionaries manned ten stations in the delta and upriver. The work included colportage, coffee-shop discussions, clinics, a hospital and schools. In 1948 trouble set in; one school was closed and another destroyed through rioting, and the number of missionaries was reduced to forty. Charles and Vivian Hoffmeier joined the Egypt General Mission, a British society, in 1950, and three years later went to the town of Herz, one hundred seventy miles south of Cairo, five miles from the Nile and five from the desert. Nearly a third of the population there were of a Christian, rather than Muslim, culture, but not necessarily of Biblical faith. The Hoffmeiers were assigned to Herz at the invitation of the Evangelical Church, which was begun almost a century before but presently was in decline.

Down the Nile, Muslim aggression throttled more of the work of the mission, and the bitter conflict over the Suez Canal in 1956 caused the expulsion of all British and Commonwealth citizens, so the remaining points of EGM ministry shut down, except that in Herz.

That lone effort might have been stopped, too, but for the plea of the pastors in Herz and surrounding villages to let the Hoffmeiers and Agnes Schirok, a German nurse, stay and work under their direction. Because it was considered a Christian area, meaning Coptic or Orthodox, contrary to the Muslim makeup of most of Egypt, the government allowed the three missionaries to stay. The mission was reorganized with the American Auxiliary Council becoming an American board. It was largely made up of residents of Lancaster, Pennsylvania, but the Egypt General Mission-USA had little financial backing. Because some members of the EGM board were also Council members of UFM, the decision was made in 1964 to merge.

The work in Herz and sixty surrounding settlements emphasized evangelism, Scripture distribution, Bible studies, children's meetings and encouragement of pastors in the small village churches. Before the government closed it in preference to one of its own, Miss Schirok's clinic helped break down the resistance of Muslims to the presence of Christian missionaries. They came eagerly for medical attention, and by the hundreds crowded into the churches and children's meetings to see the Christian films the Hoffmeiers showed.

Never easy, the mission to Egypt produced disappointments and some satisfactions. The Christians were generally indifferent and even regular church attenders showed little evidence of walking with the Lord. Sunday schools were often carried on haphazardly, with a shortage of qualified teachers. Until Hoffmeier taught them otherwise, pastors habitually called on their parishioners without carrying a Bible or making reference to it.

Among the people the sale of Bibles and New Testaments, while not phenomenal, continued with regularity. But promising were the Bible classes held for high school boys each Friday. Some sixty to ninety came to be trained in the evangelism of children. On Mondays they were dropped off in the outlying villages to put in practice what they had learned.

Agnes Schirok and Vivian Hoffmeier conducted women's meetings in several villages and visited in homes where they were invited. Miss Schirok began a school for girls. Until that time they had had no opportunity for education. And in a land of much illiteracy, the girls were delighted when they learned to read.

The Hoffmeiers were in Cairo at the outbreak of war between Egypt and Israel in 1967. Because of the United States' friendship with Israel, the Egyptians turned hostile toward Americans. Effigies of American officials decorated Cairo streets. Charles made a quick trip to Herz to get Agnes Schirok. She sailed for Germany, the Hoffmeiers for Cyprus, then England. They hoped to go back to Egypt. But the field closed permanently, so they returned to America.

The United States might not have been thought an unevangelized place, but when Walter and Beulah Kruhmin started UFM's work in New Mexico in 1965, they believed the description certainly fitted that part of the country. Their primary objective was to take the Gospel to the Spanish-speaking people of the state, particularly around the old city of Santa Fe.

They found no lack of opportunity to present the Word of God. One method to get the attention of people, thousands they might not otherwise contact, was a weekly column in the Santa Fe newspaper. Vacation Bible schools brought in the children. English-language classes put the missionaries in touch with newly-arrived immigrants. Promotion of Sunday schools received prime effort.

Shortly after their arrival in New Mexico, the Kruhmins were joined by Robert and Doris Baker, who had seen service in the Dominican Republic and thus spoke Spanish and were at home in Spanish culture. Later, Robert and Joyce Cutting became members of the team.

The Bakers concentrated on Pojoaque Valley, a small community northwest of Santa Fe. Working through the Pojoaque Valley Bible Fellowship, they entered into a full round of activities, including preaching and teaching, training elders, counseling, discipling new converts, showing films and officiating at funerals. In Santa Fe, the Cuttings cooperated with existing churches, assisting in a variety of ways before transferring to the South Africa field. The Kruhmins circulated among several locations, preaching and conducting children's ministries and Bible classes, one of the studies taking place in a center for recovering alcoholics.

The goal of this work was to discover and train local people for the pastorates and other leadership positions to replace the Kruhmins and the Bakers in their retirements in the 1990s.

A second UFM field in North America opened in 1965. French-speaking Quebec was the target of Richard and Martha Wilkinson, who for several years shared heavily in the mission's ministry in Haiti. La Croisade Evangélique had as its original thrust an outreach to students of the French-Canadian universities in Montreal. Other opportunities opened — preaching in local churches, work with children, young people's retreats and summer camps and house-to-house visitation. The goal was to establish evangelical churches among the French Canadian population.

Montreal is a cosmopolitan city, and UFM's work was soon to reflect some of that diversity. Because the animosities of war expelled them from Egypt, Charles and Vivian Hoffmeier refused to give up their effort to win Muslims to Christ. A large population of Muslims, including many Egyptians, drew them to Montreal in 1968 and thus they expanded UFM's work in that direction. Adding to the city's international air, many Haitians lived in the city, escapees from the poverty and frightful events under the Duvallier regime. By 1971 they would have their own church in Montreal.

The Quebec team expanded when Marshall and Thelma Southard arrived from Congo. They had been through the Simba uprising there. Marshall, away at a conference in Leopoldville, was separated from his family when the rebels overran Stanleyville, and for some time neither he nor Thelma and their son Larry at Kilometer 8 knew the other's situation. Free in the part of the country controlled by the government, Marshall was able to maintain communication with Bala, passing on whatever news that did filter out of Simba areas.

Herbert and Grace Harms was another couple from Congo. Speaking French fluently, the Southards and Harmses fitted in well.

A half dozen churches were established with the Quebecois, and in time they grew consistently. The congregations linked with the French Canadian section of Associated Gospel Churches, with which UFM was also affiliated. When Chapelle Evangélique Emmanuel began as UFM's first church in Montreal, many of the believers among the Haitian immigrants attended it. These folk subsequently formed their own assembly, and from it four Haitian churches were born.

The Hoffmeiers' ministry among Arab immigrants resulted in the Middle East Christian Fellowship, and when the couple retired in 1982 the witness continued without UFM personnel, and later an Arabic church was formed, in part by those who attended the Fellowship.

The UFM families kept on the move. As soon as one church became strong and stable enough to support a pastor and manage its affairs, the missionary moved on, starting a new work. Often this meant the family had to move from one community to another.

Into the 1990s the Quebec operation continued its emphasis on church planting. Some of that was definitely in a supportive role, lending a soft hand to local congregations as they moved toward maturity and in assisting the Associated Gospel Churches. In thirty years, UFM's work in Quebec was showing second-generation growth. The missionary program of the national church included three couples serving in North American evangelistic agencies and one missionary in Africa.

SOURCES, Chapter 19

Annual Reports, 1967, 1980, 1990, 1991, 1994, 1995, Bala-Cynwyd, Unevangelized Fields Mission,   UFM International

Hoffmeier, Vivian, Interview by author, 1996

Larson, Alfred and Jean, Interview by author, 1995

Pudney, Edwin and Lilian, *Miracles Multiplied*, Unpublished manuscript

Lifeline, 4th Quarter, 1958; 2nd Quarter, 1967; Summer, 1968; Fall, 1969; September, 1972;

Light & Life, Second Quarter, 1963

20
Missions in Modern Brazil

One hundred fifteen missionaries worked in the Belém field of Brazil in 1981, making it the largest operation in which UFM International had a part. By 1995, the number stood at one hundred twenty-three, of which fifty-six were supplied by the North American UFM International. The second largest number was sent by the Swiss Alliance Mission, thirty-four; followed by Britain's UFM Worldwide, eighteen; and the German Mission Fellowship, fifteen. One-third of this staff was engaged full time in church planting; fourteen per cent in theological education; thirteen per cent in Indian work and eleven per cent in specialized ministries such as radio and video production and work with street children. Ministries at the Amazon Valley Academy, the MK school, and in language training and administration employed some thirty per cent.

Roads now linked towns and villages in northeastern Brazil that a few short years before had to rely on river traffic for communication and transport. The Trans-Amazon Highway reached westward from the Atlantic Ocean; the aim was to extend it to the border with Peru. Another connected Belém with the new federal capital of Brasilia. For good or ill, these highways produced major changes in vast areas of the rain forest. Nearly impenetrable jungle had been cleared for the roads and for ranches, plantations and agribusinesses or industrial developments along their routes. Villages grew into cities. In fourteen years, Imperatriz mushroomed from a population of one thousand to eighty thousand. Altamira was a rustic village on a bend of the Xingu when the Cunninghams lived there and sent supplies to Horace Banner working upriver among the wild Kayapo. It became a bustling city with paved streets, modern shops, a university, an airport and beautiful homes sprawling in the suburbs. The little church Doug and Mary McAllister established there in 1940 had in fifty years emerged into a lively congregation housed in a beautiful building.

AICEB and MICEB, the national church and mission organizations, labored hard to match this growth with new churches. New and improved church buildings were erected in cities, suburbs, small towns and rural villages throughout the northeastern states of Brazil. A church stood at Smoke Falls, where the three Freds were killed as they pioneered an entry into the Kayapo tribe of Indians. By the mid-1990s, one hundred churches and one hundred sixty congregations in process of becoming organized churches numbered sixteen thousand believers.

The churches now had Brazilian pastors, though missionaries continued to assist wherever needed. Many of the pastors were trained at the seminary in São Luis, which was renamed the Bible College, this center of advanced theological education having started out as a simple Bible school in the interior town of Barra do Corda.

The Indian work, UFM's original purpose in Brazil, spread among the Guajajara, Canela and Kayapo tribes. The first two had the Bible in their tongues, and the Kayapo New Testament was completed. Medical ministries among the Indians filled a great need.

At one of the annual meetings of the missionaries, Earl and Ivy Trapp spoke of the changes that had come over the Kayapo. No longer were they the Big-Lip People, so seldom seen any more the protruding five-inch facial disk that had been worn by older generations. "They are no longer a wild, naked tribe roaming the jungles," the Trapps reported. "All except the children wear clothes. It isn't uncommon to see one or more men in our meetings in up-to-date suits, ties, shirts and shoes. No longer are they deceived by one or five cruzeiro notes (the Brazilian currency at the time). They are quickly beginning to realize the value of money and of their produce. Added to all this is the opening of a new road which will link our Indian villages with the outside world . . . As you can well imagine, most of the new contacts made as a result of the road are not for the spiritual good of the Kayapo."

As true everywhere with once-isolated people who suddenly discover — or are discovered by — the outside world, the Kayapo had not only to discern truth in the spiritual realm but to decide how much to be governed by the spiritual or the material. The present-day missionaries among them found that in the battle to win the Kayapo their opponent was no longer the savagery of a killer tribe but the acquired desire to live like so many of the non-Indians around them — given to drink, sensual pleasures, greed and little or no thought of God.

A hostel opened for Japanese students in Belém, as the churches in the Japanese immigrant and second and third-generation communities continued to win converts among this large ethnic group. Entrance to the families often came through the children by means of Bible classes and clubs. Nisei missionaries, already fluent in the Japanese language, were key to reaching this important segment of Brazil's population.

Radio, literature, films and video, camps and retreats, theology extension courses, youth programs, children's clubs and health education supported the work of the churches. Missionaries spearheaded much of this endeavor, increasingly shared the responsibility with national Christians and intended that someday the Brazilians would take over completely.

Seventy years of labor by missionaries who made up UFM's contingent in Brazil — some predating the mission itself —

had made a difference. One by one the pioneers fell to old age and death. Horace Banner capped a long life of service to the Kayapo by his entrance into Glory. Veteran missionaries among the Indians, river launch evangelists, teachers in the Bible schools, church planters in the cities and towns, youth specialists, administrators — all sooner or later passed the torch to capable, enthusiastic, dedicated younger workers, either foreigners or nationals, who looked on what had been accomplished as a platform on which to further build.

But some old warriors just couldn't keep away from the battle to win Brazil. In their retirement Leslie and Anita Jantz returned several times to Abaetetuba, where for many years they had lived and worked. On one such mission they began by hosting a congress of almost two hundred women in January. In February they coordinated and taught in a seminary extension course for sixty-five students from twenty-three churches. In the spring they conducted several youth retreats during the Carnival and Easter seasons and also hosted a national workers' congress, a retreat for youth leaders and a conference of the Brazilian organization for missionaries to the Indians. In May and June there was a new house to construct for a resident worker and in July two camps for lively Jet Cadet youngsters. Then there was more construction, a brief vacation with their son and his family, also UFM missionaries, and then home to Canada in time to take part in their church's missionary conference. Retirement? It was just a word.

Jessie Foulds was another who refused to quit. Remembered fondly as the bookstore lady in Belém, São Luis and Imperatriz, she had thrown herself unreservedly into every task handed her, sometimes keeping financial records, sometimes recording minutes at field council meetings, sometimes doing the things that no one else wanted to do. Nearing fifty years on the field and long past official retirement, she stayed on in Brazil, just to do the things she'd always done — or to tackle a new job for which no one else was available.

A thousand miles up the Amazon, and still farther up the Rio Branco, missionaries paddled the length of more rivers and entered more Indian settlements, all but one of them — the Maiongongs — branches of the large and diverse Yanomami tribe. Though related, these clans spoke with marked differences, necessitating a half-dozen separate language studies and translation projects.

For years now the Gospel had been communicated to the Indians of Roraima, that area of Northwest Brazil lying between British Guiana or Guyana and Venezuela. Yet, evidences of genuine belief to the point of changing lives were scarce, with clear-cut confessions to be found only here and there. The first baptism among the Shirishana, on the Mucajaí River, the second area to be invaded with the Gospel, occurred nine years after the station opened. The local chief professed salvation in Christ, but in a time of crisis fell back to calling on the old spirits to solve his problem.

Many resisted outright the missionary's message. Often the old men stood in the way of the younger, more open ones. Family feuds and bitter warfare between villages flared up frequently. Once John Peters and Bob Cable were called to a distant area to negotiate peace between two killing groups. Because of the common distrust and resulting violence, some groups ventured contact with only three or four neighboring villages out of the hundreds in the region.

Sickness, particularly virulent malaria, was unyielding. If not for his message, the missionary was welcomed by nearly all for his medicine. And for trade goods. Theft of a machete or an axe gained acceptance equal to working to earn it.

Yet, the witness continued. In just one of many such explorations, John Peters and Don Borgman, accompanied by Claude Leavitt and two Wai Wai tribesmen, trekked through the rain forest in the direction of a distant group of villages where the name of Christ had not yet been spoken. They lost the faint trail, which had not been used for years. They ran out of water, and it was the dry season when all the streams in the area had long since dried up. Leavitt, however, had learned the ways of the jungle and its Indians through his years with the Wai Wai and Trio. Some of his friends said he was more Indian than the Indians themselves. In this emergency, his instinct did not fail him. In twenty minutes he led the party to the nearest river, which was dry, except for deep, redeeming pools of water.

The Wai Wai served as contacts on several forays into the Yanomami forest. The testimony of these Christian Indians had telling effect on the pagan tribes of Roraima. Once, a man from the Mucajaí traveled to the Wai Wai home country. There he was impressed by the large number of people who crowded the church for prayer and worship services. He returned home determined to build a church for his people.

But years after many Yanomami villages in Brazil were evangelized there was not a single organized congregation. God had never promised that doing His work would be easy or accomplished rapidly.

Learning the language and culture was essential to success. As a new bride accompanying her husband to the Mucajaí for the first time, Lorraine Peters quickly learned the truth of this. On her arrival in the village, the women gathered around her, chattering incessantly. She, of course, understood nothing of this strange tongue, so they shouted directly into her ears. Surely, they believed, since she was not responding, the poor woman must be deaf.

As time went on, Bible translation and literacy took priority. Translators Sandra Cue, Edith Moreira, Sue Albright, Carole Swain, Steve Anderson and Don Borgman struggled in the various dialects to express Biblical concepts that were lacking in the Indian's world. The Yanomami had no word for love nor for gratitude. How would they express the love of God? To introduce "thank you?" Neill Hawkins was helpful here. He went to great lengths to gather from the missionaries anthropological information on the Yanomami, and then to collate and disseminate it throughout the field. His categories included, among others, witchcraft, kinships, beliefs surrounding the dead and celebrations.

As a single man, Borgman had participated in the opening of all the Yanomami stations. After his marriage, he and Barbara moved to Auaris among the Sanuma people, where he concentrated on Bible translation. At one point in his career he fell deathly ill, and for some time it was feared the field would lose an invaluable worker. He recovered, however, and his work resumed. He carried on the translation in later years after the family returned home and settled in Florida.

A trip to search out another group of people usually involved several of the young men of the tribe. These visits expanded the horizons of the travelers beyond their own village and broke the isolation that had enveloped them. After a number of such trips, the Shirishana on their own began to visit lost kin, renewing ties that had been severed for half a century.

Some visitors to the villages were not welcomed by the missionaries — gold miners. These often rough, callous, lecherous men polluted the streams with their mining operations and infected the villages with their libertine lifestyle. Other visitors were met with more openness, most often military or government officials who flew in to check on the foreigners and what they were doing among Brazil's Indians. The missionaries had nothing to hide, and were glad to demonstrate the purposes for being there — to express the love of God to a people who knew little of love and to foster a better life for them.

The local economies were aided by the purchase of handmade artifacts for resale outside. Meat and fruit were bought at one station for use at another. Basic stores were set up to provide metal tools and other goods that simplified life for the Yanomami. Schools taught reading and writing and the science of numbers. Clinics tended to physical ailments. But none of these services eclipsed the effort to present Christian faith as the workable alternative to the prevalent destructive practices.

The people were friendly, helped in construction of the stations, attended Sunday services. On the whole, they were hospitable and generous, fun-loving and nature-oriented. But they were also given to ways that imperiled their society — abortion, infanticide, subjugation of women, contempt for the elderly, disregard for the sick, drunkenness, deception, violence and revenge. Individual conversions and changed lives did occur. One powerful and much-feared witchdoctor renounced the spirits he had served and asked for Jesus' spirit to enter his chest. Others joined those who were "God's People." But it became clear that, unlike the Wai Wai or the Dani on the other side of the world, the Yanomami experienced no "people movement," or tribal conversion. Where acceptance of Christian faith did take place, the UFM missionaries were there to teach, encourage and serve, and were backed by a sensitive support staff at headquarters in Boa Vista.

The outreach in this small provincial capital depended on the initiative of individual staff members. In the frequent absences of Neill Hawkins, Rod and Tommy Lewis led field administration, and were assisted by Joseph and DiAnne Butler. In contacts for purchasing and finance and government liaison, both couples met and made friends with Brazilians who normally had no acquaintances among evangelicals. They invited these friends to the church that had been started by Wayne and Bonnie Follmar, but later came under the leadership of a Brazilian pastor. In time, churches were planted in several sections of the city, and eight of these banded together to form a cooperative link. Evening Bible studies augmented preaching in the churches.

Boa Vista became a center for the work among the partly acculturated Macushi tribe. But before the days of transportation and steady supply lines, evangelizing the Macushi meant carrying on alone in a number of nearly isolated areas.

The Macushi were Neill Hawkins' initial focus when in the

early 1940s he entered the frontier territory by means of the Rio Branco. Pressing on with his brother Robert to contact the Wai Wai, he turned the school he had started over to another brother, Rader. The school was later ceded to the Baptists and Rader and his wife Ann went to Georgetown, on the coast of British Guiana, to open a school and boarding home there as well as to be the support center for UFM's inland ministries. Primarily, the school served Macushi children of the Rupununi District of British Guiana. In 1956, the mission was permitted to open a school near the village of Nappi on the country's wide savanna. Three years later, Patrick and June Foster joined three women missionaries at the school, Elizabeth Weeks, Jean McCracken and Kathryn Pierce. Pat engaged in language work and June taught in the school. As the women moved to other stations, Darrell and Betty Teeter joined the staff.

In 1960, a major innovation opened several areas to the Gospel. Dr. and Mrs. Frank Davis were UFM missionaries in Lethem, the leading town of the area. Dr. Davis put together a medical-evangelistic team which, by MAF plane, made monthly visits to nine communities. After he left the field in 1967, Miriam Abbott, a nurse, continued the clinics. But two years later, all Macushi work was interrupted by a serious but failed attempt by local ranchers to rebel against the government, which in 1966 had won its independence from Great Britain. The missionaries were expelled by the leftist government that then came to power. Many of the Macushi believers moved to Brazil with them. The Christian Brethren Church picked up what remained of the savanna work and the Lord blessed their efforts.

The Macushi straddle the border between Guyana and Brazil. What was successful on the Guyana side became a very effective ministry in Brazil. Dr. Charles Patton, an MAF doctor, began fly-in clinics in the Roraima region in 1966. For a nurse he had Bernita Gutenberger, a Brazilian, and as evangelist, Jaoa Batista. Dr. Patton eventually was succeeded by a Brazilian, Dr. Dankwart Schreen. Five local churches resulted from the work of the team.

Moving to the Brazil side, Pat and June Foster continued Bible translation and preparation of teaching materials. They also engaged in evangelism, and Pat pushed the witness to the Macushi into the Pacaraima Mountains near the Venezuela border. Debra Bratcher assumed responsibility for the medical-evangelistic outreach, while Miriam Abbott and her nurse partner, Jane Burns, went from village to village training Macushi as health agents for their villages.

The number of Christians grew. The believers at Napoleao invited all who would come to a Bible conference in 1967. So many responded, including a truckload of Indians from Guyana, and enjoyed the gathering so much that the conference became an annual event. Church leadership took advantage of Bible extension classes. Land near Boa Vista was purchased for a future center that was planned to include a training school for young Macushi men and women and a hospital for all Indians.

After Guyana's political turmoil quieted, UFM worked with another tribe on the savanna, the Wapishana. Following her work at the Waica station among the Yanomami, Frances Tracy stayed with them for many years, teaching and translating, working in partnership with Beverly Dawson, of Wycliffe Bible Translators. In Fran's last year before retirement, the Wapishana Christians staged a week-long Christmas celebration. The villagers built a large house for their visitors — Macushi from the savanna and Wai Wai from the jungle, as well as other Wapishana, and Fran as special guest.

Guyana's population is cosmopolitan — African descendants, East Indians, English, Chinese, American Indians and mixed. Especially is this seen in Georgetown. From the original Kitty Bible Church, which later affiliated with the Baptists, UFM's church-planting increased to eight congregations, all held together by the Association of Bible Churches. The Bible school was started by another mission in 1954, and given to UFM in

1966. During the attempted revolution it ceased to function, but in 1983 was reorganized under a national board as the Guyana Bible College. The student body grew to about seventy-five, with Donald Kearns their teacher for several years.

The Georgetown ministry traces back to Rader and Ann Hawkins, who also worked in Lethem and in years when retirement could be expected still stayed at their post in Santerem, on the Amazon River. A Guyanese couple who likewise gave full measure whenever and wherever needed were Lionel and Iris Gordon.

Neill Hawkins traveled annually to the south of Brazil to promote the Indian work and to recruit young people as missionaries to Amazonia. He taught mission courses at the Word of Life Bible Institute in São Paulo. In 1971 he injured his back, requiring him to relinquish the leadership of Roraima to Rod Lewis and to undergo medical treatment in the United States for two years. On his return to Brazil, he joined the faculty of Word of Life, teaching missions. For the next seven years he and Mary shepherded selected students to Roraima and set them up in short-term internships among the various Indian groups, and many an internship turned into career service.

This resourceful, untiring, challenging, encouraging servant of God and leader of His people contracted hepatitis and died in the summer of 1982, forty years from the time he pledged his life to the Lord for the Indians of South America. Mary stayed on in the accounting department of Word of Life for another four years.

Two of Neill's former students were Milton Camargo and Curt Kirsch. They were among those who interned, then in 1980 yielded their lives to serve among the Yanomami. A task they tackled with enthusiasm was an eight-day canoe trip up the Uraricoera River to the remote Maithas region. Their purpose was to deliver the canoe to a mission station on the river and then to continue on to be the first to take much-needed health care and, all-important, the Gospel to the Maithas Indians.

The river was swollen from seasonal rains, but an outboard motor sent them confidently into the current.

"Intrepid, that's us!" exclaimed Milton. "This trip's going to be a blast!"

On the third day the first mishap occurred — in a difficult cataract the canoe capsized. They raised it, after having lost a camera and shotgun. They went on, through difficult stretches of river and spending short, uncomfortable nights on shore. On the fifth day, bone-weary and each hour facing tougher conditions, they reached a part of the river that divided into innumerable branches, resembling a giant labyrinth of puzzling canals, islands, streams and swamps — and always rapids. They did not make it through. The propeller caught on a submerged vine, flipping the canoe, which in the force of the water folded in half, throwing men and gear into the sucking waters of a whirlpool. Two Indians who had been their guides escaped the river, looked around and saw nothing of the missionaries. They went on foot to the mission station upstream and in a couple of days reported the two were at the bottom of the river. The missionaries did not drown, however, but miraculously managed to beach themselves, and for the next five days lived in torture as they tried to survive in the jungle without food or a knife and with little hope.

The report of the Indians alerted the entire mission. In the hope that the men had somehow survived and could be spotted, the MAF plane flew sortie after sortie, but discouragingly over a jungle of thousands of square miles and thousands of places the current could have carried them. Most important, people prayed, not only their families and colleagues in Brazil, but a network of prayer warriors throughout UFM's constituency.

Camargo and Kirsch were found, finally seen from the air in the canoe which they had pounded back into usable shape.

255

Exhausted, they followed the lead of the plane overhead and eventually reached a rescue party.

One night as they had tried sleeping, realizing that survival chances were minimal, they both acknowledged they were incapable of saving themselves.

"I had started out on this trip feeling I was God's 'Indiana Jones,'" said Milton to his rescuers, describing that night's feelings. "But now I realized I really was more like 'Balaam's Ass.'"

The Lord had saved them. He had a purpose in saving them. Curt Kirsch went back to his jungle post among the Yanomami. Milton Camargo answered the call of his co-workers. He became president of MisSão Evangélica da Amazonia (MEVA), the mission organization that since 1969 encompassed all UFM and Brazilian missionaries on an equal basis in the work throughout Roraima.

In the rain forest far to the southeast of Boa Vista, the Wai Wai made a valiant effort to interact with the deadly Atrowari people. They aimed to live alongside the killer tribe in order to learn their language and then tell them about God. More than two dozen contacts had been made, but with limited achievement of their goals. The only results seemed to be recollections of walking along the brink of death and two orphaned brothers who had asked Jesus to enter the pits of their stomachs.

The boys were in their teens. One went back to his own people, but reports were heard that he stood true to God. The other chose to live with the Wai Wai and in a few years married one of the Wai Wai girls.

The Wai Wai had often said to the Atrowari, as they had said to other pagan tribes, "Come live with us and you will learn what it means to be a Companion of Jesus."

In a surprise drop-in one day, ninety-two nearly naked, whooping Atrowari did just that. They moved in, warriors, women and children — with their dogs, pet monkeys, parrots and macaws and chickens, bows and arrows, cooking pots, wooden stools and smoked ham joints. The population of the village had about doubled. Those wishing to study the visitors' language got their opportunity. But before real progress was made, the Atrowari departed as suddenly as they had come.

Another time a few men arrived at the Wai Wai village for a friendly visit. They were followed by another group whose intent was not friendly. The second batch had come to kill an enemy in the first. Their intended prey, however, had gone with some Wai Wai for a long hunt in the forest. So the belligerent Atrowari became lustful Atrowari and turned their attention to the Wai Wai women.

"No!" the Wai Wai men protested. But how long could they hold off these hot-blooded, wild warriors? Likely, they'd kill the men first, then take the women as they pleased.

"Sing! They like to sing!" one of the Wai Wai leaders shouted to his tribesmen. "Round them up and get them into the church!"

Both Wai Wai men and Atrowari herded into the oblong, leafy structure that served the village well as its house of worship. At the same time, the women and children ran off into the forest.

The chorus inside the building was loud and in no particular key. But to the men whose wives and daughters they were desperately trying to protect it was a joyful noise. The song had been made up on the spot, consisting of the one word the song leader knew of the visitor's tongue — *Maarye*, good.

"Again!" he shouted. "Louder!" Again and again and again they sang, the Wai Wai to give their women time to escape and the Atrowari because it was fun. Once their emotions were spent, the Atrowari cooled down. Then the man they had come to kill appeared with the hunters, but after another "sing" or two and with their carrying baskets filled with Wai Wai food, the Atrowari were content to leave for home

The Wai Wai made more visits to the Atrowari than they received. Two families tried to settle in an Atrowari village, but after a couple of weeks were driven off. The government erected a fence of threatening soldiers between the two tribes. The Wai Wai were ordered to stay out of Atrowari territory. A giant hydro-electric project began in the Atrowari area of the jungle, and those whose project it was did not want the Indians Christianized. They would be much more pliable if not bothered with principles and integrity and were made dependent through gifts of food, clothing, motors for their canoes — and especially intoxicating drink. For twenty five years the Wai Wai had prayed and attempted to evangelize their forest brothers. Now, all that was left to them was to pray.

There were few other tribes remaining in the Wai Wai region of the jungle, perhaps only one, but this one that they believed was out there became the object of intensive search. The people were eventually found, a stone-age tribe that in its aimless wanderings over a generation had been greatly reduced in size and purpose. They, too, came into the fold of the Wai Wai, as six or eight other tribes had, and most of their members also entered God's family. To accommodate them, because they were uneasy living in a settlement that numbered over a thousand, and to scour the forest for any stragglers, a number of the Wai Wai moved away and formed a new village on the Jatapuzinho River. Among them was Elka, the first Wai Wai Christian and the man who had led his people to be the people of God as no other Indian in the Amazon had done. He was now retired as chief and in poor health. He died in 1994, and his obituary appeared in Christian publications of the United States.

A new set of leaders — chiefs, elders of the church, deacons, work captains — governed the Wai Wai, sons of the early Christian stalwarts. After nearly forty years the church was still the center of village life. In some of the younger generation, it was true, the zeal of their parents was lacking. Seldom did second-generation believers fully plumb the depths of fear, degradation and deprivation from which their forebearers had been

258

delivered. Flights out to city hospitals and motors making trips easier and quicker upriver or down, depending on the village, introduced the people to Brazilian towns. The wall of isolation had largely disappeared. Wrist watches, plastic toys for the children, aluminum pots, radios, shotguns — these were the trophies of trips to the outside world. Often a young man chose to stay out, and like as not fell victim to those who looked on Indians as easy game. To some of these youths home looked pretty good when they discovered that in the Brazilian's world you had to pay over money if you wanted to eat, or when they got sick and no one around seemed to care.

Irene Benson remained as the only North American missionary to live among the Wai Wai. For more than three decades she had been their teacher, and had trained a large staff of villagers to run the schools. Before her retirement after thirty-four years, Florence Riedle established a tradition of competent medical care. Bob Hawkins completed translation of the Old and New Testaments and periodically he and Florine flew in from their home in Texas to check the accuracy and readability of the work, and to introduce the new hymns Florine had translated or written, and to teach and counsel with the tribal leaders.

Claude and Barbara Leavitt kept up direct interest in two South American tribes, the Wai Wai and the Trio, the latter in southern Surinam. Over many years, they had served them both, originating the work among the Trio. Like the Wai Wai, the Trio had matured in their Christian commitment. They hosted a Bible conference, to which Wai Wai, Macushi, Wapishana, Hishkaryena and other tribes made pilgrimages each year.

In 1995, hope revived for evangelizing the Atrowari. Three times that year the once-fierce tribe made friendly visits to the Wai Wai, led by their one-time haughty, cruel, self-loving chief, who himself issued an invitation for the Wai Wai to return the visit.

To get to the Wai Wai, the Atrowari had journeyed neither by stealth through the forest nor by canoe, as they once did, but as far as the roads extended they came in vehicles supplied and driven by a government that a few years before had decisively cut off all contact between the two tribes.

SOURCES, Chapter 20

Annual Reports, 1967, 1980, 1990, 1991, 1994, 1995, Bala-Cynwyd, Unevangelized Fields Mission, UFM International

Foster, Patrick, 1996, *A Brief Description of the Work of UFM Among the Macushi Indians*

Hawkins, Mary, Chronology, Brazil-Roraima field, 1944 - 1983

------------------, Roster, UFM missionaries in North Amazon/Guiana field, 1996

_____, Letters to author, 1995 - 96

Hawkins, Neill, Prayer letters, 1955 - 1981

Hill, Joseph, Letter to author, 1996

Jantz, Leslie and Anita, Letter to author, 1995

Larson, Alfred and Jean, Interview by author, 1995

Lewis, Rodney, Letter to author, 1995

_____, Prayer letters, 1957 - 1960

_____, Notes on early draft, 1996

Lifeline, 4th Quarter, 1958; 2nd Quarter, 1967; Summer, 1968; Fall, 1969; September, 1972;

Light & Life, lst Quarter, 2nd Quarter, 1963

Lubkemann, Frieda, *Rain Forest Rescue*, Undated, UFM International

McAllister, Mary, Letters to author, with enclosures, 1995

Miesel, John, Report on Trip to North Amazon, 1979

North Amazon Field Conference, 1979, Minutes

Peters, John, 1996, Untitled manuscript on Yanomami Indians

Pudney, Edwin and Lilian, *Miracles Multiplied*, Unpublished manuscript

Station Log, Waica (Yanomami Indians), Brazil, 1958 - 1968

Trapp, Earl, Prayer letter, 1964

21

The UEBH

In 1977, UFM turned the administration of the Haiti field over to the Union Evangélique Baptiste d'Haiti (UEBH). While not yet completely achieving the goal set by Edwin Pudney, that every missionary should work himself out of a job, this arrangement nevertheless fulfilled the dream of Florent Toirac, that the national would become an equal partner with the foreign missionary. In reality, this move went a step further. The missionary from outside Haiti, as on several UFM fields, now received his invitation to come, assignment and job description from the Haitian church. More and more, missionary work consisted of training national workers, advising, exercising the Scriptural gift of helping — *those able to help others.* UEBH was the reorganized Mission Evangélique Baptiste d'Haiti. An independent association of churches, its aim was to spread the Gospel throughout Haiti and the world, establish and strengthen believers, develop spiritual ties between member churches of the UEBH and work for the spiritual and material development of the country.

The final step in the transition occurred when Walter L. Wilson, Jr., wrote a check that settled all financial matters and presented it to representatives of UEBH.

Wilson had first come to Haiti in 1956 with his father, the noted Bible teacher of Kansas City, for the Spiritual Life Conference of missionaries, "the Haiti Keswick," as it was known. He met Ralph and Majil Odman at that time and was impressed with Ralph's charitable nature. Eight years after Ralph died, Walter and Majil were married, and thus began a new career for the retired businessman — that took him and Majil to eleven UFM fields over the next thirteen years.

In Haiti, Wilson helped UEBH set up an accounting system and trained its staff. To alleviate constant pressures on the general fund, Wilson advised that a small percentage of all cash flow be applied to administration. The plan worked well, bringing welcome relief to the budget and gratitude to Wilson for his counsel.

At La Pointe, Majil Odman Wilson saw a reminder of the ten years she and Ralph had spent in Haiti. It was the large modern tabernacle built in 1968 for the crowds that thronged to the annual Béraca Convention. The Ralph Odman Memorial Tabernacle was an appropriate tribute to the decade the late UFM general director had labored as field leader in Haiti. Odman had supervised the building of the first tabernacle. Before he left to take up his post at Bala-Cynwyd, he remarked that the old auditorium needed replacing; he was afraid it would someday fall with unhappy results.

Gifts to his memory and volunteer labor from America built the concrete and steel replacement. Holding five thousand worshipers as opposed to the two thousand of the old building, it still was overrun some years, but was closer to the sea whose cooling breezes were so welcomed by the packed audiences. If the convention continued to assemble each year over the expected life of the new tabernacle, it would extend well beyond the lifetime of any of its present happy constituency.

The Bible institute and the seminary in Port-au-Prince kept on turning out capable workers for Haiti's churches and other institutions. Attendance at either the Ecole Evangélique de la Bible or the Séminaire de Théologie Evangélique de Port-au-Prince, which shared the same faculty but had separate buildings, commanded respect. From a first-year student body of thirteen, the EEB had grown to number one hundred thirty-three in 1995, with twenty-seven graduates. That year the seminary, STEP, graduated twenty of its ninety-two students.

Graduates of both schools went on to head several missions in Haiti and to fill other responsible positions. Several of the faculty of sixteen held degrees from Dallas Theological Seminary in Texas. Duthène Joseph, founder of STEP and former president of EEB, earned his master's degree from Dallas and later received an honorary doctorate from the Union of Private Universities of Haiti.. Joseph's home village lay near St. Marc. His theological training began when as a boy he read the Bible to an illiterate local pastor. Though he filled many important posts in education, the church was never far from his mind. Besides supervising the two institutions on the hills overlooking the capital, he also pastored the Bolosse church, the large, active church at the lower entrance to the mission campus.

By example the Bible school taught its students that an agency of God was not simply something to which people came. It also went out to the people. Before the end of each school year, the entire student body was sent throughout Port-au-Prince and the nation's villages for Evangelistic Week. One year the capital was blitzed with tract distribution to ten thousand homes. Every year there was the Evangelistic Walk. Students and professors alike hiked fifty miles through the countryside, stopping wherever they found people to witness to them of Christ, and in Haiti fifty miles encompassed a lot of people.

Music became an avenue for evangelism. Before called to the States to help in mission administration, John and Helen Beerley trained an institute choir for concerts that appealed to music lovers of all economic and social classes. Beerley conducted the school's radio program over a Port-au-Prince commercial station, while outside the capital Donald Weaver aimed his message through a Christian broadcaster, Radio Lumiere, an effective ministry founded by David Hartt of World Team.

There was no letup in the medical work at La Pointe and in other centers in the north. The clinic at La Coma, started by Caroline Bradshaw in the parched northwest peninsula, concentrated on the care of mothers and children, with food distributions to three hundred malnourished children and some elderly folk. The hospital at La Pointe now counted forty beds, and a surgery building replaced the makeshift facility that once had been a storage area. For six years La Pointe boasted its own missionary surgeon, Dr. William Piepgrass. He was one of several second-generation missionaries, most of whom had grown up in Haiti. Another son of a missionary might have served with his father, except that John Schmid, the father, was killed in a road accident. John and Jackie Schmid had been co-workers with Florent Toirac and came into UFM with the merger in 1949. John served Haiti in numerous capacities, but mainly as a pastor. One night in 1978 he traveled the dark, twisting road between Gonaives and Port-au-Prince and a truck collided with his station wagon. After his father's death and mother's eventual retirement, David Schmid kept the family name on the roster of Haiti missionaries, becoming one in a series of UFM leaders of this large and historic field.

One from the merger who was still active more than forty years later was Catherine Froh. A Bible teacher for much of her tenure, she returned to Haiti again and again for short-term ministry, even when well past the age of seventy. Others served the burgeoning population of Haitians in the United States. Among these were nationals who fled the country during the appalling dictatorships and the chaos that followed. Those days of repression and reprisal were noted for their necklaces of burning rubber tires and other forms of torture and killing, which sometimes were administered for no discernable reason.

In his various positions in mission and church ministries, Dr. Claude Noel became widely known; because of this, he could expect threats against his life from some quarter. Years earlier, after his graduation from the Bible institute, Noel continued his studies at Providence College in Rhode Island, then returned to Haiti to pastor the large Bolosse Baptist Chruch, to serve as president of UEBH and later to found the Conseil des Eglises Evangéliques d'Haiti. As leader of CEEH, Noel united in purpose and cooperation the Bible-centered churches of the country and represented Haiti in the World Evangelical Fellowship. For safety's sake in the political turbulence, he took refuge in Florida as did tens of thousands of his countrymen, but his Christian effort continued with much success among Haiti's diaspora up and down the east coast of the United States.

To reach Haitian refugees and immigrants to the U.S., UFM missionary teachers from the seminary at Bolosse opened a Bible school in New Jersey and also began systematic Bible teaching and youth ministries in Florida. Curriculum from the Bible school in Haiti was used, and the ministries were carried on in both French and Creole.

At Bolosse, Maranatha College was upgraded from a secondary school to junior college in 1993. UEBH operated four high schools, a trade school at La Pointe and an agricultural school at Verrettes. Its three hundred elementary schools, attached to local churches and chapels, enrolled twenty thousand pupils. For the children of missionaries and English-speaking nationals, UFM helped found Quisqueya Christian School in Port-au-Prince, an inter-mission school whose student body grew to three hundred. Caribbean Christian Academy at La Pointe was also established for the children of missionaries serving in the medical work in the north.

Under the direction of Boxley Boggs and an able assistant, Madame André Roseville, the printing and literature ministry, La Presse Evangélique, greatly expanded. It paid substantial income to UEBH and its various mission projects. A large building on a main boulevard of Port-au-Prince was acquired, giving the operation better visibility and room for expansion. Branch bookstores in St. Marc, Cap Haitien, Les Cayes and La Pointe were supplied by the parent store. Large amounts of evangelical literature, both imported and published by La Press Evangélique, were produced and distributed across Haiti, providing a foundation for Biblical teaching in the churches of many missions. To reach Haiti's professional class, a building for a modern bookstore was purchased in the affluent suburb of Pétionville. Space there was made available for studios of the Christian radio station, Radio Lumière, operated by another mission, and for a language and culture school for new missionaries, which was directed by Professor Edward Jeanty.

Born of necessity, community development became an activity requiring the involvement of both missionaries and nationals. Northwest Haiti for years has been an arid region, but one nine-year stretch of drought left it nearly devastated. Famine called for food programs. Water was scarce, so conduits, cisterns and irrigation projects became practical manifestations of Christian love, alongside the verbal Gospel. Latrines were built, nude land was reforested and roads were repaired. Much of the funding came from agencies that had money but no connections with the communities nor people to do the work.

This was the church in action, but that term also applied to a program of church growth and encouragement that emphasized evangelism, prayer cells, discipleship and leadership training. Seminars, rallies and visits to local congregations stimulated the one hundred twelve churches of UEBH, plus five among Haitian laborers in the Dominican Republic, to press toward their Year 2000 goal of one hundred twenty-five churches and one hundred thousand members.

In addition to the full-fledged churches, UEBH counted two hundred forty other preaching points, fifty-two ordained pastors and two hundred twelve lay pastors. On the rolls in the mid-1990s were almost twenty-two thousand baptized members and a total of thirty-eight thousand believers. In Port-au-Prince, Fellowship House ministered primarily to business people and professionals of Haiti's upper class. Sunday morning worship, prayer and Bible study, along with warm fellowship, counseling and a radio broadcast made up the program. Alabanza Productions began in 1987 as a Christian music group that performed concerts and produced video and audio tapes. Theological Education by Extension reached into seventeen communities. Witness at the university level was hoped for, but depended on adequate personnel.

Besides schools provided by the churches, Good News Clubs, Vacation Bible Schools and Sunday schools carried the message of God's love to children. Translation of English-language curriculum materials and teacher manuals into French or Creole boosted these efforts.

In 1995, talks began with Mission Biblique, which had offices in France and Switzerland. The Europeans had already sent missionaries and project funding to Haiti, and both that society and UEBH drew up a covenant that would link the two organizations.

The Haitian churches began taking seriously their responsibility toward world evangelism. Jean Edner Jeanty, Jr., and his wife were sent by UEBH as missionaries to Africa. Like his father who had held key positions in Christian education in his homeland, the younger Jeanty went to Zaire to teach in the Bunia Theological Seminary. Four Haitian missionaries crossed over the mountains into the Dominican Republic. Six went to the impoverished northwest. Missions did appear important in the church's future.

Advances of Christ's Kingdom in Haiti seemingly came in spite of the horrendous conditions that gripped the nation. That 1994 was the most emotional, traumatic and suspenseful year in memory could scarcely be doubted. The country's infrastructure collapsed, crime spiraled, hunger spread. Danger stalked everywhere. Several Haitian pastors and lay leaders were forced to flee their homes because of the lawlessness in their areas. Some church members lost their lives. The foreign missionaries were asked to leave the country, which all but a small group of men did. Some families returned within six months, the rest in eight.

For a year and a half the nation struggled to survive under a punishing embargo that left cupboards bare, transport gravely interrupted and day-to-day life a mass of confusion. The likelihood of a bloody intervention by the international community frightened everyone. Even when the outside forces arrived without bloodshed, violence and persecution continued in the countryside, and in some areas mounted.

The sadness and despair that marks the history, especially the recent history of Haiti, were no obstacle to the life and growth of the church. With desperation all around them, many members, in fact, became more faithful in attending worship services and prayer meetings, and throughout the region unbelievers prayed to receive Jesus Christ as their Savior and Lord.

SOURCES, Chapter 21

Annual Reports, 1967, 1980, 1990, 1991, 1994, 1995, Bala-Cynwyd, Unevangelized Fields Mission, UFM International

Annual Report, UFM International, Haiti Field, 1995

Beerley, John, Letters to author, 1996

_____, Notes on early draft, 1996

Bitner, Robert, Letters to author, 1996

_____, Notes on early draft, 1996

Boggs, Boxley, notes on draft, 1996

Brown, Joy, Prayer Letter, 1951

_____, Letters to author, 1996

_____, Notes on early draft, 1996

Courier Evangélique, Le, February 1979; UEBH, Port-au-Prince, Haiti

Donor, Ethel, Paper, Beginnings at La Pointe, Undated

Fact Sheet, Collège Evangélique Maranatha (Haiti), Undated

Group interview by author, 1996, retired Haiti missionaries, Lancaster, PA

Haiti, Pearl of the Antilles, Undated, Script for slide presentation

Hawkins, Neill, Prayer letters, 1955 - 1981

Hill, Joseph, Letter to author, 1996

Larson, Alfred and Jean, Interview by author, 1995

Lifeline, 4th Quarter, 1958; 1st Quarter, 1966; 2nd Quarter, 1967; Summer, 1968; Fall, 1969; September, 1972;

Light & Life, Second Quarter, 1963

Pudney, Edwin and Lilian, Miracles Multiplied, Unpublished manuscript

Wilkinson, Richard, Audio tape, 1996

Wilson, Majil Odman, Letter to author, 1996

_____, Notes on early draft

22

"Work Yourself Out of a Job"

The church among the Dani people in Irian Jaya faced what new-born churches throughout history have faced — second-generation problems.

Like the Wai Wai in Amazonia — and the churches of Asia in the First Century — the children of Dani believers only heard about, but did not experience, the power of faith that delivered their parents from the tragedies of the old life. Inevitable contact with the outside world posed the question of how to balance the spiritual with the material. Which of the old customs should be kept and which changed or discarded in this new, more complex mode of living in every tribe and village?

At Mulia, the number of believers dropped from a probable ninety-five per cent of the population around the time of the fetish burnings to perhaps eighty some twenty years later. At one time decisions were made by group agreement; but as government and other influences penetrated the Dani mind, it became acceptable to dissent, and some did.

But a strength of conviction undergirded the massive display of Christian commitment. This became evident at the first gathering of tribal leaders from thirteen stations of four mission agencies three years after the initial turning of Dani to Christ. The men meeting there tackled basic questions relating to their new-found faith and pushed through until they found answers. By 1967, the Dani in UFM's area had completely abandoned demonism and warfare, formerly the two main elements of their way of life.

In that year, UFM counted thirty-five churches and thirty pastors, twenty-nine hundred baptized members and some twenty thousand adherents. Many thousands had learned to read and hundreds could write in their own language. Programs to improve the food supply and economy were many and varied.

The Witness Schools conveyed Biblical truths to new believers at a critical time in their development. One couple from each village learned Bible content during the week and on week ends went home to teach what they had learned to their fellow villagers. The favorite lesson was of Christ overcoming Satan and his temptations in the wilderness. The students also took to heart the building of the tabernacle by the Israelites.

"We can do that," one couple said. They went back home and led the Christians in constructing a house of worship.

Experience enriched ministry as occasional revivals deepened the dedication of leaders. The Dani became missionaries before they became an organized church. They had accompanied UFM missionaries to the Kimyal in the "T" or Naltja Valley and to other tribes and were seeing the fruit of their labor. There was no breakthrough in the Naltja, such as occurred among the Dani, but the Kimyal believers grew in number and spiritual depth. So did those among the Nggalum at Kiwi, who now had the New Testament and part of the Old in their language, and the Kentengmban. Good leadership was in large measure responsible for progressing churches. Dagai was one of the newer stations, Nabire another. The Terablu area, with several language groups, was yet another outreach. The churches of the Kimyal and Kentengmban were heavily involved.

In the 1980s and 1990s, all stations benefited from mission medicine. Immanuel Hospital at Mulia provided professional care for a region of one hundred thousand population. Mulia was a likely place for a hospital to develop. In its pre-Christian days, cretinism and goiters plagued the village. While the Mulians treated their retarded children with tenderness, outsiders shunned the village. With improved nutrition, medicine and better living conditions introduced by the missionaries, both problems cleared away. Mulia became the place to go when sickness struck.

The Indonesian government established schools in many areas. Mission programs were blended with them. Literacy increased. Sunday schools aided in the spiritual development of children, and classes were held for women and young people, though youth always needed more attention than they received.

Bible schools played important roles in fitting people to become pastors, evangelists and leaders in other fields. One school each served the Dani, Nggalum, Ketengmban and Kimyal. The Indonesian Bible and Vocational Training Center was set up as an inter-mission effort in Sentani, and besides its spiritual ministry helped move the once naked, stone-age people along toward the Indonesian culture. Missionaries and nationals alike learned to speak Indonesian.

In the 1990's, the mission emphasized church planting in the cities and rural lowlands on the coast. Congregations in the Sentani-Jayapura area were officially recognized by the Gereja Injili Di Indonesia, the Evangelical Church of Indonesia. Plans announced by the government alerted the field to coming changes. Over the next ten years five million Javanese families were to be relocated to Irian Jaya.

As the work in the valleys of Irian Jaya grew and matured, numerous tensions arose. Not all tensions are bad; not a few aid in the development of strength and endurance. Yet, all must be dealt with.

There was the tension of time. How many years ahead did UFM have in a land that, at best, tolerated Christian missionaries and increasingly made it harder for them to obtain visas? The field determined to make careful plans and to stick to priorities.

Theology. The national church did not always see issues quite like the missionaries. As one who observed such differences once wrote, "They approach theology from a position of sitting cross-legged around the fire, dressed in a gourd and grass skirt, stomach hurting due to infestation of worms, and reading only a portion of the truth of God, not the intellectual prosperous bastions of Western thought. In turn, we have a tendency to minimize their input and press on to do our own thing. Like flies to be waved off, they are an annoyance."

Complete translations of the Bible and greater literacy in the Word promised broader understanding and agreement. Patience would be required while spiritual children found themselves in the field of theology and in doctrinal issues.

Finance. Robert Bitner, once field leader in Haiti, raised an issue in *Light and Life* that missioners before and after him wrestled with, and which was pertinent to Irian Jaya. How far does the mission organization go in financially supporting nationals and their projects of church planting, education and community development? Should the mission put money into church buildings, schools, hiring of teachers, scholarships and support of pastors? This question has probably caused more rifts between missionaries and nationals than any other. UFM's position was that the use of money on any field should stimulate and build incentives for the church there and establish a secure base for the church's future rather than create a dependence on the foreign giver.

Economic Development. Often present was the Scriptural command to get involved with hurting brothers, not by bidding them to depart in peace and trust that somehow they'd be warmed and filled, but by sharing both in the suffering and in the alleviation of it. Yet, threatening also was the usurpation of priorities by economic projects that would steal from spiritual objectives. Turn to government or to other agencies for economic enhancement, or should the mission shoulder such responsibilities until the local church took over?

Leadership. In Irian Jaya, tribalism as well as nationalism had to be recognized. The former houseboys and gardeners had become the pastors and Bible school teachers and national church officers. They had stepped into the driver's seat. Wasn't that what the missionary force had been waiting for? Wasn't Edwin Pudney's dictum to "work yourself out of a job" happily becoming reality? The missionary's assertive tendencies, honed by necessity, and programs and practices that evolved over many years could hardly be put in a bottle and capped without a struggle with the ego. Yet, the present-day missionary had to work at doing just that, work hard at it, and attune himself to the fact that more and more he was the teacher, the demonstrator, the mentor, the discipler, the helper, the encourager. From pulling, someone once said, to pushing.

For the most part the tensions were approached by both missionaries and nationals with grace. Relations remained warm and good. Once in a while a key leader would be dropped from office for sin in his life, and this caused somewhat of a crisis in the church, pointing up the need for more qualified, spiritual men. Criticism sometimes came from some quarters because the mission did not do as much financially as hoped for. A few considered their national chairman too pliant in regard to the mission. But Ferdinand Ayomi stood straight and tall, a godly man and a recognized good pastor. Not without his weaknesses, he worked on those areas, and UFM did whatever possible to support him.

In 1984, UFM moved into Java, one of the most densely populated places in the world. One of sprawling Indonesia's thirteen thousand islands, Java contains Jakarta, the capital, and is the commercial heart of the nation. David and Julie Ray studied the language, then moved to Jogjakarta to teach at the Evangelical Theological Seminary of Indonesia and to work toward planting churches among the Javanese Muslims.

Their outreach profited from an invaluable partnership with a team of Christians from Irian Jaya who were the fruit of UFM's ministry among the Dani. Led by the Rev. Paul Tabuni, the team skillfully turned public curiosity about them into a testimony of Christ's power to transform.

Repeatedly, they would walk through an area that had resisted any Gospel witness and the villagers would notice their dark skin, holes through the septum of their noses and, in the leader's case, half of an ear cut off.

"Hey, you!" the people would call, "Are you from Irian?"

An affirmative answer brought great excitement, because the Javanese had seen the mysterious Irianese on television, but never in person. After all, Irian Jaya, while a part of their nation, lay three thousand miles to the east. The people of that land were greatly different from any they knew.

Inviting the Irianese into their homes, they would ask, "Is it true that you eat people in Irian?"

Their guests would answer, "Yes, it is true that we used to kill and make war and burn down houses with women and children inside, and we ate our victims right up until the missionaries came. Then we stopped all that immediately."

"You did? What difference did the coming of the missionaries make?"

The Irianese would then tell in detail how the Gospel's ability to transform lives had changed them, changed whole villages and even tribes. How strange! This was something the Javanese Muslims had never heard of.

Within six years, twelve congregations were started.

David Scovill, long-time field leader in Irian Jaya, and his wife Esther, who together had translated the Dani New Testament and taught thousands to read, moved to Java in 1987, focusing on church planting and government liaison work in Jakarta. Working with nationals as evangelists, they recorded nine new congregations in eight years in the Jakarta area and on the neighboring island of Sumatra. Week-end schools, like those among the Dani, reinforced believers. The scheduling left the students free to pursue their usual routines during the week.

Other missionaries joined the UFM family on Java, serving as teachers, translators, pastoral trainers and children's workers. One couple devoted themselves to the fourteen million Madurese who occupy the island east of Java. Another assembled teams to use the Javanese art form of *wayang*, or shadow puppetry, as a tool for evangelism. Called the Bible of Java, *wayang* was the means by which the Javanese learned spiritual values. Typically, every person identified himself with one or another of the puppetry's characters. *Wayang* was seen as an entrance to Javanese hearts.

The one issue through out Indonesia that appeared most intractable was that of missionaries obtaining visas. While not the only UFM field to have this problem, Indonesia presented the longest delays and most adamant refusals. Sometimes visas came through, and a missionary's worries were over for either a short or long term. But in contemplating future work in Irian Jaya, Java or one of the other islands, bi-professionalism appeared to be the key. Teaching, business, economic development, medicine, engineering —these professions would be most likely to be admitted. The holder of such a position then could, after hours and as a helper to a local church, minister in the way that God and the Indonesian Christians led him.

SOURCES, Chapter 22

Annual Reports, 1967, 1980, 1990, 1991, 1994, 1995, Bala-Cynwyd, Unevangelized Fields Mission, UFM International

Dillinger, Leon and Lorraine, *Experiences of Leon and Lorraine Dillinger in Dutch New Guinea / Irian Jaya,* Undated paper

Hively, James, 1996, Audio tapes

Larson, Alfred and Jean, Interview by author, 1995

Lifeline, 4th Quarter, 1958; 2nd Quarter, 4th Quarter, 1963; 1st Quarter, 1964; 2nd Quarter, 1967; Summer, 1968; Fall, 1969; September, 1972;

Light & Life, 4th Quarter, 1958; 2nd Quarter, 1963

Maynard, Ralph and Melba, 1996, Letter to author

Pudney, Edwin and Lilian, *Miracles Multiplied,* Unpublished manuscript

23

Limbo in Zaire

The reunion of twin brothers Assani Benedict and Bo Martin after the Simbas were largely cleared out of Congo brought immense joy. Assani had returned from Uganda, where he and his family happened to be during the rebels' murderous sweep of Northeast Congo. Bo returned from an executioner's kangaroo court.

The brothers had grown up in rather pleasant circumstances in the town of Banalia where they were free to tramp the forest and to learn in the village school. An old saintly believer led them both to accept Christ as Savior. As youths, they yielded their lives in service to God.

Happy days at the Bongondza Bible school were followed by productive years of traveling, preaching, exhorting around village campfires, organizing groups of believers into small churches, training preachers for outlying areas. The whole region where they labored heard the Gospel, and hundreds responded to it. A central church was established at Bopepe and a score of satellite churches sprang up.

Bopepe became a station of the UFM mission, with Mary Baker as the first resident missionary. Bopepe centered upon the church, built by the hands of the people. It was a Christian village, a peaceful, happy place with church, school and dispensary. The people took Mary Baker and Margaret Hayes, who had joined her, into their hearts. Then the Simbas came. The two women, one American, the other English, were marched away to Banalia. Bo walked voluntarily alongside them and in vain fought for their release. The people of Bopepe cried so desperately for their teacher and their nurse that the Simbas finally relented and permitted Margaret to go back to care for them. Mary, however, died with other prisoners at Banalia.

Bo returned to Bopepe. Hearing of the horrible massacre at Banalia and figuring that Bopepe would be next, he whisked Margaret off into the forest, built her a small leaf shelter. For a month she remained in hiding, receiving food and her Bible from loving friends who were careful to leave no trail to betray her to the enemy. But on learning that the Simbas had arrived in Bopepe and burned all the homes and killed two Christians, and that they threatened to kill a hundred more unless the white woman were found, Margaret made her way out of the jungle and surrendered.

Unlike those at Banalia, her life was spared, for how long she could only guess. At the moment, the Simbas needed her to nurse their sick and wounded. Bo, by this time also a fugitive, gave himself up. A mimic of a court sentenced him to die.

The day of his execution was set, then postponed, set again, postponed. This went on for a month, the vacillating actions always interspersed with beatings, threats and long, exhausting interrogations.

"Why did you shelter the white woman?" he was asked over and over.

"Because she is my sister in Christ, the child of my own Heavenly Father."

As they had done so many mornings before, the guards entered his cell once again. This time, instead of pushing him out with guns or spears to the river, where executions occurred, they took him by the arm and led him to the house where their commanding officer lived. There, the major treated his prisoner with civility. The previous night he had had, he said, a terrifying dream in which a voice told him that if he killed Pastor Bo he himself would die. He dropped to his knees and begged forgiveness. Bo spoke to him about God's forgiveness. The Simba leader wrote out a safe-conduct pass. This obtained Bo's release in the three times he was re-arrested. After Stanleyville was freed of rebel control, the reunion with his brother Assani took place.

In post-Simba Congo and into the period in which the country was renamed Zaire, both men were greatly used by the Lord to win souls. Assani reported that in a recent tour more than eight hundred believed and twenty backsliders were restored at Wanie Rukula, two hundred eleven believed at Ponthierville and in Kisangani, the former Stanleyville, four hundred forty-six accepted Christ.

But administration rather than evangelism began taking more of the attention and time of the church's top leader.

At home in England, Kinso asked prayer for Assani. "It would appear," he wrote to friends, "that his administrative duties are proving to be a heavy burden and are causing him to do things which the missionaries do not agree with, and this is causing friction."

A number of pastors and other church leaders did not agree with some of his decisions, either. But African culture prompted them to respect and obey those over them, and in pyramid fashion this went all the way to Assani at the top.

Much of the problem stemmed from the Zairian government ordering that all religions going by the name of Christian be grouped together in a single entity. To be included were Protestants, Catholics and Kimbanguists, the latter a national movement. The Protestant arm, the Church of Christ of Zaire (CCZ in English, ECZ in French) forged an alliance with the World Council of Churches. That made a problem for UFM and other missions which saw in the ecumenical factor a threat to Bible-centered theology.

To the consternation of missionaries and national believers, Assani became a district superintendent for the CCZ. They believed he was beginning to show a desire for power that was contrary to the work of a shepherd of the flock. The Evangelical Church of Christ in Upper Zaire, the association of local churches started by UFM, asked for delegations from the United States and Great Britain to come to Zaire to try to iron out some of the problems.

Kinso led the group from Britain and Al Larson from North America. A compromise was worked out that said UFM would submit to the government of Zaire by recognizing CCZ as the umbrella Protestant organization, but because of Bible-based convictions in the area of relationships, the church in Upper Zaire would not actively support the program of the government entity but participate only to the least amount the law allowed. The church in Upper Zaire would continue to demonstrate local autonomy by the church's faith and practice.

The statement was approved by all present, including Assani, and it was felt that the matter was settled. It was not. Assani was appointed a bishop in the CCZ and a good many in the local churches believed he was behaving more like a dictator than a shepherd and his actions were contrary to the wishes of a vast majority of the members. Tribal instinct, however, prevented rebellion.

Nevertheless, a few pastors objected to some of his dealings and for their dissent fell out of official favor. They believed their leader — to them, he was president of their association, not a bishop of the state organization — was pushing them into a debt that the church could not afford. No one thought that Assani enriched himself, though as a government-recognized leader he enjoyed a number of material perks. But it was Assani's way to spend money he did not have, to give money to any deserving person coming before him — money that was his own until it gave out, then money that was not his to give.

At times he admitted that the chief reason he had become so active in the CCZ was for the economic benefits that its tie to the World Council could bring. His churches, as he saw it, would reap new buildings, and pastors would enjoy decent salaries. He preferred not to discuss the likelihood that with the largesse would come persuasion to liberalize theology and possibly threats of benefit denials if persuasion failed.

As general director, Alfred Larson informed the UFM North American missionaries to Zaire that the Home Council on July 7, 1977, had ordered the withdrawal of the mission. The decision came after a meeting between Assani and mission officials in New York. To Larson, it seemed that in the meeting his group was trying to speak of spiritual matters while Assani was thinking politically and continually expressing a need for money.

Of four UFM couples and two single women, only one was in Zaire at the time. Donald Muchmore was sent to Zaire to express the Council's position. Larson made it clear that the Americans were not suggesting that their British brethren or other missions should follow UFM out of Zaire. But because there was no perception that the pressure for ecumenicity had lightened, the last of the British missionaries was gone a year later.

E. J. Pudney had laid the foundation for UFM's rejection of compromise in doctrinal issues and affiliations. Ralph Odman articulated the mission's position against yoking with unbelievers in his widely-noted monograph. It fell to Al Larson to apply principle to practice. There was trauma in withdrawing from a field that had been an original for the mission, where nineteen of its people had met a martyr's death, in pulling away from a work whose fruits could so readily be seen. It was especially difficult for Larson who, with Jean, had been on the scene for much of the church's growth and during the tragic Simba days.

The church in Upper Zaire chafed under Assani. A large segment came to the point where they wished to break away. But once again Assani was elected president of the region — because no one else wanted his position. Relationships within the church deteriorated. Masini, pastor of a large church in

Kisingani, became openly critical and he and Assani worked against each other, their ecclesiastical conflicts amplified by their being sons of different tribes. Several churches canceled their contributions to the association's treasury. Assani grew more adamant in imposing his will on the church. Yet, despite all the disturbing influences, the local churches continued to thrive.

After several years of anti-missionary, anti-West rhetoric, CCZ, the government-sponsored alliance, turned around and began calling for missionaries to return. To determine the wishes of their former colleagues, and if favorable to return, to set conditions under which the missions would operate, UFM International in 1989 sent Delbert Carper, who had been UFM's field leader when withdrawal came, and UFM Worldwide sent its beloved old Congo warhorse, Herbert Jenkinson — Kinso.

Willing parties all around worked to produce reconciliation. Because there had been no bad feelings at the time of withdrawal, the church and the missionaries were able to pick up their friendly relationship again. More difficult to repair was the breach within the church. But because no local congregation had pulled out — except Masini's in Kisingani — no back-tracking was necessary. Nor had there been deviations in doctrines — only Assani's haughty conduct and his eagerness for financial handouts seemed to comprise the differences. Assani now spoke with humility. That the golden eggs were never as numerous nor as lustrous as anticipated perhaps aided in lowering his attraction for world ecumenicity and helped him to abandon affiliation with the World Council. At the meeting of reconciliation in Kisingani all agreed to forget the past and, with eyes fixed on Jesus Christ, to go forward. It was good news that later was flashed from Zaire to Bala: "We are hearing good reports from Kisingani. Masini is working with Assani."

Despite new unity in the northeast, the Zaire of the future would be a troubled country. The improvements that held promise for easier living twenty-five years earlier were now scarcely found. Inflation rose to three thousand percent. When salaries went unpaid, school teachers had to raise their own food. Many children were kept from school for lack of tuition money. Family after family, having no cash, fell back to bartering to obtain their needs.

Still, the church progressed. No missionaries today as pastors. Only a few specialized roles awaited foreigners. From America, Mary Rutt returned for a literature ministry; Donald and Eleanor Muchmore to teach at the seminary moved from Banjwadi to Bunia and conducted jointly with the Africa Inland Mission; Herbert and Grace Harms, Del and Lois Carper and Bill and Coral Snyder to Kisingani for whatever they might be assigned to. Others, it was expected, would be dispatched when Zaire called for them. Two sons of the slain Hector McMillan were in training, as was the son of Robert McAllister, the father having stood next to Hector the day he was shot by Simbas.

While in some ways forced by circumstances, the indigenous principle worked in Zaire. More than one hundred thirty thousand persons had been won to Christ in the period of UFM's most prolific service, and from them arose the leaders and workers needed to sustain the church and to take it on to greater heights. In an otherwise unstable situation, the church in Northeast Congo had become, as the end of the millennium neared, the sturdiest element of society.

Except as a subject for prayer, Zaire remained in limbo for nearly half of Larson's tenure as UFM's director. That period, however, was crammed with the launching of new fields around the world. Mexico began in 1971; Italy, 1974; Germany, 1976; South Africa, 1979; Ireland, 1980; Sweden and Austria, 1984; Spain and the Philippines, 1985; Puerto Rico, 1986.

UFM's sixtieth anniversary and Larson's twenty-fifth year in the general director's office would converge in 1991. Two years before that date the call went out to the fields to nominate his successor. This conformed to the mission's rule to first search within for its leadership and to go outside only if no appropriate candidate could be found. The fields presented their choices and after extensive evaluations James Nesbitt, having served in France, was the unanimous choice as UFM's next director.

During the anniversary year, it was natural to look back to see from where UFM had come, and how much it had gone forward. The measurements came in many areas.

The number of missionaries grew from the original thirty-two in 1931, and only one of them from North America, to 384 on the fields from North America in 1993, with an additional eighteen short-termers. The high point occurred in 1990, with 415 individuals in active service. Total "family," which included home staff, appointees, retirees and those on leave of absence, reached 571 in 1990.

In candidates attending Orientation, the number increased from sixteen in 1966, Larson's first administrative year, to thirty-nine in 1991, with a high of forty-three in 1983 and a total of 731, and an annual average of twenty-eight.

Mission income rose from $96,794 as a total for the first ten years, to $9,983,658 in the single year of 1991, the larger amount recorded in 56,078 receipts.

Estimates of the number of believers varied, some reflecting only baptized church members, others including professions of faith without regard to baptism or formal church rolls. The range certainly was a quarter of a million and upward.

Dollars received and dollars spent, reports, statistics, averages, trends — these were one side of a mission. The purpose and intended practice of UFM in North America was stated clearly by Al Larson a few years into his leadership. Writing in *Lifeline* in the Summer of 1970, he said:

The imperative which Christ gave us after the resurrection was to *make disciples*. UFM accepts this command as a primary goal and seeks to follow the Biblical principle of the centrality of the local church. Whether this local church we are establishing is found in an urban center, a town, a jungle village, or in the midst of a primitive tribe, developing an effective thrust of evangelism is essential for its growth.

Recognizing the changing times and patterns of missionary service in today's world, it is our firm conviction that all programs for evangelism and church planting must flow from a solid doctrinal position. We accept the absolute message which Jesus Christ gave — "I am the way, the truth, and the life, no man cometh unto the Father but by me." We believe this is the message for this hour in history.

Changing times do not change our belief in the divine and verbal-plenary inspiration of the Scriptures. We continue to uphold the inerrancy and historical accuracy of the original writings as well as their infallibility for faith and practice.

Communicating this message is our challenge. It must be presented in the framework of the local culture of each country in which we serve, making it meaningful to the hearer. The churches which are being established throughout the world must be culturally oriented in expression of worship and music, for we recognize that a church is established, consolidated, and perpetuated in a society through its culture. Some organizations may use politics, trickery, suppression, or even violence to achieve their ideological and practical ends but the Church must communicate Christ and the deep truths of the Gospel simply by informing and persuading men, trusting God through the Holy Spirit to convict of sin and accomplish the work of regeneration in lives.

In our outreach we are not dealing with abstracts but with individuals (psychological aspect) who live in a given society (sociological aspect) and share a common way of life (cultural aspect).

God has outlined our program for reaching this world with the Gospel in Luke 4: 16 - 19 — the Word of God, through the man of God, blessed by the Spirit of God.

It was a statement that on his retirement in 1991 to take care of a risky heart condition but to continue to serve the mission through deputational representation, Larson did not have to change. Faithfulness to principle over long years was a characteristic of UFM.

SOURCES, Chapter 23

A *Congo Miracle*, Pamphlet, Undated, Bala-Cynwyd, Unevangelized Fields Mission

Annual Reports, 1967, 1980, 1990, 1991, 1994, 1995, Bala-Cynwyd, Unevangelized Fields Mission, UFM International

Jenkinson, Herbert, Prayer Letters, 1995 - 1988

_____, Trip Diary, 1968-69

Larson, Alfred and Jean, Interview by author, 1995

Lifeline, 2nd Quarter, 1967; Summer, 1968; Fall, 1969; September, 1972; December, 1995; June, 1996

Morris, Edward, Report on Kisangani Trip, 1989

Pudney, Edwin and Lilian, *Miracles Multiplied*, Unpublished manuscript

24

Decades of Growth

The 1970s and 1980s were decades of growth for UFM International, particularly in the opening of new fields. The mission's mandate was to present Christ to the *unevangelized* and nurture new converts through churches and schools until they were able to stand alone. Much of the world had yet to hear the Gospel. Openings in Europe, Africa, the Western Hemisphere and Asia would give additional tens of thousands the opportunity to believe.

In Mexico, UFM's presence dated from 1971, though the work it received from the Mexican Indian Mission began in 1930. As on some other fields, the small pioneering mission was unable to build a strong home base of support, so its good work was preserved by merging with UFM.

Dr. James Dale and his wife Katherine went to Mexico in 1899. Except for the time of the violent Mexican revolution, they ministered for thirty years in Rio Verde and Tampico. About 1927, an Aztec Indian, Martin Mendoza, found his way to the Dales' home and asked to be instructed in the Bible. For two years he studied with Dale, then went home to Tamazunchale to teach his people. The response was overwhelming, so he begged the Dales to come and help him. The mission they represented was feeling the financial squeeze of the Great Depression, so could not expand into Indian work.

With the mission's approval, the Dales resigned, moved to Aztec country and with absolute dependence on God, began ministering to the Indians, Katherine, who was a physician, devoting herself to the medical needs of the people, and James establishing a Bible school for them. Two years later, their son, John T. Dale, founded the Mexican Indian Mission. He became known for his mastery of the Aztec language and the Bible training he gave to Indians.

The Dales, parents and son, were deeply concerned lest any church begun in Mexico be seen as a building or an organization; rather, it should be regarded as part of the Body of Christ. They gave careful consideration to the culture of the people. They began by meeting in the home of a believer or of a person willing to listen to the Gospel. As the group grew, a larger home was needed. Eventually, from the believers came the idea of a church building to house the growing congregation.

Within the first twenty-five years, more than a hundred centers were established with buildings occupied and the work supported solely by the believers themselves. Each group was autonomous, with elders to govern and teach. Each local church enjoyed fellowship with other churches. The churches multiplied. In 1946 the Association of Evangelical Mexican Churches was founded. After UFM entered the work, completely in accord with the Dales' principles, the missionaries came under the association, which was governed by an executive committee of Mexican believers.

The ministry spread over the years to seven areas, stretching from San Luis Potosi north of Mexico City to Oaxaca southeast of the capital. Much of the work centered on the Indians, but the Spanish-speaking Mexican was also included. Evangelism and church planting, Bible teaching, children's work, literature and literacy training, health and agronomy constituted the assignments of twenty missionaries and scores of national workers in 1994. Indians were among the millions who migrated to Mexico City to make it the largest urban complex in

the world. UFM also went to Mexico City and other burgeoning urban centers, specifically to minister to the transplanted
Totonac and Aztec and members or descendants of other ancient tribes.

While yet serving in France, James Nesbitt surveyed Italy
for a possible role for UFM. He was a natural choice for the
task, since he not only spoke French and German, but was studying Italian as well. He discovered that the strategic northern
city of Milan had no evangelical mission. With a population of
one and a half million, Milan in itself constituted a likely field.

The evangelization of Milan began in 1974 under direction
of Ray and Lois Whitlock, college classmates of the Larsons
and missionaries with twenty years of experience in central Italy.
With the help of a summer team of young people, they distributed forty thousand tracts the first year. From this effort developed three Bible study groups. Bible studies led to home visitations and children's classes, and later came contacts with university students, literature distribution and church planting.

Ronald and Rosa Fisher, who felt a great burden for Italy,
moved from France to Milan to assist the Whitlocks. The missionary force grew with the arrival of William and Deborah
Peach, Al and Billie Nucciarone and Sam and Joan Fiore. This
expansion enabled the development of study groups into
churches and the launching of a Christian FM radio station.

By 1991, the team numbered ten couples and two single
women, all of them engaged in evangelism and church planting. A half-dozen zones, strategically spaced around the city,
were targeted for churches. For the most part, the seed fell in
good ground and the planting succeeded. One ministry had a
dual fellowship — Italian and Arab. Another served the substantial English-speaking community; although its congregation
was made up largely of transients, attendance stabilized at around
eighty. Emphasis on youth, market-square literature distribu-

tion, one-on-one discipling, the dramatic presentations of mimes and puppeteers, concerts, Bible studies tailored to women, men and children, evangelistic campaigns — all were on the agendas of the churches. Reaching beyond Milan, a fellowship was formed in Bergamo, the center of a region having a population of one million.

The movement in all the UFM-originated churches was toward full Italian leadership. The churches affiliated with the Brethren, a group with which UFM found it comfortable to associate.

As Ernst Maier studied theology at Grace Seminary in Indiana, he and his wife Ilse became convinced that the greatest need of their native Germany was for Bible-believing churches. Skeptics told them to forget it. Plant an evangelical church in Germany? An impossible dream!

Less than ten years later, a church the Maiers started in Germany claimed sixteen members — minuscule, perhaps, but an embryo that would grow, and by the same process more would be produced.

Settling in the Bavarian city of Pfullingen in 1976, the couple bought a building and renovated it for living quarters for themselves and their three sons, and for an office, a print shop and a meeting room. They invited people they met to what they called an Evening Bible Institute. In four years three men completed the study cycle, and attendance at the sessions grew to about twenty-five. Clubs for boys and girls reached a few children, but also served as a contact with parents. Attendance at women's meetings was irregular. Decisions for salvation were slow in coming. But the Bible-believing church — it was in place.

Eric and Terri Stricker arrived to help the Maiers. They were sent to the larger city of Reutlingen. With the small but steadily growing church in Pfullingen a reality, the missionaries concentrated on starting a second church, this one in Reutlingen. Tract distribution, open-air evangelism and another Evening Bible Institute proved productive, and their method was to work hand-in-hand with German believers. In three years the church begun there had tripled in size.

Ernst Maier was a persuasive as well as a prolific writer. His booklets on Biblical subjects aided in the teaching done by other churches besides their own. He published an evangelistic magazine. He led German pastors to form an association promoting new churches nationwide. Every fall, the association sponsored a three-day seminar on church planting, and produced a quarterly journal that became a major tool to influence more than one hundred German Christians to serve on church-planting teams.

Ilse assisted Ernst in the translation of American Sunday school material into German. There was great demand throughout the country for the literature. The couple conducted tent campaigns and introduced church-family retreats as a Summer activity aimed at fellowship and unity of believers. More missionaries joined the team — Karl and Donna Faehling, Jonas and Sadie Stoltzfus, Terry and Ellen Miller and Susan Barrett among them. The Millers opened work in Augsburg, the Faehlings in Cologne, Karl's birthplace. Shortly after West Germany and East Germany were united, Harvey and Selma Boldt moved to Cottbus to minister in this former Communist community. Jonas and Sadie Stoltzful made plans to start a church in Leipzig, an important city in the former East Germany. The possibilities were ample; most East Germans professed to be atheists.

The tools used in missionary work in Germany were universal. Karl Faehling advertised his Bible study group in a Cologne newspaper. But that wasn't the tool, only the means to take a tool off the workbench and make use of it. Interest in people, love, the sharing of hope — these became the instruments to win a distraught new widow to the Lord. She answered his ad, came around to talk, poured out her life as he listened.

Emmy's husband had died, and she still was angry for the coldness with which the hospital staff and doctors had treated her. The priest, too, was indifferent, telling her, "After all, it's all over, he's dead." There was nothing he could do, nothing he could say to ease her pain.

Her four grown children forsook her. The woman felt she had nothing left, and so decided to take her life. That is when she read the ad about the Bible study. What hope, she asked, could the Bible give? The Faehlings shared with her the life and hope that is in Jesus Christ. She came to the study week after week, asking questions and receiving answers. After four weeks, she gave her heart to Christ, and then was baptized and became a member of the church in Cologne. Her fear and anger and mourning gave way to an inner peace and outward joy. She continued to have problems, but she knew she was loved. Her emptiness was filled.

The old Emmy, Faehling related, was a picture of Germany. Almost half the Germans did not believe in the existence of God and more than ninety per cent rejected the Bible as the Word of God, so how could they be expected to taste the fruit of God's spirit? More than eighty percent remained beyond the current reach of the Gospel. *Unevangelized* — the mandate applied to this intellectual and economic power of Europe.

The dynamic leader of the German field was called home to Heaven in 1994. The men Ernst Maier had taught carried on his work, as did Ilse and their son Andreas and his family. Susan Barrett moved into the print shop to continue that important aspect of the witness. Walter and Pat Stuart, former field leaders in France, began the International Family and Church Growth Institute. Its aim was to train German and French leaders in the skills of Bible-based counseling.

In 1983 UFM sent its first missionaries to serve on the staff of the Black Forest Academy, a school for the children of missionaries. Among those since have been a chaplain, teachers and houseparents.

UFM entered South Africa when it was politic to shun that nation, to boycott it in every sphere, whether business investment, sports, cultural interests, diplomacy or social intercourse. Against such a backdrop, and knowing that violence, turmoil and hatred were rampant, UFM went to South Africa. It went because it recognized that people there needed Christ and that only the application of Biblical principles to the problems would bring long-lasting peace and heart-felt acceptance of one person by another.

The first task facing Ray and Millie van Pletsen when they arrived in the Transvaal in 1979 was to determine what specific needs existed, geographically and according to people groups. A significant amount of Christian work was being done in the rural black communities. The newer white neighborhoods around the cities were almost devoid of churches. The high cost of gasoline inhibited even once-faithful members from traveling to their old churches, many of which had turned liberal. Some denominational effort was waged in the new areas, but little accomplishment appeared, and this at a time when there was a receptive mood toward "religion" and Bible study.

The van Pletsens began the Weltevreden Chapel in a Johannesburg suburb their first year. It started as a home Bible study, with attendees finding the Lord almost every week. Four years later the chapel moved to its own five-acre property.

John and Christine French succeeded the original couple at Weltevreden, but by 1991 the chapel had called its own pastor and part-time youth leader, and was thoroughly South African in every respect. The church offered a full range of ministries, and in its missions program supported three families in Christian service and another five in Bible college and seminary preparation.

A second church was started in 1985, at Midrand, which

sat directly between Pretoria, the national capital, and Johannesburg. Gordon and Beth Gregory joined the Frenches in Midrand, and together they found in the country's fastest growing area great opportunities for the Gospel. Located there were a cross-section of South African society, culture and language groups and a new campus of the University of South Africa.

Donald Orr relinquished his work in France to younger people and went home to Ireland. Supposedly retired, he did not cease, however, to labor for the Lord. He earnestly petitioned UFM to include his native Emerald Island in its fields of ministry.

At about the same time, Ernest and Nancy Tromsness indicated in Candidate Orientation that they longed to take the Gospel to Ireland, perhaps recalling St. Patrick's missionary endeavors that transformed Ireland and equipped it to give the light of Christian faith to spiritually darkened Europe. Physically, the land lies under cloudy skies for long periods, with the sun breaking through now and then to throw its beams over the cool green fields. For centuries since Patrick, spiritual darkness has hovered as well, and the breakthroughs have been few.

UFM sent Jim Nesbitt, who was then European administrator, William Sifft, chairman of UFM's Canadian board, John Beerley, associate director for Europe, and Tromsness to check out the possibilities for service. As a result, Ernie and Nancy were dispatched to Cork. There they worked with the pastor of the Baptist church, the Rev. Ted Kelly, who did much to orient and encourage the new missionaries and get the work off the ground.

In time, the Republic of Ireland became a UFM field. Besides Cork, places with a familiar ring to their names, such as Ballincollig, Limerick and Douglas, responded to the efforts of the expanded mission team. Two churches were born and grew in good health. Another neared a start. The team assisted national Christians in camping for youth. Various ones taught the Bible through adult education in the public schools. Other ministries centered on children's work, outreach to university students, contacts with young adults and open-air and door-to-door evangelism.

Not everyone in this predominately Catholic country appreciated Protestant missionaries and their message. Preaching and individual witnessing took place in front of pubs and in the parks. Sometimes eggs and tomatoes flew through the air, often as not finding their mark. Opposition was expected and expectations were generously fulfilled.

The adult school Bible classes stimulated some participants to delve deeper in the Word of God through small-group studies. Some members of these home circles invited friends and family to study with them. A few of these then began meeting for Sunday morning worship services. By this process the churches came into being. Essential to the means was the continual building of personal relationships. Knocking on doors, inviting neighbors in to dinner, taking time to sympathize with the grieving — there seemed to be no limit to the way it could be done.

Sweden was not yet an official field of UFM, though the mission's two representatives to Scandinavia worked as intensively as if it were. Ten missionaries were required to constitute a field; John and Kris Voss looked around at what in their time in Sweden they had been able to accomplish and compared it to what remained. They concluded the land they served needed to be a field, needed ten missionaries, or perhaps twenty, or forty.

On entering in 1984, they found Sweden a difficult country to penetrate, both with the Gospel and with any Biblical concept of independent, or non-State, church life. The spiritual, social and moral condition of Swedish society, in their view, raised a natural antipathy to Biblical standards of worship and life. They accepted the secular climate as a challenge.

UFM's entry into Sweden came under the auspices of the Uppsala Biblical Theological Seminary. An independent, graduate-level school, it trained Swedish men and women for effective ministry, aiming to equip them theologically and to actively involve them in planting local churches. Cooperating in this vision was Fishers of Men, an independent Swedish church-planting organization.

In Gothenburg, location of the seminary, the Vosses worked both in the school and in the community. John taught at the seminary and the Christian Counseling Center, and through the church that he and Kris attended discipled those they hoped would be future church leaders. He also helped in the founding of a new church. He traveled on teaching missions from Norway to Romania, while Kris taught in a local Christian school. Together, they led a lively young people's group and conducted marriage seminars and other types of workshops.

Jim Beerley, an MK from Haiti, and his wife Mary went to another land where God seemed safely hidden away on a shelf. Monte Carlo, the Mediterranean playground of princes and other beautiful people, permitted one English-language Protestant church, and it was to this church that the Beerleys were called. Not having a building of their own, but borrowing time from a French congregation, the evangelicals met on Sundays at an hour the sanctuary became available. Much of the population was transient, so leadership in the church was difficult to sustain. But as pastor, Jim Beerley knew he had the privilege, as well as the responsibility, of preaching Christ to eighty or so persons who in several months might be scattered throughout the world. Who could predict the end of the chain of succession that began in the little glittering, but spiritually jaded, jewel on the Riviera?

Austria became another European thrust in 1984. Tied in with the Vienna Christian School, the effort there spawned Grace Church, which Andrew and Cheryl White worked to produce and which came under the pastorate of Al and Billie Nucciarone, who helped pioneer UFM's church planting in Italy. Other UFM personnel served from time to time on the faculty and staff of the Christian school.

The Apostle Paul intended to visit Spain. It is not known whether he carried out his plan, but no known vestige of such a contact exists. The Moors, however, crossed into Spain from North Africa in 711 and conquered the land in the name of Allah. Not until 1492 were the Muslims driven out, though the imprint of Islam is still on southern Spain.

At the time that the Reformation brought a resurgence of personal faith to much of Europe, the Inquisition instead gripped Spain, and for hundreds of years no faith but Catholicism was permitted. Following the bloody civil war that devastated the country from 1936 to 1939, the fascist Francisco Franco became firmly entrenched. For almost forty years his iron rule strongly opposed any but the recognized church. It was not until after his death in 1975 that religious freedom appeared; evangelicals gained full equality in 1992. Less than one per cent of the population claimed to be evangelical — but the door indeed was open.

In the Summer of 1977, *Decision* magazine and the Pocket Testament League sponsored a series of Christian films in the southern coastal town of San Pedro. This produced a tiny band of believers who were placed under the care of a small independent church in Malaga. In 1979, the Rev. Robert Peabody, a nineteen-year veteran of mission work in Morocco, started a Sunday ministry in San Pedro. Believers from two neighboring cities, Estepona and Marbella, joined this fellowship.

In preparing for retirement, Peabody asked UFM to carry

on with the believers. Ronald Fisher, who was now the mission's European administrator, surveyed the potential, then requested a couple of missionaries experienced in other fields to give their assessment. They expressed an eagerness to reach out to the southern coastal region, an area experiencing population growth. Moises Mariscal was a Mexican who, after becoming a Christian, attended seminary in Guatamala. Returning to Mexico, he pastored the UFM-related church in Puebla. There he met Maria, who ministered to the country's Indians. After they were married, they moved to Washington, D. C. While attending Capital Seminary, he led a Spanish-speaking church in the Washington area. They prayed about the future and felt called to Spain.

Maria was from Boston, of Portuguese ancestry. She entered missionary service by working among the Indians of Brazil, then represented UFM on American college campuses. Her next assignment was Mexico. And then with her husband to Spain.

They built up the little group of believers in San Pedro and, turning the work over to newcomers, entered the larger city of Almeria. There they launched a Sunday morning worship service, which was attended by middle-class residents. In Marbella, Curtis and Donna Edwards began Hospitality House, a center where Muslims who migrated from North Africa received special attention. Features of the house included a multi-lingual Christian bookstore, audio tape and book lending library, counseling, short-term lodging, second-hand clothing and cultural programs.

Moises Mariscal also helped the Fellowship of Independent Churches with a correspondence school ministry.

The Association of Bible Churches of the Philippines invited UFM into that Pacific country in 1985. For three years the mission's two families lived under aegis of SEND, an American faith mission that was begun by former World War II servicemen who had served in the Philippines and Japan. One of the UFM families was employed in church planting, the other taught missionary children at Faith Academy in Manila. The more extensive work which UFM was to assume started earlier by one-time classmates of Liberty University. Glenn Kurka and James O'Neill had surveyed the Philippines in 1978 and determined that Bohol was a place to begin a Gospel witness. Bohol is one of the larger of the Visayan group of islands that make up the central portion of the Philippines. It has a population of about a million people, most of them scattered in fifty-two major towns, with over twenty-five thousand population each, and more than a thousand barrio villages.

In 1980 Kurka led a Summer team of Liberty students in evangelism on Bohol, and that same year Kurka and O'Neill set up the International Asian Mission. In 1981 Glenn and his wife Sandy moved to Tagbilaran, the capital of Bohol and began IAM's work, organizing the Calvary Baptist Church the next year with about forty adults as members. Jim and Sterling O'Neill and Paul Halsey, the third ex-classmate, and his wife Kimberly joined them.

Another team of Liberty University students assisted in evangelistic meetings in sixteen towns that Summer, and from the group came other full-time missionaries. Typhoon Nitang hit the island in 1984, and the resulting relief work carried out by IAM resulted in the beginning of two new churches.

Churches were born in other towns on the island, and it became necessary to open a school to train leadership for them. The International Asian Mission Discipleship Seminary held its first classes in August of 1986.

A merger proposal by the International Asian Mission in 1987 was accepted by UFM, and the two were joined in April of 1988. This opened a well-defined field of service and ministry for UFM and a solid administrative and financial structure for IAM. It was now up to UFM to continue plowing the field and to plant the seed of the Gospel.

As in UFM's other fields, Bible studies became the root of church planting. Developing relationships was the life-sustaining fluid. John and Rachael Sherwood discovered that a small loaf of banana bread, given in friendship, opened doors for them. They delivered this home-baked gift to a number of new acquaintances one Christmas, among them the mayor of Tagbilaran. In return, he invited the couple to his party that evening at the local cultural center. They attended, and of the five hundred guests present, they were the ones the mayor escorted to the head table where they shared roast pig, fish, shish-ka-bob and chicken. What quicker means to be introduced to the movers and shakers of the town?

Jim O'Neill taught Bible prophecy to employees of a successful business in the city. A month later Iraq invaded Kuwait, and the impact panicked the economy of the Philippines. O'Neill was bombarded with questions by shaken Filipino friends. Were these the end times? Was Saddam Hussein the Antichrist? Was Christ ready to return? What will happen to us?

The owners of the business asked Jim to teach the Bible to a group of professional friends. For months Jim had sought an opening to this group. Now the doors opened overnight. After six months, perhaps half of the fifteen regulars at the Bible study became believers.

"I am convinced," said O'Neill, "that it is possible to reach Heaven through Iraq!"

Bible study and the Lord's timing. Who could tell how far that combination might go?

By the mid 1990s churches had been started and were beginning to grow in four cities. Calvary Baptist Church of Tagbilaran, the provincial capital, the oldest and largest of the four, targeted three nearby villages for evangelism. Another effort was aimed at professionals in Tagbilaran, with good prospects that some day there would be a church among the educated leadership of the island. Cebu City, second to Manila as the nation's largest urban center, came within the sights of those planning for the future. To gain a beachhead on this important island, which lay next to Bohol, would be a major step toward winning the central Philippines for Christ.

Children's Bible classes, pastoral training, discipleship, music and sports were utilized to advance church planting and maturing of young congregations. The Bohol Wisdom School provided an opportunity to teach Bible in a private school for the children of professional families. The Institute of Missions and Discipleship in the Philippines, the new name for the former seminary, offered four years of training for future pastors and other Christian workers. A majority of the governing board were Filipinos and the goal of sixty per cent of operating costs coming from national supporters has nearly been met.

Income-generating projects were instituted in 1989 to assist pastors and their parishioners in meeting their family financial needs. A part of this program was a pilot farm demonstrating how agriculture can be adapted to sloping land.

The name of the former board, International Asian Mission, was kept and applied to the missionary endeavor of the local churches. Four men were assisted financially in their ministries, and it was hoped that a fishing boat project and a rice field would produce income to support these and others.

As on several UFM fields, the short-term workers and summer interns on Bohol extended the reach of career missionaries. Much of what they did was evangelistic in nature, including vacation Bible schools for children. Some groups of young people attracted the youth of the country through sports clinics and were able to share with them their love for God. Others utilized drama and mime to get their message across. It was not unusual for short-termers or summer interns to be more affected by their service overseas than the people to whom they went to minister. The experiences of some of these volunteers led to their becoming life-time missionaries, with UFM or some other mission society.

Differing from all other UFM fields, Puerto Rico came into being to serve the United States military. The Safe Harbor Christian Servicemen's Center was founded to evangelize and disciple men and women at the Roosevelt Roads Naval Base at the east end of the U. S. commonwealth in the Caribbean Sea. The work was begun by Donald and Brigette Farley who brought the center with them when they joined UFM in 1986. Several couples and a few single missionaries manned the center, a number of them for two-year terms. Navy personnel made up the board of directors of the center.

Ministries varied from time to time, but included hospitality, Bible studies, personal witnessing, literature distribution, children's Bible classes and a Friday meal and worship service at the center. More than six hundred men and women passed through Safe Harbor in a year. In addition to those professing faith in Christ, numerous service people recommitted their lives to the Lord, some going on to full-time Christian service.

When Alfred Larson retired as general director in May of 1991, UFM International occupied twenty fields on five continents and in the Caribbean, besides work with Haitian refugees in eastern United States. His successor, UFM's fourth director, assumed office in July of that year. James H. Nesbitt continued the outreach to more unevangelized countries and cultures, with the emphasis still on church planting.

Dr. Nesbitt and his wife Nancy joined UFM in 1964. Assigned first to Ambérieu in France, they spent their second term starting a church in Valence. He became field leader for France and later European administrator, helping initiate UFM's new ministries in Italy, Germany and Ireland. The Nesbitts returned to the United States in 1981, he to direct the modern languages department of Grace College at Winona Lake, Indiana. At the same time, he served as Midwest representative for UFM.

He came by his two doctorates (Th.D. and D.M.L.) with a solid and extensive education, receiving degrees from Princeton University, the University of Paris, Grace and Dallas Theological Seminaries and Middlebury College. Nancy Nesbitt held a nursing degree.

Already familiar with most of the fields and attuned to areas yet with limited or no witness, Nesbitt lost no time in moving eastward in Europe as the Soviet empire crumbled, releasing its people and the millions in satellite nations from two generations of communist despotism.

Romania, the two parts of the former Czechoslovakia and Russia itself became the target nations.

Prior to the 1989 revolution, missionaries in Western Europe made occasional teaching treks into Romania, usually clandestinely. They used only first names for themselves so if a believer were questioned by the authorities he could truthfully say he knew only a "Dan" or "Grig" and had no other information about him. After the overthrow of Nicolae Ceausescu, UFM missionaries in Western Europe took short trips into Romania for evangelism or teaching and for "surveying the land." The mission then appointed Americans Karl and Jo Ann Kosobucki and a Romanian couple, Constantin and Elena Alexandrescu, as its first team there.

The Alexandrescus had left their country in 1991 to attend Dallas Theological Seminary. Constantin often prayed for a Bible school to be opened in the city of Iasi, where they lived before moving to the United States. He and Elena and the Kosobuckis went to Romania in 1993 to help begin the Bethlehem Bible Training Center. More than fifty students enrolled the first year.

Besides teaching at the Bible school, Constantin taught

English at the Iasi Institute of Agronomy. Elena was a speech therapist for children. Her day was hardly over when she left her job; she had a ministry of encouragement and counsel to the Christian women of Iasi and an evangelistic outreach to neighbors and friends, including hospitality to their many visitors. Constantin was always an evangelist at heart, preaching on Sundays and reaching out to give God's Good News to any who would receive it. He nurtured friendships with students and faculty at the university and brought some into Bible studies. Iasi lies in the northeast corner of Romania near the Republic of Moldova, another breakaway from the former Soviet Union. He made frequent trips to Moldova to encourage Christians and to evangelize, particularly the Jews, guiding a number of them in their turning to Jesus Christ as their Messiah and personal savior.

Before the revolution, the Alexandrescus worshipped in nonregistered house churches. Baptisms took place in a household bathtub. When the old regime was toppled and openness replaced it, baptisms took place as a public witness.

Language study and search for Christian partners preceded ministry in Slovakia, and limited amounts of preaching and evangelizing were done. In the Czech Republic, UFM provided a teacher of Hebrew and Old Testament theology for the Prague Bible School.

In Russia, UFM missionaries were both students and teachers, mixing Russian language study with the teaching of English. Surveys indicated Izhevsk, about six hundred miles east of Moscow, and cities of the Volga River basin would be fruitful places to begin church planting. Sam and Karen Puckett, who previously served in Mexico, relied on friendships to open doors to the lives of their students at the Russian Christian Professional Institute in Izhevsk. That relationships could be fluctuating, the Pucketts soon found out. Friendships could move in a few short weeks from cool indifference on the part of the Russian to an intensity that demanded almost more than the missionary could give. But it was in personal friendships that hope for their ministry resided.

Like the mercurial relationships between individuals, the uncertainty of the future had to be dealt with in any ministry in Eastern Europe. Political situations were clouded, particularly in Russia. How long before apathy and resistance set in was a concern. Another apprehension loomed large as reactionary forces gathered strength. How long would the door remain open to the Gospel?

SOURCES, Chapter 24

Annual Reports, 1967, 1980, 1990, 1991, 1994, 1995, Bala-Cynwyd, Unevangelized Fields Mission, UFM International

Banquet Brochure, 60th Anniversary, 1991, Bala-Cynwyd, Unevangelized Fields Mission

Beerley, John, 1996, Letter to author

Fisher, Ronald, 1996, Letter to author

Joseph, Charlene, 1996, Letter to author

Halsey, Paul C., 1996, Letter to author

Kosobucki, Karl, 1996, Letter to author

Larson, Alfred and Jean, 1996, Interview by author

Lifeline, February, 1981; April, 1991; September, 1995; December, 1995; March, 1996; June, 1996

Nesbitt, James H., 1996, Notes on draft

Scovill, David, A Very Brief History of UFM Java, Undated paper

Stoltzfus, Jonas, History of UFM Germany, Undated paper

25

After the Modern World

The old beech tree on the grounds at Bala-Cynwyd had stood since Colonial days. Beeches grow to be very large, and this one was said to be the largest in Pennsylvania. For forty years its immense shade sheltered missionary candidates and returning missionary families as they held their picnics under it, and children climbed among the branches and built forts in them and from the sturdy limbs swung to their heart's content.

But even the durable grow old. Weaker each year, the huge tree was no match for the unkind storms that teased and whipped it and the contrary summer heat and winter freezes that tortured it, and possibly the suburban pollution that cut off its breathing. Branches fell. Cracks widened. Warnings to keep out from under had to be issued. At Christmas of 1995 the old tree was brought down. It fell, but certainly not without a chuckle at the puny saws, the longest anyone could find, that sliced only part way through its hulking trunk. Picks, axes, ropes, wedges, chain saws — a logger's complete arsenal — were pressed into use to slay the giant.

Easy to look back with nostalgia and yearn for the old beech. But it was gone forever. Its death inevitable, some benefit issued from its decease. Its legacy was a mountain of magnificent hardwood, the broadest and best fit for a cabinet maker's use, the scraps good for warming many a room. The sun now flooded an area that for three centuries had been dark. And, favoring the many who crossed and recrossed the UFM campus each day, the danger of a calamitous fall was past.

As if an old friend were buried and life was to go on, the mission turned to refitting its grounds and buildings at Bala-Cynwyd for efficient service in the twenty-first century.

For almost two years, the UFM Board of Directors had examined the mission's long-term growth potential and what consequences that would have for headquarters. Other missions had abandoned their historic headquarters for new sites; UFM looked into this possibility. It was decided, in the end, that while growth for the mission was most definitely contemplated in the next ten years, the present facilities would do for the next five, though alterations and upgrading would be needed for current use and for any eventual sale of the property.

With more than five hundred missionaries working in twenty countries or retired, demands on the home staff increased year by year. Financial accountability — annually handling 60,000 receipts an example of one operation — required an efficient accounting department, and its people and their equipment had to have space. Room was needed for those who communicated prayer requests to constituents and encouragement to missionaries. More personnel were added to meet the requirements of governments for immigration and tax laws, and to conform to new regulations regarding international, non-profit, mission organizations. Visas, passports, travel documents, shipping invoices and multitudinous other papers flowed through the offices every day. All this meant people at work in the offices, and to house them one-time homes on the campus were turned into work places.

The old days when the beech lived were fine. So it was in the pioneering days of the mission. Adventurous, self-reliant trail-blazers were necessary for the opening of physically and spiritually dark areas of the world to the Gospel. It was essential for Kinso to walk into the heart of Africa, for Ernest Wootten to penetrate the ominous Amazon jungle on foot, for Hans Veldhuis to trek over the mountains and through the deep valleys of Dutch New Guinea. The original missionaries who broke away from a situation they could no longer support and formed UFM as a new mission exhibited courage and faithfulness to their calling. The three Freds, the Congo martyrs, Fenton Hall, Ron Combs, Donadene Dawson, Fernand Albert, Neill Hawkins, John Schmid, Ralph Odman and others who died in service and the hundreds who suffered disease and privation provided models for their contemporaries or for those who came after them.

Fenton Hall inspired Fred Dawson and helped propel him to Brazil. Fred Dawson, Fred Wright and Fred Roberts became heroes to a younger generation, and it can only be imagined how many became missionaries because of the willingness of these three to pay out their lives for the Gospel. Among them was Neill Hawkins, who influenced Ralph Odman's decision to join UFM, and in his relatively short life Ralph recruited a number who still serve on one field or another. Edwin and Lilian Pudney and George Thomas drew many by life and witness into the mission family. Sons and daughters of UFM missionaries followed in the footsteps of their parents, often serving on the field where they grew up, sometimes striking out to open a new area.

The old inspired the young. And the older and younger alike equipped new generations to carry on the work, particularly among the nationals.

UFM International shared many traits with fellow members of the Interdenominational Foreign Mission Association: Conservative in its theology, administration and financial practices (of each dollar sent by supporters for a missionary, ninety-four cents went overseas or into the missionary's personal benefits), centered around the importance of the family, seeking to be innovative in its policies, given much to prayer, dedicated to winning people to Christ. In assessing the distinctions of UFM, General Director James Nesbitt placed above all others the discipleship it had practiced.

"UFM has always been characterized by the importance it places on good Biblical and theological training," he once wrote. "Many who come to UFM are drawn to the organization because of its conservative stance and its emphasis on theology. Conservative evangelical theology is important to UFM because its leadership has always understood that the training of disciples and the building of church leadership must be established on foundational Christian truth. This requires good study and training in recognized conservative institutions."

Discipling led to indigenous leadership. When they were won to Christ and taught in God's Word and then served an apprenticeship in practical doing, nationals were able to replace the foreign missionary, which fulfilled E. J. Pudney's dictum, Work yourself out of a job.

In Zaire, Brazil, Haiti — all the older fields — the number of UFM missionaries diminished while the roster of national workers grew. The Yanomami, the Kayapo, the Wai Wai and other Amazon tribes; the Dani, the Kemyal, the Ngalum and the Ketengmban in Irian Jaya; the Babari and the Pygmy in Zaire — all had been helped by missionaries to comprehend the outside world and to prepare for assimilation in it. Forosha, a second-generation Christian, became chief of a Wai Wai village of a thousand people. With dignity and competency he dealt with government officials, visiting anthropologists, poaching miners, doctors, pilots and curious writers and photographers, as well as with a broad spectrum of developing levels among his own people.

Constantin and Elena Alexandrescu had no strange language to learn when they returned to their native Romania to preach and teach. Donald Orr helped the first missionaries to Ireland because it was to the land of his birth that he returned for his retirement. In most of the countries where UFM worked, however, leadership was built up slowly over many years, by patient teaching and day-to-day demonstration of what the Christian life is about. On every one of its fields, UFM established training institutions once local churches were founded. After evangelization and conversion and church establishment, the need for Biblical leadership became one of the final steps in assuring a mature, healthy national church. After the first or second generation of missionaries had vacated the pastorates in Zaire, Brazil, Irian Jaya and Haiti, Bible schools and theological seminaries were still staffed, at least in part, by missionaries whose sole purpose was building up national leadership. The results have been significant. UFM fields generally have organized national denominations with skilled leaders. In Haiti, UFM schools provided leadership for other groups who themselves were not able to establish schools like the Bible Institute or Theological Seminary in Port-au-Prince.

Teachers, too, need continuing education. It is normal for UFM missionaries on home assignment (the modern term for furlough) to undertake advanced Biblical studies or graduate work. More than thirty earned doctorates were held by active-service UFM missionaries in the mid-1990s, many of them having turned Bible school diplomas into seminary degrees. A Continuing Education Committee was set up among Board members to encourage and monitor requests for graduate studies, with a dozen missionaries pursuing such education every year. Upgrades in language skills, translation methods, medicine and other technical areas have been provided through seminars, workshops, conferences and special courses. Feeding direct benefits to national churches, these deeper understandings and expanded skills are passed on to national workers as missionaries return to the field and teach their brothers and sisters what they themselves have learned.

UFM has been dependent on and appreciative of the colleges, Bible institutes and seminaries that year after year provide it with a majority of its missionaries. Together, Moody Bible Institute and Philadelphia College of the Bible have sent the most graduates to UFM. Dallas Theological Seminary and Grace Theological Seminary have supplied more than fifty men and women. The Princeton Evangelical Fellowship has for more than sixty-five years been a Christian witness on the Ivy League university campus; it was the instrument of conversion of one-third of the 1990s UFM Board of Directors, and Jim Nesbitt and several of his contemporaries on the field, first became acquainted with UFM while at Princeton and active in PEF.

Donald B. Fullerton held no position with the university, yet was for some of the students their principal teacher. He tutored them in Bible on Sunday afternoons and mid-week, and, being a man of deep convictions and strong opinions, taught them to avoid the snares of liberalism, neo-orthodoxy, ecumenism, relativism, secular humanism and evolutionist thought. A gifted man in relationships, he prodded "his boys" with a startling wake-up call.

Having been a missionary for a few years, smuggling Bibles into Afghanistan while stationed in India, he returned home to the United States because of a heart condition and also because F. B. Meyer, the famed London clergyman, convinced him that his calling was to multiply himself through the recruitment of university students for missionary work.

As the agency with which to serve, UFM became Fullerton's number one recommendation.

In the Winter of 1996, a delegation from Bala heard Assani Benedict recount the history of the Gospel in Northeast Zaire. UFM missionaries had brought God's Word to the people, led many to Christ and trained them well in the Scriptures, Assani said. On leaving, they bequeathed schools and seminaries and built-up pastors, elders and deacons. But, unlike some others, they had left no monuments behind.

Perhaps it was ironic that the Zairian bishop spoke just outside the "cathedral" built by missionary Timothy Kauffman.

There were substantial churches and schools and clinics all throughout the Ituri Forest that, if not built by missionaries, were the products of their encouragement and oversight. UFM had erected imposing structures at La Pointe and Bolosse in Haiti and La Bégude de Mazenc in France, and in other lands where it worked. But Assani was right. The monuments UFM left behind were not buildings, but people and the changes in heart and mind and sometimes body that God had wrought in them.

Along with winning men and women to Jesus Christ and grounding them in the Word of God, UFM staunchly believed in cooperative efforts in advancing the Kingdom of God. This included national groups and sending agencies. In Zaire, the Caribbean and Guyana, UFM's work with Bible schools, seminaries and churches benefited not only the churches that resulted from its ministry, but churches of like faith, including denominations, throughout the country. Difficult to match was the working relationship practiced in Brazil, with members of the mission coming from Switzerland, Germany, the United Kingdom, Canada and the United States, all equals on a single team. In a visit to Belém and its outlying fields, George Peters, former professor at Dallas Seminary, considered it the most unusual cooperative effort he had ever seen in missions.

Ordinarily, the tendency is for national groups of missionaries to find it easier to work alone, avoiding cultural and linguistic misunderstandings. But in Brazil, UFM found strength in international cooperation, cutting across language and cultural and denominational lines. The arrangement worked well in other places besides Brazil. In Georgetown, Guyana, and Zaire UFM workers even came under the supervision and accountability of other missions. This cooperative mode was seen as providing great flexibility and necessary for future moves into other presumably inaccessible countries.

International comity of believers extended to the national churches. Haitian church members sent money to France for

312

the printing and distribution of Gospel tracts. As these were taken door to door and their origin explained, the distributors encountered astonishment.

"For me? From the Caribbean with love from some poor Haitians?"

How could they refuse? Every tract, Gospel booklet and Bible was accepted with thanks.

Irian Jayans, Haitians, Brazilians, Amazon Indians, Europeans — all took on the responsibility of penetrating lands foreign to them with the Gospel. For some of these missionaries, it meant adapting to more sophisticated cultures. Which perhaps was easier to accomplish than for today's citizens of industrialized nations to adapt to less developed countries.

The gap between developed and underdeveloped nations seemed to expand each year. Travel by North Americans increased, but despite this exposure to global culture, the modern American exhibited less capacity for overseas living. By the time the average American was professionally qualified and financially equipped, he or she was usually locked into the North American way of thinking and living.

Their education failed to enable North Americans to learn foreign languages readily and to adjust to cultural change. Because foreign languages largely disappeared from high schools and from college requirements, the average missionary candidate arrived at Orientation with no language-learning experience. And while modern techniques shortened the time for language acquisition, the candidate had to shake off the illusion that he likely would arrive at a level of good understanding or speaking after a course or two on the field.

Where a resource was lacking, missions always had had to somehow work around the deficiency and get on with the job. So all was not lost in the downgrading of language learning in American schools. English had become the world's second language where it was not the first. And that was a useful bridge.

In South Africa, between Pretoria and Johannesburg, UFM

missionaries worked closely with Pastor Gilbert, a South African who spoke Shangan, Zulu and Xhosa. The latter, a complicated click-strewn tongue, was mastered by very few North Americans. But Pastor Gilbert, speaking the languages of the people, was able to enter rapidly developing townships and enhance the establishment of new churches, dispensaries, clinics and family stations. He became the link between the new churches and the missionaries, passing on to the congregations the benefits of the missionaries' training and experience.

In some of the current internationalization of the Gospel, missionaries do not attempt to learn the native dialects, but function in English where that is the people's second language. In the former Soviet Union, missionaries from many agencies work exclusively in English with Russian workers who then translate the material into the local tongue. It would take years for a North American to function at a high level of teaching or discipling if first he had to master a Central Asian tongue — and perhaps by the time he did the day of opportunity might well have come and gone.

As the new millennium with its new environment approached, Jim Nesbitt assembled a team of associate directors at Bala to take the places of the men who had served worthily over the past quarter of a century and who now had retired. Each new executive was an experienced missionary, had served in a leadership capacity and shared the vision of evangelizing an unevangelized world. Yet, they were young enough to serve well into the new century.

Boxley Boggs came in from Haiti. Ronald Fisher had worked in both Italy and France before assuming responsibility for all of UFM's European fields. Larry Sharp had served in the Belém field of Brazil. John Sherwood was drawn in from the Philippines.

The 1990s was sometimes called the Post-Modern World. To meet the challenges of such an uncertain, frequently confusing era, the missionary had to be a person with a particular mindset and skills. Jim Nesbitt described him and his calling thus:

"A jack-of-all-trades and master of some."

Now the average missionary often has great work experience, ability in planning and management and familiarity with modern techniques, computers and communications. These are skills that are desperately needed by the church in every developing country. But the average North American is used to a high level of living with all the amenities and comforts that are missing in the third-world countries. A post-modern missionary is older, experienced, used to movement, project-oriented but less able to fix himself or his family in a primitive church-planting situation. For first-world countries found in Europe or South Africa or parts of Asia, it is less difficult, but cultural subtleties are often the undoing of the modern missionary.

New developments have shown mission leaders the strengths of the post-modern candidate. He can help the church cope with many of the necessities of modern life. Being accustomed to change and to travel, the post-modernist is well-adapted for short-term ministries and coming and going into church situations where there is a need for discipleship and leadership training. This is a strength of many North American missions that should be built on for the developing churches overseas. Those churches do not need the old-style pioneer missionary. They are often third-and fourth-generation Christians, and the requests that constantly come to modern mission organizations is "please send over the right kind of missionary to help us . . . ones that will help us develop and cope with government standards, training necessities for our leaders and managerial expertise that will show us how to organize our own churches and institutions."

Post modernism carries derogatory connotations. Many think of post-modern as meaning uncommitted, unattached to objective truth, changing, and everything that is bad in academia. In spite of these negative connotations, the post-modern world still recognizes integrity, faithfulness and availability for meeting desperate human needs. Missionaries today must no longer be colonialists or kingdom builders. Very few areas are left in the world that require or appreciate such rugged individuals. Furthermore, no "lone rangers" are needed; that is, missionaries who go out and work alone with no team work and no accountability and no relationships to local churches. The modern missionary must understand that churches overseas are looking for men and women who can network with them and cooperate with their programs, building them up and making them viable under modern tensions and stress. In Zaire, for example, recently church leaders said, "You are our fathers and mothers. Missionaries came and won us to the Lord Jesus, they gave us the Gospel, they built us up in the faith, they helped us organize our churches, they showed us how to evangelize. We consider ourselves as your children. But now we are teen-agers. We need your help. Please come over and help us as we enter the twenty-first century. We do not know how to organize ourselves. We do no know how to train ourselves. We do not know how to manage what we have already established."

Therefore, just as in 1931, when missionaries formed UFM from their Brazil and Congo fields, so today the needs are greater than ever with even more opportunity than we experienced before World War II. Indeed, as the Scriptures indicate, *An open door and effectual is given to us and there are many adversaries*. But the adversaries are there to show how mighty is the power and provision of our Lord Jesus Christ.

Lest it be mistakenly thought that the current missionary or candidate substitutes e-mail and faxes for prayer and sits behind a desk polishing his prose on a computer, a report from Java illustrates that the new missionary has the same dedication and sense of servanthood that marked the old.

The Weiss family, said the report, was teaching at the Wesley International School and was involved in church planting.

Phil and Kay Myers were discipling church leaders at the Evangelical Theological Seminary, sharing the goal of a church in every Indonesian village in one generation.

David and Julie Ray were spearheading a ministry to an unreached people group of fourteen million in which there were only about four hundred known believers.

Veteran missionaries David and Esther Scovill were leading a church-planting ministry in the capital of Jakarta and another in the south of Sumatra.

Frank and Karren Fosdahl were evangelizing through the traditional Indonesian art of shadow puppets.

Through teamwork with Indonesian believers, ten churches were established in ten years and numerous outposts opened. But as in all other fields, so much more needed to be done.

In France, Joe Mellon found a way to pierce the self-protective armor of indifference or the hostility the French people show toward the Gospel. Unable to get past the high hedges and snarling dogs of the relatively few who live in separate houses or to get beyond the lobbies of high-rise apartments, in which most of the residents of Chambéry live, he sat down and wrote out short tracts on topics the French are interested in — reincarnation, death, loneliness, AIDS, Christmas (whose birthday?), the Bible (an unread book). Since all had a mailbox, regardless of how isolated they wished to live, he reached thousands with the Gospel. Each of his mailings brought response.

In Brazil, a new ministry began in the teeming cities. The target was the children who live, sometimes play and work, often engage in crime and too frequently die in the streets — ten million of them.

Along the Atlantic Coast, four couples worked in the mission field that came to the United States. Ronald and Eleanor Lawson and James and Martha Straubel ministered to Haitians who fled the violence of their country and settled in the New York area. James and Jean Montgomery and Scott and Dorie Nelson did the same among the thousands of Haitians in south

Florida.

Wherever Christians are found today — in South Africa, the Dominican Republic, Mexico, Spain or North America — they appear to be a counter current to the world rushing past them toward destruction. As Jim Nesbitt aptly phrased it, "Today, even though things seem to be disastrous in many parts of the world, the church moves ahead as the missionary outlook carries people toward Heaven and toward saving others with the wonderful good news of Jesus' death and resurrection with forgiveness of sins through faith in His accomplished work."

"Missions," he says, "are the dynamic heart of all Scripture. When the last person is reached, when the last soul is saved, then the Church of Christ will be completed. The metaphor of the Church as a building under construction is an explanation why missionary zeal pushes believers to reach out with the Gospel so that the last person or "stone" may be added to the Church, completing God's plans for the ages. No matter what the circumstances, no matter what conditions surround us, evangelization gives sense in a senseless world. That is why believers and Christians everywhere can be optimistic — because their efforts will have eternal, lasting and secure results in Heaven. Missions, then, is the dynamic force that encourages and propels Christians in their ministry to the lost that surround them. That is why Christians, in general, can be optimistic about the future. Their lives make sense, and all their efforts tied in to the missionary movement have eternal meaning."

For the sake of brevity in a culture that tolerates only short spans, Unevangelized Fields Mission became UFM International. Regardless of the name, the mission is still the same. Reaching the *unevangelized*. When Christ returns and removes the negative prefix from the word, UFM's work will be done.

Until then, there are jobs to be filled. There is much yet to do.

The End

SOURCES, Chapter 25

Lifeline, September, 1994; September, 1995; March, 1996; June, 1996, Bala-Cynwyd, UFM   International

Nesbitt, James H., 1996, Unpublished paper

_____, 1996, Notes on draft

Peters, John, 1996, Untitled manuscript on Yanomami Indians

Seetoo, Lee, 1996, Reprint, *A Brief History of the Princeton Evangelical Fellowship*

UFM International, 1996, Pamphlet, *A Growing Mission*

The Original 36

*(The Founding Missionaries of UFM,
Listed in "Life & Light," Volume I, Number 1, August/
September, 1931)* *

Congo
G. F. Buckley
D. V. Evening
Meyer

(On furlough from Congo):

Miss F. Allan
Mrs. G. F. Buckley
Mr. and Mrs. A. W. Davies
Mrs. D. V. Evening
Mr. and Mrs. George Kerrigan
Miss M. Millington
Mr. and Mrs. Edwin J. Pudney
Mr. and Mrs. A. Voyle

Brazil
Mr. and Mrs. Leonard Harris
Miss M. McKnight
Horace Banner
Robert Story
Fred Roberts
George Thomas

J. Glenn
Mr. and Mrs. Harry Heath
Miss A. Persse
Mr. and Mrs. Ernest J. Wootton
Myrddin Thomas
D. Black

(On furlough from Brazil):

W. McComb
Joseph C. Wright
Patrick Symes
G. Stears

**Central Asia
(Kashmir, India)**

Mr. and Mrs. R. Bavington

*Neither D. Black nor G. Stears is listed in Volume I, Number 2.
India last appears as an active field in Volume II, Number 2.

Those Serving a Term or More with UFM in the Past

(This list does not include active members and staff.)

(N.B. Also <u>includes </u>those listed on 1996 Personnel Directory under the headings <u>Associate Membership, Leave of Absence & Retired</u>)

Abel, Sheri

Abel, Glenn & Dorothy

Adkins, Myrna

Ager, Joyce

Albert, Fernon & Althlea

Albert, Michael & Cheryl

Albright, Susan

Allen, Anna May

Alves Ferreira (Hawkins), Mary

Anderson, Douglas & Dawn

Anderson, Lloyd & Marion

Anderson, Stephen & Dawn

Archer, Norma

Arnott, Margery

Aubin, Judy

Aylor, Margaret

Backman, Samuel & Shirley

Baker, Harold & Margaret

Baker, Mary

Baker, Robert & Doris

Baker, Walter & Dorothy

Bakker (Weber), Irene

Barre, Stephen & Marilyn

Bartel, Leona

Beard, Kenneth & Flora

Bernardo, Jane

Binzel, John

Binzel, Catherine

Bitner, Robert & Nona

Bjerkseth, Olive

Bohlin, Ruth

Bound, Jim & Bonnie

Boyes, Herbert & Marjorie

Bradshaw, Caroline

Brant, Patrick & Margaret

Brown, Helen

Brown, John & Jennifer

Brown, Rod & Joyce

Brown, Vance & Joy

Browne (Watts), Lois

Bruce, David & Eleanor

Brumagin, David & Dolores

Burk, Chester & Dolena

Bushre, Vincent & Alberta
Butler, Joe & DiAnne

Canfield, John & Bonnie
Canfield, Judith
Carne, William & Judith
Carper, Delbert & Lois
Castijon (Rumpf), Carol
Chester, Raymond & Susan
Chastain, James & Alta
Combs, Ronald & Lois
Cole, Clifford & Dorothy
Cole, David & Dina
Cole, Larry & Erica
Collett, Joan
Cook, John & Bessie
Coulbourn, Sonia
Cowger, Janet
Crecraft, Rhoda
Crew, May
Crouch, Eugene & Jan
Cue, Sandra
Cunningham, Angus & Rosemary
Cuthbertson, Mary Dean
Cutting, Robert & Joyce

Dale, John & Louise
D'Amico, Anthony & April
Dancy, Charlotte
Davies, Rowland & Eva
Dawson, John & Kathleen
Dawson, Larry & Marcellyn
Doepp, George & Davina
Doner, Ethel
Downey, Thomas & Lucy

Ebel, Frank & Isobel
Eberly, Loretta
Eby, Hazel
Ediger, Loren & Betty
Emery, Wilfred & Jean
Evans, Donald & Florence

Farley, Donald & Brigitte
Fay, William & Laura
Faulkner, Raymond & Jean
Fickinger, Theodore & Carol
Follmar, Wayne & Bonnie
Folmar, Dennis & Judith
Foreman, Howard & Debbie
Fowler, Gary & Johanna
French, Joseph & Dawn
Froh, Catherine

Garrick, Debbie
Gegner, Philip & Nancy
Gibbs (Lufkin), Ethelle
Glover, Larry & Claudia
Golinski, Peter & Luana
Grant, David & Sonia
Grasley, Jean
Green (Schade), Verna
Greenfield, John & Rie
Greer, Robert & Patti
Groff, Lynn & Dorothy
Groman, Thomas & Virginia
Gulick, Wilfred & Jean
Gutierrez, Manuel & Jane

Hamner (Wegner), Lois
Hanson, Stanley & Gladys

Harding, George & Eleanor
Harland, Thomas & Freda
Harms, Herbert & Grace
Harrell, Delbert & Marguerite
Harter, Frederick & Joyce
Haslam, Doris
Hawkins, Neill & Mary
Hayward, Douglas & Joanne
Heider, William & Alene
Heppner, Gertrude
Hess, Clara
Hiles, Pearl
Hinchman, Sharon
Hoffmeier, Charles & Vivian
Holley, Philip & Marian
Holley, Raymond & Florence
Hough, Florence
Houghton (Stevenson), Jean
Husmann, George & Ruth
Hutchison, Marion

Ige, Elaine
Irland (Prescott), Ethel

Jack, William & Siri
Jackson (Laughlin), Dorothy
Jantz, Leslie & Anita
Johnson, David & Arlene
Joiner, Bruce & Judy
Jones, Delmas & Marda
Jones, Nannie
Jose, Martin & Sarah

Kauffman, Timothy & Wanda
Kearns, Donald & Miriam

Keener, Lehman & Louella
Ketchum, Henry & Janet
Kettleson, Ed & Elsie Mae
Kiehl, Clarence & Joy
Knight, Donald & Frances
Knight (Clements), Leesa
Kruhmin, Walter & Beulah
Kunihiro, Kenneth
Kurka, Glenn & Sandra
Kvigstad, Irene

Lanzillo (Gilbert), Donna
Laskowski, Ted & Janet
Leavitt, Claude & Barbara
Leavitt, Steven & Donna
Leverett, Cletus & Judy
Lewis, Rod & Louise
Lewis (Nelson), Saralie
Lilly, David & Patricia
Linton, Ella
Lockhart, Austin & Ellora
Logan, Thomas & Peggy
Longley, Frances
Loyer, Ben & Gloria
Ludlow, Wilma
Ludwig, Mr. & Mrs. Fred

McAllister, Douglas & Mary
McCallum, Thomas & Lynn
McCracken, Jean
McDougall, Willy
McGann, Robert & Karen
McIver, Murdeen
McMillan, David & Rebecca
McMillan, Hector & Ione

McMillan, Paul & Linda
McNutt, James & Julia

MacLean, Sutherland & Rodina
Maier, Ernest & Ilse
Maistros, Robert & Barbara
Mann, Charles & Stephanie
Masson, Raymond & Dottie
Masterson, Jack & Linda
Matthews, Donald & Wilma
Matz (Hafer), Evelyn
Maynard, Ralph & Melba
Mersdorf, Alexander & Mary
Messer, Larry & Judith
Middleton, Richard & Sherlyn
Miesel, John & Janice
Miller, Douglas & Kaye
Mills, Eva
Mills, Grady & Marjorie
Minehart, Richard & Catherine
Moffet, Ruth
Moree, James
Muchmore, Donald & Eleanor
Mulder, James & Joan

Nebel, Caroline
Nelson, Ralph & Martha
Newton, John & Darcie
Nicholls, Stanley & Iris
Nicholls, Thomas & Karen
Nishimura, Jon

Odman, Ralph & Majil
Ogilvie, Margaret
O'Neill, James & Sterling

O'Neill, Russell & Cheryl
Ordway, Cynthia
Orr, Donald & Olive
Ouren, Bernice

Parker, Ethel
Parker, Horace & Joyce
Paul, Martin & Lois
Peach, William & Deborah
Pearson, Orin & Margaret
Personett, Janet
Peters, John & Lorraine
Petersen, John & Shirley
Pickett, Faith
Piepgrass, Charles & Arlene
Piepgrass, William & Marcia
Pierce, Kathryn
Powell, Jerry & Carol
Puckett, Larry & Doris
Pudney, Edwin & Lilian

Randell (Thompson), Jane
Redman, Mary
Redner (Shade), Bonnie
Regier, William & Dahna
Reinke, Leonard & Margaret
Riedle, Florence
Roche, Dorothy
Ruchti, Harold & Ruth
Rudolph, Mamie
Rudy, Kenneth & Donna
Rutt, Mary

Sadlier, Stanley & Barbara
Sakata, Evelyn

Sands, Russel & Audrey
Sarginson, Charles & Effie
Sasscer, Russell & Patsy
Schell, Harold & Dorothy
Schirok, Agnes
Schmid, John & Emma
Schmid, Melvin & Marsha
Schmidt, Henry & Sarah
Schmidt, Steve & Cathleen
Schmidt, Sue
Schneider, George & Jean
Scholten, William & Dorothy
See, Glenn & Wilma
Sessoms, John & Olive
Sewell, Bruce & Alba
Shreve, Edgar & Jessie
Sigg, Richard & Amelia
Snider, Neoma
Snyder, Dale & Mary
Snyder, George & Coral
Southard, Marshall & Thelma
Spade, Rodney & Carole
Sparling (Davidson), Dorothy
Sparling, Norman & Hilda
Spears, Benjamin & Barbara
Sperring, Michael & Cheryl
Stanszus, Gerd & Maria
Starring, Malcolm & Jan
Stensvad, Allan & Margaret
Stevenson, John & Susan
Streight, Evelyn
Streight, Norman & Norah
Stricker, Eric & Terri
Swain, Richard & Lois
Sweatman, Gareth & Carole

Sykes, Thomas & Ruby

Taylor, Lynn & Ruth Ann
Tew, Roger & Karen
Thomas, George & Blanche
Thomas, Margaret
Thompson, Elizabeth
Timbers, Lillie
Timmerman, Eleanor
Tippens (Cordero), Tabitha
Tofflemire, Stella
Toirac, Florent & Dorothy
Toirac, Juanita
Tracy, Frances

Umenhofer, Naomi

Vandermeer, Ed & Marion
van Pletsen, Raymond & Mildred
Veldhuis, Johannes & Eleanor
Verderame, John & Catherine

Walker, Viola
Walsh, Thomas & Marsha
Weber, Mark & Jolene
Weeks, Gary & Claudette
Weeks, Elizabeth
Welsford, St. John & Joy
Wenger, Mabel
Wesley, Robert & Margaret
Westcott, Dr. & Mrs. George
White, Paul & Carol Ann
Whitlock, Raymond & Lois
Wiebe, Helen